Morality and Moral Reasoning

Morality and Moral Reasoning

Five Essays in Ethics

Edited by
John Casey

Methuen & Co Ltd
11 New Fetter Lane London EC4

First published 1971
by Methuen & Co. Ltd
11 New Fetter Lane, London EC4
© *1971 Methuen & Co. Ltd*
Printed in Great Britain by
Richard Clay (The Chaucer Press) Ltd
Bungay, Suffolk

SBN 416 16340 8

Distributed in the U.S.A.
by Barnes & Noble Inc.

Contents

ERRATA

p. 111, line 27: The sentence beginning on this line should read:

But this is exactly what does not happen with moral truth, where we are asked to make intelligible the notion of a state of affairs subject to the constraint that its existence does not follow from the naturalistic facts being as they are, but its continued existence follows from the naturalistic facts staying as they are.

p. 119, line 28: For cannot *read* can

Contents

Preface

The following essays concentrate upon two important questions in ethical theory: 'What is it to judge morally?' and 'What makes a reason a moral reason?' The first question is discussed in the essays by Bernard Williams, Roger Scruton, S. W. Blackburn and J. E. J. Altham. There is some extended discussion of the relation of moral judgements to attitudes, emotions and beliefs, and of the question whether moral utterances are to be construed as expressions of belief, or of feelings or attitudes. This leads to consideration of the notion of expression, and of the relation of the evaluative 'speech act' to the mental state which might be thought to be its 'sincerity condition'.[1] In fact the first four essays, taken together, can be seen as a varied and sustained defence of ethical emotivism. The question is approached from different points of view, but the arguments tend in a common direction.

The second question – 'What makes a reason a moral reason?' – is a topic both of my own contribution and of Part II of Mr Scruton's 'Attitudes, Beliefs and Reasons'. Much of the discussion centres on the notion of 'moral relevance': when is a fact or feature of a situation relevant to a moral judgement? When does the mention of some fact or feature provide a morally relevant reason? Is it possible to dismiss a whole category of moral principles – for instance, those of an absolutist sort – on the grounds that they are committed to a false notion of moral relevance? This discussion proceeds into the area of agency and moral responsibility, and touches on the relation between the grounds for making moral distinctions and the grounds for making distinctions of responsibility and agency.

With the exception of Professor Williams's 'Morality and the Emotions', none of the essays has been previously published. All of the authors are (or were until recently) in Cambridge, and most of the essays owe a good deal to informal discussion among the contributors. Williams's essay in particular has had considerable influence upon several of the other pieces.

John Casey
Cambridge 1970

---

[1] Cf. J. R. Searle, *Speech Acts* (Cambridge, 1969), p. 64 n.

1 Morality and the Emotions[1]
Bernard Williams

Recent moral philosophy in Britain has not had much to say about the emotions. Its descriptions of the moral agent, its analyses of moral choice and moral judgement, have made free use of such notions as attitude, principle and policy, but have found no essential place for the agent's emotions, except perhaps for recognizing them in one of their traditional roles as possible motives to backsliding, and thus potentially destructive of moral rationality and consistency. Much the same is true when one turns to what has been said about the *objects* of moral judgement: here there is much discussion of what it is to judge favourably or unfavourably actions, decisions, principles, states of affairs, intentions; indeed, men and men's characters. There is less, however, about what a man ought or ought not to feel in certain circumstances, or, more broadly, about the ways in which various emotions may be considered as destructive, mean or hateful, while others appear as creative, generous, admirable, or – merely – such as one would hope for from a decent human being. Considerations like these certainly play a large part in moral thought, except perhaps in that of the most restricted and legalistic kind; but it is my impression that the part they play has not adequately been mirrored in the recent concerns of moral philosophers.

There are a number of reasons for this neglect. Some of the reasons are no doubt of mainly historical or sociological interest, but others are of more direct concern to philosophical theory; and of these, there are two that seem to me particularly significant. The first is connected with questions about language. The second consists in a combination of two things – a rather simple view of the emotions, and a deeply Kantian view of morality. The first part of what I have to say will be about language; this will lead into those other issues, about which I shall try to say something in the latter part.

[1] This is a reprint of an Inaugural Lecture delivered at Bedford College, University of London, on 4 May 1965, and originally published by the College. I have left out two paragraphs and made one or two minor revisions.

The first reason, then, for the neglect of the emotions lies in some considerations about language. In these years philosophy has found its way to lie in reflection on language, and moral philosophy in reflection on the language of morality. Now this tendency, in itself, does not exclude much; for the diversity of what can be called 'reflection on language' is equalled by the diversity of what can be called 'the language of morality', and there was no basic reason why a generous approach to the linguistic endeavour should not have embraced those features of our speech about morality that reveal or suggest the parts played by the emotions; such features, as I shall try to show, certainly exist. What has largely inhibited this development is something over and above the linguistic programme itself: this is the preoccupation with the distinction between fact and value. This preoccupation has been inevitable. It has also, in many respects, been valuable. But there is no doubt that some of its consequences have been unfortunate. Since the preoccupation is one with fact and value as such, it has imposed on the linguistic enterprise a concentration on the most general features of moral language, or indeed, yet more widely, of evaluative language. Thus the attention goes to such very general linguistic activities as 'commendation', 'evaluation' and 'prescription', and to such very general terms as 'good', 'right' and 'ought', and the more specific notions in terms of which people a lot of the time think and speak about their own and others' conduct have, with the exception of one or two writers, largely gone by default.

This concentration has helped to push the emotions out of the picture. If you aim to state the most general characteristics and connections of moral language, you will not find much to say about the emotions; because there are few, if any, *highly general* connections between the emotions and moral language. It has been all the easier for recent analytical philosophy to accept this truth (as I take it to be) because of the evident failings of a theory, itself one of the first in the linguistic style, which claimed precisely the contrary. This was emotivism, which offered a connection between moral language and the emotions as straightforward and as general as could be conceived, in the form of the thesis that the function and nature of moral judgements was to express the emotions of the speaker and to arouse similar emotions in his hearers. This theory not proving very plausible, and the interest in the highly general questions remaining, it was natural enough to look to things quite other than the emotions for the answers.

Not that emotivism has ceased to be mentioned. It is mentioned in order to be refuted, and indeed the demolition of emotivism has almost come to take the place in undergraduate exercises that used to be held (as Stephen Spender comically recalls in his autobiography *World Within World*) by the equally mechanical dismembering of Mill's *Utilitarianism*. The emotivist is specially suitable for this role of sacrificial victim because he is at once somewhat disreputable (emotivism being regarded as irrationalist) and at the same time embarrassingly likely to be taken for a close relative. But there are things to be learned from emotivism which do not always emerge in the course of the ritual exercises; and it is some of these that I shall now go on to consider. My aim will not be to reconstruct emotivism, but to steal from it; not to rebuild the pagan temple, but to put its ruins to a holier purpose.

Emotivism held that there were two purposes of moral judgements: to express the emotions of the speaker, and to influence the emotions of his hearers. I want to concentrate on the first of these. Now it was clearly the intention of emotivism, in referring to the expression of emotions, to offer a view about the nature of moral judgements, a view of their logical and linguistic character; it was not offering merely an empirical claim to the effect that moral judgements (themselves identified in some other way) always do express the emotions of their utterers. This being so, it must be part of an emotivist thesis that there are some kinds of linguistic rule associating moral judgements with the expression of emotion. What form might such linguistic rules take? Here there are two importantly different possibilities, which must be distinguished. On the one hand, they might be rules about the correct use of certain sentences or forms of words – those forms of words, namely, in uttering which we make a moral judgement; and the rules would state that unless those forms of words were used in expression of emotion, they were being misused. In this form, the rules would be about the correct use of the sentences that we use in making moral judgements, laying it down about those sentences that their correct use lies partly in the expression of emotion. The second possibility is that the linguistic rules should concern not the correct or incorrect use of those sentences, but should rather regulate the application of the expression 'moral judgement'. In this form, the rules would not lay it down that a speaker would be guilty of a misuse of certain sentences if he used them not in expression of his emotions; it would merely lay down that if he did so use them, he would not count as making a moral judgement. In slightly more technical terms, one might say that the first possibility concerns the semantics of a certain class of sentences, while the second possibility concerns the definition of a certain speech-act, the speech-act of *making a moral judgement*. I shall consider these two possibilities in turn.

On the first possibility, that the requirement for expression of emotion actually enters into the semantic rules of sentences employed in moral judgements, it might be wondered whether there are any sentences at all whose use was governed by semantic rules of this type. There certainly are. I shall leave out the case of sentences which also say something explicitly about the speaker's emotional state, e.g.

I am extremely angry with you;

these raise interesting problems about the relations between statement and expression,[1] but they are not likely to provide much direct help in the present question. But consider a sentence like

He has broken his tricycle again, blast him.

Here it seems reasonable to say that the use of this sentence is governed by the requirement that the speaker be expressing irritation, or some feeling of that sort. We encounter here the matter of intonation in utterances of this sort; it is notable that there is a large range of intonations in which the sentence would be inappropriate, and others in which it would be appropriate, and if the latter were employed when the speaker was not irritated, his utterance would be misleading, even deceitful.

In this case, these features of the sentence of course centre on one word, the expletive; and this backs up the account of these features in terms of the semantics of the sentence, for they are features connected with the use of this expression: if someone did not know that the expression worked like this, he would be ignorant of a fact about the English language. That the features centre on this expression makes this example particularly simple in a certain way; the inclusion of the expletive merely adds something to what, without it, would be a straightforward statement of fact. That statement by itself could of

[1] For a helpful discussion of this and related issues, see W. P. Alston, 'Expressing', in Max Black (Ed.), *Philosophy in America* (London, 1965).

course also be made in a manner expressive of irritation, but it does not have to be; the addition of the expletive gives a way of making that same statement of fact which is restricted to cases in which its utterance is to be taken as expressive of irritation. This is the sort of case to which one can straightforwardly apply the old *New Yorker* request: Just Stick to the Facts, Please.

The most primitive type of emotivist theory assimilated moral judgements to this type of utterance: statement of fact plus expletive addition. This, as has been often pointed out, will not do. It is only too obvious that the moral judgement

He did wrong in not going to the appointment

is not necessarily expressive of indignation or any other emotion; though of course a particular utterance of it may be expressive of some emotion, just as a statement of fact may be. Apart from this, expletives are not logically manoeuvrable enough to provide a model for moral, or any other value judgements. To adapt to this question an argument that has been used by J. R. Searle[1] against a more sophisticated thesis, it is notable that you cannot *make conditional* the expressive functions of an expletive. Thus the sentence

If he has broken his tricycle again, blast him, he'll go without his pocket money

obeys the same sorts of rules as the simpler sentence considered before; it can be appropriately used only by someone who is *already* irritated. But even if I shall be indignant if I believe that he did wrong in not going to his appointment, it is clear that the sentence, uttered when I am still in doubt about the circumstances,

If he did wrong in not going to the appointment, I shall have something to say to him,

does not express existing indignation, my indignation remaining as

---

[1] 'Meaning and speech-acts', *Philosophical Review* (1962), pp. 423–32. Although the principle of Searle's argument and of mine is the same, the arguments proceed in contrary directions. His point is that there is not a meaning-link between a certain sentence and the performance of a certain speech-act, since the speech-act is not performed when the sentence occurs in contexts other than that of simple assertion. My argument rather suggests that there is a meaning-link between the expletive and its expressive function, since the expressive function is preserved in such contexts.

hypothetical as the truth of the antecedent. A similar point can be shown with negation. If A asks

Has he broken his tricycle again, blast him?

and B replies

No, he has not broken his tricycle again, blast him

either B is himself irritated, or (just possibly) he is sarcastically *quoting* A's expletive.

The same consideration can be applied to cases more sophisticated than the simple occurrence of expletives. If my infatuated friend says

Lisa looks incomparable lovely tonight

it scarcely seems open to me, even if I wish to disagree with his estimate of Lisa's appearance, to do so by just denying his assertion in its own terms:

No, she does not look incomparably lovely tonight

would be an odd thing to say, and would have a place, I suspect, only if I were in effect quoting him, as above – and thus being very rude – or possibly, and more interestingly, if I were myself fairly infatuated, and disagreeing only about the incomparability of her loveliness tonight; in which case, paradoxically, the denied expressive terms are still doing their expressive job. This resistance to losing their force in conditional, negative, etc., contexts may well be a mark of sentences which *semantically incorporate* the expression of emotion. Those sentences which are used to make moral judgements do not in general have this peculiarity, and the first possibility for a general emotivist link between moral language and the emotions fails.

While this is so, it is not the end even of this part of the story. While those sentences that are used to make moral judgements do not in general semantically incorporate the expression of emotion, it seems clear that some of them do. For instance,

Of course, he went back on his agreement when he got to the meeting, the little coward

seems to be reserved for use in circumstances where certain emotions, such as contempt, are felt by the speaker. What else does the utterance of this sentence do? First, it states or implies certain facts, as that he made an agreement, and went back on it at the meeting; and second, it imports an explanation, since 'cowardice' is an explanatory notion (the speaker would be taking a different view of what had happened if, equally unamiably, he called the man an 'ambitious little crook'). Is this all? If so, we can analyse the utterance into statement of fact, suggestion of explanation and (something like an) expletive addition: i.e. as merely a slightly more complex example of the 'blast him' sort. But this seems to leave something out, since one would be naturally disposed to think that the original remark also embodied some moral opinion or assessment of the man's behaviour. On the present analysis, it looks as though this function will be borne only by the expletive addition – that is to say we shall be accepting for this case the primitive emotivist account which has been in general rejected. If this is not acceptable, it seems that there should be some way of representing the moral assessment feature independently of the expletive addition; so that the removal of the expletive addition will leave us with a triple core, of stating facts, suggesting explanation and making a moral assessment. If this is so, we should be able in principle to isolate this care without the expletive trimmings – obeying, as it were, an amplified *New Yorker* instruction: Just Stick to the Facts, Explanations and Moral Assessments, Please.

What would the isolated core look like? Here there are difficulties which particularly centre on the expression 'little coward'. While 'coward' is an explanatory term, it is not a very unemotional one; and if 'little' refers to the man's moral, rather than his physical stature, it is not (at least in this collocation) a very unemotional way of making a moral assessment. This phrase seems inextricably linked to the expletive addition, and so cannot appear in the core. The core is, then, going to look something like this:

> As might have been predicted, he went back on his agreement at the meeting through fear; which he ought not to have done (*or* this was a bad thing).

This sentence is supposed to stand in the same relation to its earlier emotional counterpart as 'he broke his tricycle' does to 'he broke his tricycle, blast him'; i.e. in this more complex case, it states the same facts, suggests the same explanation and makes the same moral assessment. All that the replacement sentence has supposedly lost are the expletive additions. But is this in fact so?

It is made a little easier to agree to this by my having introduced a term that is sometimes introduced in this sort of connection, viz. 'moral *assessment*', since there is a satisfactory sense of 'assessment' in which you and I give the same assessment merely if we are both 'pro' or both 'con' or, perhaps, both 'neutral'. Certainly in the present case both the original sentence and its non-emotional replacement equally reveal the speaker as 'con'. In one sense of the phrase 'moral judgement', the notion of 'same moral judgement' might be adequately modelled on this very skeletal pattern of 'assessment'; this is where 'judgement' is something offered by a judge, one who applies such labels as 'pass' or 'fail', 'first', 'second', 'highly commended' and so forth. In this sense, we might say that the original sentence and its replacement embodied the same moral judgement. But, as has been quite often pointed out, the technical phrase 'moral judgement' has other overtones, being virtually the only survivor into contemporary philosophical vocabulary of that Idealist usage by which beliefs and opinions, roughly, were called 'judgements'. And these overtones have to be preserved if the phrase 'moral judgement' is to have any hope of doing adequate work in its exposed position in moral philosophy; since, in being interested in a person's moral judgement, so called, we are in fact not merely interested in whether he is pro this and con that, whether he grades these men in one order or in another. We are interested in what moral view he takes of the situations, how those situations look to him in the light of his moral outlook. Could we in this broader sense of 'moral judgement' say – to revert to our example – that the replacement sentence expressed the same moral judgement as the first one? Does it lay before us the same moral view of the situation? Scarcely so. To agree to this would commit us to saying that the contempt (or something like it) that the speaker of the first sentence felt and put into his words was not an integral part of his moral view of the situation; that contempt was an adventitious addition to his low rating of the man's behaviour at the committee, as my irritation is no doubt an adventitious reaction to my learning that Tommy has broken his tricycle again. Something like this *could* be true; but very obviously, it need not be so. Indeed, it is far from clear what content is to be assigned, in the moral connection, to the bare notion of 'grading low'; this is an idea which seems much more at home in highly structured professional or technical kinds of comparison. In the present case, the mode in which this man's behaviour appeared bad may precisely have been that of its being contemptible; and if the person who made the remark comes not to think of it in those terms, he will cease to take the same moral view as before of this man's behaviour. Where this is so, we may not be able to isolate the moral-judgement content of the utterances from what makes them expressive of emotion.

We shall get back to this area again. Now, however, let me take up what I mentioned earlier as the second line by which an emotivist type of theory might seek to make a direct link between the making of moral judgements, and the expression of emotion. This was the suggestion that the expression of emotion might be logically involved, not in the semantics of certain sentences that people utter, but in the description that we give of their uttering them: that a speaker's expressing emotions should be regarded as a necessary condition of his utterance's counting as the making of a moral judgement. This was the 'speech-act' thesis. I think we shall see that this suggestion, while no less false than the last one, also raises some questions that lead us, by a rather different route, to entanglements of the emotions with moral judgement.

The 'speech-act thesis' takes 'moral judgement', or more precisely 'making or expressing a moral judgement', as the name of a certain type of speech-act; that is to say, as a member of the class that includes also such items as 'giving a warning', 'making a promise', 'stating an intention', 'making an apology', 'expressing regret', 'describing what happened' and so forth. Interest in such speech-acts, promoted by the work of the late J. L. Austin, has been prominent in recent philosophy, not least in moral philosophy, where particularly such linguistic activities as 'commending' have been to the fore. I think that valuable light has been shed by these studies, and that this will continue to be so.

We shall be able to see the possible relations of emotions to the speech-act of making a moral judgement, only if we get clearer about a somewhat complex question, which is the role of *sincerity* in different speech-acts. The category of sincerity and insincerity is of fundamental importance for the understanding of linguistic activities; for it is a necessary feature of linguistic behaviour that it can be deliberately inappropriate, designed to mislead, etc. This does not mean, however, that the notions of sincerity and insincerity apply equally to all speech-acts, or in the same way to all. I shall try to distinguish very briefly six different types of case; this will be only a very rough exercise, designed to clear a bit of the undergrowth round our present problem.

B

(1) There are some highly conventionalized speech-acts which cannot be sincere or insincere at all: such as greetings (or at least very simple ones). Just saying 'hello' cannot in itself be done sincerely or insincerely, though certain accompaniments, such as a tone of warm enthusiasm, may admit the notions. Similarly, saying 'How are you?' cannot be insincere, if regarded as a greeting; if regarded as an *expression of concern for the man's health*, it can be.

(2) Orders cannot be sincere or insincere. However, there are some associated conditions on the speaker and his situation which get us nearer to the realm of sincerity, without actually reaching it. These concern whether the speaker wants the hearer to do the thing ordered or not; and – perhaps differently – whether he means the speaker to do the thing or not.

(3) Consider now certain sorts of judgement: grading and (in one sense) commending, as where a man gives his judgement, allocates an order of merit, etc., at a dog show or examination. It could be said (though it would be an unnatural thing to say) that a man does these things 'sincerely' or 'insincerely'; and there is more than one way of doing them 'insincerely' (there are important differences between his having been bribed and his conscientiously applying official standards which he himself regards as inappropriate). But when he judges or commends insincerely, he really does judge or commend – the act is performed, though 'insincerely'.

(4) In this respect, there is a similarity between these acts and that of promising: an insincere promise is quite certainly a promise. Promising, however, has the feature not present in the last case, that the application of 'sincere' and 'insincere' is absolutely clear and well established – an insincere promise is a promise made without the intention of carrying it out. Yet, one may perhaps repeat, it is quite certainly made: in the phrase 'insincere promise', the word 'insincere' is not what the scholastics called an *alienans*[1] term, that is to say a qualification which weakens or removes the force of the term that it qualifies (as 'bogus', 'imitation', 'pretend', etc.).

(5) Equally well established is the application of 'sincere' and 'insincere' to expressions of intention and of belief (which can be regarded together in this connection). But here it looks as though 'insincere' has a rather different effect: here it does appear to be *alienans*, for an

[1] For the use of this term, cf. P. T. Geach, 'Good and evil,' *Analysis*, vol. 17 (1956), p. 33.

insincere expression of intention is surely not an expression of intention, nor an insincere expression of belief an expression of belief. Perhaps if we are to be accurate, we cannot say anything quite as simple as that; we can indeed speak of the deceiving man, even after we have discovered his deceit, as 'having expressed an intention to . . . ', meaning that he used a formula usually taken as an expression of intention, and meant it to be so taken. But, though that may be so, he certainly did not express *his* intentions, nor does the man who misleads us about his beliefs, express *his* belief. This 'his' is perhaps significant. His greetings, his orders, his commendations, his promises are *his*, basically, just in that it is he who utters them; his expressions of intention or belief are *his* not only in this way, but because they are expressions of *his* intentions or *his* beliefs, and these latter lie below the level of the speech-act.

(6) Expressions of feeling or emotion are obviously to be regarded in general in the light of what has just been said: he is not expressing his feelings if his remarks are insincere. However, there are at least a few cases in which the steady flow of human pretence has shaped the language, and worn a semantic gap between formula and feeling. 'Expression of regret', for instance, seems to be the name of a type of utterance conventionally identified, and an insincere expression of regret is still an expression of regret. Similarly, perhaps, with expressions of concern. Both, it may be noticed, are among the sorts of items frequently sent by one government to another.

Let me now try to put together what has just been said with the question of moral utterances. There has been a tendency in recent work to assimilate the speech-acts involved in the making of moral utterances – 'making a moral judgement' and so forth – to the sorts of speech-act considered in (2) and (3): the giving of orders, and grading, commending, etc. This assimilation tends to conceal the many and vital respects in which speech-acts associated with moral utterances belong rather to types (5) and (6). It inclines us to forget that a man who sincerely makes some moral utterance expresses his judgement of the situation, his beliefs about its merits, his moral outlook, his opinion, his feelings on the matter – possibly his intentions. A man who makes an insincere moral utterance does not do these things, but hides his belief and his real feelings. But it is these that chiefly concern us: the moral cast of the man lies below the level of the speech-act.

This is not to say that to concentrate on models in classes (2) and

(3) for understanding of moral language necessarily leaves out the notions of sincerity and insincerity. We have already seen that there is some room for them there, if rather less directly than elsewhere; and case (4) – promising – shows that there can be a straightforward use of these terms to qualify speech-acts which, like those others and unlike those grouped in (5), can be expressed by what Austin called an 'explicit performative'.[1] The trouble is not so much that concentration on the models in (2) and (3) displaces the notion of sincerity, as that it misplaces it, and tends to conceal from us the basic, if not simple, truth that one who misleads us about his moral view is, in this respect, like one who misleads us about his factual beliefs or about his feelings – he says something other than what he really thinks or feels.

Consider the grading or commending model (2). We remarked there that a man may grade or commend certain things or persons contrary to his real opinion of their merits, and that could be a form of 'insincerity' (though it need not be: it may not be his job to bring his own opinions into it). But now what does 'his real opinion of their merits' mean? If activities like grading and commending are to be the clue to moral thought, it is *this* that must itself be explained, and presumably explained in terms of grading and commending. Here the line that has been actually pursued, perhaps the only possible one, is that of saying that 'his real opinion of their merits' is to be explained in terms of the gradings or commendations that he gives or would give in accordance with *his own* standards. This in turn has to be explained; and although strenuous efforts have been made to cash this notion merely in terms of systematic action, I myself am convinced that we could not in fact attach much content to it if men did not do such things as express their enthusiasm, admiration, hope, boredom, contempt, dislike, scepticism – that is to say, express views and feelings about the objects or persons that they grade or commend, and not merely go about grading or commending them.

I said earlier that our emotivist suggestion, that the possession of certain emotions might be a necessary condition of performing the speech-act of making a moral judgement, would turn out to be false. We can now see why this is so. First of all, there is certainly *a* sense

---

[1] Neither 'I intend' nor 'I believe' is, of course, an explicit performative. Loose talk about a 'performative' analysis of these expressions (as opposed, presumably, to an 'autobiographical' analysis of them) obscures this obvious fact.

of 'expressing a moral judgement' in which an insincere moral judgement is still a moral judgement: the sense in which a man who, quite
insincerely and to please an illiberal host, says 'homosexuals ought to
be flogged', has expressed the moral judgement that homosexuals
ought to be flogged. This sense may encourage the assimilation of
'making a moral judgement' to the types of speech-act (2) and (3),
which we have already noticed. But it should not do so. What rather
it is like is the sense – noted under (5) – in which a man who insincerely
says that he intends to do a certain thing has expressed an intention.
In this sense of 'expressing a moral judgement' the emotivist thesis
must obviously be false; if one can perform this act without even being
sincere, how can it be a necessary condition of performing it that one
has feelings appropriate to the content of the judgement?

If we turn now to the notion of a man's expressing *his* moral
judgement on a situation, that by which his moral judgement, like his
factual and other beliefs, lies below the level of the speech act; is the
presence of appropriate feelings a necessary condition of a man's
doing this? This question comes to much, if not exactly, the same as
asking: are appropriate feelings a necessary condition of sincerity in
expressing a moral judgement in the first sense? To this question,
again, the answer seems to be 'no': the facts stand firmly against any
simple and general connection of feelings and sincerity. Thus the
general emotivist thesis again fails. Nevertheless, feelings make some
contribution to the notion of sincerity: and this in more than one way.
I shall now try to consider this contribution.

The first part of the contribution is to be found in this, that there
are *some* moral utterances which, if they are to be sincere, must be
expressive of emotions or feelings that the speaker has. For instance,
there are those moral utterances that are expressed in strong terms.
These will include the cases that we were led to before, at the end of
our discussion of the first emotivist suggestion, namely those cases in
which the moral utterance involves terms that are semantically linked
to the emotions. But these will not be the only cases; for it is perfectly
possible for a man to express himself on a moral matter in a way which
uses no such terms, but makes it perfectly clear that he feels strongly
about the matter. He does not have to use expressions like 'little
coward', 'outrageous', 'appalling', 'ghastly mess', 'crook', 'disgusting'
and so forth, nor yet the vocabulary of ordinary obscenities and swear-
words: though it is worth remembering that violent language and

obscenities play a larger part in people's remarks in appraisal of human conduct than one would gather from a textbook on moral philosophy. But the speaker, as I said, may not express himself like this; he may just, in few and moderate words, make it clear that he is shocked, disappointed, indignant or (conversely) full of admiration, for instance. It is certainly a condition of his speaking sincerely in all these cases that he should feel those things that we are given to understand he does feel.

It may be said here that this is obvious enough, but that it has nothing particularly to do with the sincerity of moral utterances. It is merely that we are here dealing with those moral utterances which are expressed in terms, or in a manner, expressive of emotion, just as other sorts of utterances may be; and that the link of sincerity and the emotions exists merely in respect of those features, and not in respect of the moral utterance as such. But this objection will have force only if it further claims that we can isolate the content of the moral judgement, as such, from the rest. I have already argued, for the cases where there is a semantic link of what is said to emotion, that this is an unrealistic idea. I think that the new perspective that we now have on the question, from the point of view of sincerity, shows a more general point of the same kind.

It cannot be denied that an intrinsic feature of moral thought are the distinctions between taking a serious view and a less serious view; having strong convictions and less strong convictions, and so forth. It would be a mark of insanity to regard all moral issues as on the same level. Now the man who expresses himself in strong terms, such as we are considering, can usually be taken as indicating that he takes a strong or serious view of the matter in question.[1] This is not inevitably so: sometimes a man may himself be clear, and make it clear to others, that the moral view he is expressing with strong feelings is not a very serious moral view, and that the strong feeling is, for instance, merely personal irritation. But this is certainly a special case; in general, the display of feeling and the moral utterance will be taken together, and the strength of feeling displayed about the matter is generally taken as *one* criterion of the man's having a strong or serious moral view about it.

It is not, of course, *the* criterion, nor an infallible one. Thus it is

[1] Some points bearing on this are made by D. Braybrooke, 'How are moral judgements connected with displays of emotion?', *Dialogue*, IV (1965), pp. 206–23.

possible for a man to express strong feelings in his moral remarks about a matter, himself regard the feelings as related to the moral issue, and yet not really take a very serious view of it. It may be, for instance, that his feelings (as we may see, or he may see later) are merely those of hurt pride, or fear, made over for the moment into moral indignation or altruistic upset; in such cases we may speak of self-deception. Again, and differently, his moral reactions may be in general so freely laced with emotion and so little borne out in action or by serious inquiry into the facts that we come to doubt whether he has any serious moral views at all: here we may think in terms of self-indulgent moral frivolity, particularly if the emotion he so generously indulges is indignation. In these cases, what is in a real sense a genuine emotional expression does not guarantee that a strong moral view is really taken. Conversely, it is even possible for a man to give a genuinely strong moral view an insincerely emotional expression: an 'un-emotional' practical man, seriously devoted to some moral end, may find it helpful, in persuading others, to lay on a display of anger or sentiment which does not come spontaneously.

These cases, and many others, are commonplaces in the complex relations between the emotions and moral seriousness. While there are these commonplaces, few of them are likely to lie beyond all dispute, since these are obviously matters on which one's views cannot be independent of particular outlooks, values, and even fashions. The charge of insincerity has been exchanged many times in the last two centuries between the practical and the Romantic, both in morals and politics, and the notion of sincerity is consequently unsettled in a way which represents sets of perfectly real and very basic divergences – divergences which exist, obviously, not only between but inside individuals.

The variety of cases, however, and the systematic differences in their interpretation, all exist against a background in which there is some connection taken for granted between strength of feeling displayed on moral issues, and the strength of the moral view taken. This connection appears to me basic enough for the strength of feeling to be called *a* criterion of taking a strong moral view, rather than saying that there is a mere empirical correlation between them. If it were a mere empirical correlation, we could imagine a world in which people had strong moral views, and strong emotions, and their emotions were not in the least engaged in their morality. Some moral theories certainly involve the conclusion that such a world is conceivable; but I do not think that it is.

The difficulties in such a conception are both psychological and logical. I shall consider just one, logical, difficulty. I shall try to show a point of involvement of the emotions in what may seem an independent criterion of moral sincerity – the only one, I imagine, which is likely to be thought capable of carrying the weight of the concept by itself. This is the criterion of appropriate action. That consistent or appropriate action is the criterion of moral sincerity is an idea that has been constantly stressed in recent discussion. The point I want to make is that the *appropriate action* which is demanded by this conception of moral sincerity is itself something which, often, is not independent of the emotional elements in a man's moral outlook.

It is an essential feature of the action-criterion as it has figured in the discussion of moral sincerity that reference is made to a *class* of appropriate actions; what provides the backing for the sincerity of a particular moral judgement or decision is a disposition on the part of the agent to do a certain type of action in certain types of circumstances. This requirement of generality is imposed for at least three reasons. First, it is only a small class of moral utterances that directly indicate a particular action, performance or non-performance of which by the utterer could constitute a test of his sincerity; those utterances expressing a moral decision in favour of some particular future action by the agent himself (e.g. 'I ought to give back the money'). By contrast with these, judgements about the past, other people's actions, etc., do not point to any relevant particular action on the agent's part; here appeal moves to his disposition to do or refrain from actions similar to those that he is commenting on. Second, it is held that even the cases where some particular action by the speaker is in view call for a general disposition to do things of that sort, if his comment or decision is to count as a moral one: this in virtue of the universalizability requirement on moral judgements. Third, the relevance of a general disposition to the question of attributions of sincerity is also supported by a more general doctrine in the philosophy of mind, that the truth-conditions of the claim that a man was sincere in what he said on a particular occasion are not in general to be found in features of that particular occasion (for instance, in some internal psychological state of the man on that occasion), but to be found rather in some broader pattern into which this occasion fits; this can, though it does not have to, take the form of a general disposition to action of a certain sort. All these considerations need considerable qualification; I shall not try to discuss that here. I shall assume that a general disposition to do actions *of a certain type* is of at least some relevance to the question of a man's sincerity in making a particular moral judgement. The question that concerns us is rather: how is the relevant type of actions determined? What holds together the class of actions?

My suggestion is that, in some cases, the relevant unity in a man's behaviour, the pattern into which his judgements and actions together fit, must be understood in terms of an emotional structure underlying them, and that understanding of this kind may be essential. Thus we may understand a man's particular moral remark as being, if sincere, an expression of compassion. This may then be seen as part of a general current in his behaviour which, taken together, reveals his quality of being a compassionate man; and it may be that it is only in the light of seeing him as a compassionate man that *those* actions, judgements, even gestures, will be naturally taken together at all. It is understanding this set of things as expressions of a certain emotional structure of behaviour that constitutes our understanding them as a set.

A special, but very central, case of this sort of understanding is that which concerns the emotions of remorse or guilt. The relevance of this emotion to moral sincerity is, one would have supposed, fairly obvious; the comparative neglect of this basic moral phenomenon in recent work may be partly explained as a liberal and Utilitarian reaction against the destructive emphasis placed upon it in the more sadistic styles of education. Those uncreative aspects of guilt that motivate the Utilitarian moral objection may indeed at the same time encourage philosophical scepticism about the relevance of the emotion; unproductive self-punishment may be seen as precisely *not* an expression of those principles that ought to have issued in action, but rather as a misdirected substitute for action. In these reactions there may be much that is true. But they neglect the possibly creative aspects of guilt, and overlook that distinction which presents itself in Kleinian psychoanalytical work as that between persecutory and reparative guilt. That is to say, he who thinks he has done wrong may not just torment himself, he may seek to put things together again. In this rather evident possibility, we not only have in general a connection between the emotions and the moral life, we also have something that illustrates the point I have been trying to make about the interpretation of a set of actions in terms of an emotional structure. For it is highly probable that the very diverse things that such a man will go on to do and say can be interpreted as one pattern of behaviour only because we understand that the man feels that he has to take reparative action, because we see these activities of his as in various ways expressions of his feeling bad about what he has done or failed to do in the past.

I am suggesting, then, that reference to a man's emotions has a significance for our understanding of his moral sincerity, not as a substitute for, or just an addition to, the considerations drawn from how he acts, but as, on occasion, underlying our understanding of how he acts. But now it may be objected that no such reference to his emotions can ever be essential for the interpretation of his action. For his actions will be relevant to our understanding of his moral outlook and disposition not if they are merely any actions produced by compassion or remorse, but only if they are appropriately done in situations that provide *grounds* for acting in a compassionate manner, or – in the other case – are actions the *reason* for doing which is that they constitute reparative conduct. It is in the light of these grounds and reasons that his conduct is to be viewed; and this makes no essential reference to his emotions. The short answer to this objection is that what is relevant for our understanding of his moral disposition is not whether there are (in our view) grounds or reasons for action of that sort, but whether he takes there to be; whether he sees the situation in a certain light. And there is no reason to suppose that we can necessarily understand him as seeing it in that light without reference to the emotional structure of his thought and action. But this is a very short answer. A more adequate response to the issues presented here can come, I think, only from a more direct confrontation with the nature of the emotions than I have attempted so far.

In what I have said so far I have moved gradually from talking about the sincerity of particular moral judgements to more general considerations about the interpretation of a man's pattern of moral activity. I have progressively tended to discuss the emotions as motives, as states expressed in action; at the same time, I have continued to concentrate on the external point of view, that is to say, on an observer's assessment or understanding of another man's actions and judgements. For the rest of what I have to say, I shall turn the subject round in two dimensions: stop talking about assessments of moral agency and talk rather about moral agency; stop talking about the emotions merely as

motives and admit their other aspect, that under which they un-
doubtedly must be regarded as things that happen to us, to which we
are subject, with respect to which we are passive.

That the emotions must be regarded both as productive of action,
and also as states to which we are subject, is an important point, which
has been stressed by a number of writers.[1] Even in their latter aspect,
of course, they are not, as the same writers have pointed out, blank
occurrences like certain kinds of bodily sensation; for they have in-
built – usually, if not inevitably – a reference to an object, and may be
said to involve a thought. This helps to explain – or, perhaps, it would
be fairer to say, it shows the place at which one would start to explain –
how it is that a sane man can, on occasion, control his emotions, and
how they can be appropriately directed. Some reports that the cruder
moralists have brought back from the weary battleground of Reason
and the Emotions seem to suggest that the only known ways of a
man's keeping his emotions under control is either to deny them
expression when the occasion is not appropriate – here the disciplinary
activities of the Will are very important – or else, as a longer-term
investment, train himself to have less of them, or to have only those of
the more amiable kind. But these pieces of tactical and strategic advice
seem to omit the most obvious influence of rational thought or advice
on the emotions: that of convincing one that a given object is no proper
or appropriate object of that emotion. As the phenomenologists have
constantly stressed, to feel a certain emotion towards a given object
is to see it in a certain light; it may be wrong, incorrect, inappropriate
to see it in that light, and I may become convinced of this. When I am
convinced, the emotion may go away; and it is wrong to forget the
numbers of cases in which it *does* just go away or turn into something
quite different, as when my fear of the impending car journey evapor-
ates on learning that Miss X is not in fact going to be the driver; or my
reserve and suspicion towards this man dissolve when something
shows that his manner does not mean what it appeared to mean; or
my passionate loyalty to the partisan leader suddenly cracks when I am
convinced that his actions can only mean betrayal.

Of course, it may be that no thoughts about the object shift the
emotion; because they fail to convince (which, notoriously enough,

[1] See, for instance, R. S. Peters, 'Emotions and the category of passivity', *Proceedings
of the Aristotelian Society* (1961–2), pp. 116–34; and A. Kenny, *Action, Emotion and Will*
(London, 1963), ch. 3.

may be a function of the emotion itself) or because, although they in a way convince, the emotional structure persists. The phenomenology, psychology and indeed the logic, of such situations is highly complex and various. But the important point now is this: that when considerations which show the emotion to be inappropriate fail to displace it, this is not because it is an emotion but because it is an irrational emotion.

The notions of appropriateness, correctness and so forth in the object of course cry out for examination; and they wear on their front the fact that they are in some part evaluative. What should be feared or hoped for, and so forth, is obviously, to some extent, a matter in which disagreements of value between societies and individuals come out. Equally this is a central matter of moral education. If such education does not revolve round such issues as what to fear, what to be angry about, what – if anything – to despise, where to draw the line between kindness and a stupid sentimentality – I do not know what it is. The phrase 'inculcation of principles' is often used in connection with moral education. There are indeed areas in which the 'inculcation of principles' is an appropriate phrase for the business of moral education: truth-telling, for example, and the sphere of justice. But more broadly, as Aristotle perceived, we are concerned with something not so aptly called the inculcation of principles, but rather the education of the emotions.

In this, there also lies something important for the question of fact and value. For while, as I have said, in the notion of an appropriate object of an emotion and in the less central issue of what emotions one should feel at all, there is obviously a valuational element that can differ from society to society, there are natural and indeed logical limits to the range of what objects given emotions can take, and what emotions a human being is expected to feel or, alternatively, to dispense with. Reflection on these limits evidently could not in itself decide the merits of any existing system of human values as against another; for any existing system must exist within these limits. But it opens one way to something which many who feel the force of some distinction between fact and value have nevertheless thought should not and cannot be destroyed by the pressure of that distinction: the possibility of thinking through a moral outlook and reaching its presuppositions, in terms other than those merely of the logical consistency of its principles. It is the points of intersection between the more purely evaluational elements in a moral outlook, and an associated view of human nature, that provide most fruitfully both the sources of under-standing, and the focus of criticism. Such a point of intersection will be found quite crucially in the moral significance of the emotions.

It is time, finally, to face up to Kant. For, if one is going to suggest that those things that a man does as the expression of certain emotions, can contribute to our view of him as a moral agent; if, further, one is going to say (as I have perhaps not yet said explicitly, but am very happy to) that one's conception of an admirable human being implies that he should be disposed to certain kinds of emotional response, and not to others; one has to try to answer the very powerful claim of Kant that this is impossible. Nor is this just a claim that turns up in some books sent out from Koenigsberg a long time ago; unless one has been very unusually brought up, it is a claim to be felt in oneself. It is a claim deep enough to make what I can hope to say now very inade-quate; but I shall make one or two rather brisk suggestions that may help.

The Kantian objections to the idea that any emotionally governed action by a man can contribute to our assessment of him as a moral agent – or be a contribution, as Kant put it, to his moral worth – are, I think, basically three: that the emotions are too capricious; that they are passively experienced; that a man's proneness to experience them or not is the product of natural causation and (in that sense) fortuitously distributed.

First, they are too capricious. I may feel benevolent towards this man, not towards that, for all sorts of causes or reasons, some lying in my own changing moods. To act in accordance with these promptings is to act irrationally and (possibly) unjustly; but moral action is con-sistent action, done on principle. This is partly true; but in so far as it is, it tells only against the view that emotional motivation has every-thing to do with moral worth, not against the view that it has some-thing to do with it. But in any case the point is partly wrong. For, first, it posits a crude view of the emotions themselves; it suggests that there is no way of adjusting one's emotional response in the light of other considerations, of applying some sense of proportion, without aban-doning emotional motivation altogether; and this is certainly false, as can be seen from any sane man's attempts to distance and comprehend his emotions in matters which are not directly of moral concern, but are of emotional concern, to him. Moreover, I think – in a contrary

direction now – that there is a certain moral woodenness or even in-
solence in this blank regard for consistency, in any case. It smacks of
what I believe Maynard Keynes used to call, with reference to the
deliberations of academic bodies, the Principle of Equal Unfairness:
that if you can't do a good turn to everybody in a certain situation,
you shouldn't do it to anybody. There are indeed human activities
and relations in which impartiality and consistency are very much the
point. But to raise on these notions a model of all moral relations is, just
as Kant said it was, to make us each into a Supreme Legislator; a fan-
tasy which represents, not the moral ideal, but the deification of man.

Next, the emotions are passively experienced; they happen to us.
But moral worth can attach only to what we freely do, to those respects in which we are rationally active. Here there is everything to be
said; and I shall not try to take up the most immediate points, that
emotionally motivated action can itself be free, if any is, and – against
Kant himself – that his account leaves it largely unclear how bad action
can be morally assessed. I shall make just two suggestions. The first is
that we should not dismiss too hastily the idea that some element of
passivity, some sense in which moral impulses prompt us, and courses
of action are impressed on us, may itself make a vital contribution to the
notion of moral sincerity. There are, after all, some points of resemblance between moral and factual convictions; and I suspect it to be
true of moral, as it certainly is of factual, convictions that we cannot
take very seriously a profession of them if we are given to understand
that the speaker has just *decided* to adopt them. The idea that people
decide to adopt their moral principles seems to me a myth, a psychological shadow thrown by a logical distinction; and if someone did
claim to have done this, I think one would be justified in doubting
either the truth of what he said or the reality of those moral principles.
We see a man's genuine convictions as coming from somewhere deeper
in him than that; and, by what is only an apparent paradox, what we see
as coming from deeper in him, he – that is, the deciding 'he' – may see
as coming from outside him. So it is with the emotions.

My second suggestion here is, once more, a moral thought, and a
banal one: is it certain that one who receives good treatment from
another more appreciates it, thinks the better of the giver, if he knows
it to be the result of the application of principle, rather than the product of an emotional response? He may have needed, not the benefits of
universal law, but some human gesture. It may be said that this is

obviously true enough in many cases, but it has nothing to do with morality; it just shows that people place other sorts of value on human conduct besides moral value. Well, this may be said, and Kant indeed said it, but it leads to an uncomfortable dilemma. Either the recipient *ought* to prefer the ministrations of the moral man to the human gesture, which seems a mildly insane requirement; or, alternatively, if it be admitted that it is perfectly proper and rational of the recipient to have the preference he has, the value of moral men becomes an open question, and we can reasonably entertain the proposal that we should not seek to produce moral men, or very many of them, but rather those, whatever their inconsistencies, who make the human gesture. While there might be something in that conclusion, I feel fairly sure that this very restrictive, typological use of the word 'moral' is not the best use to make of it.

Lastly, Kant urges that men differ very much in their emotional make-up, as a result of many natural factors. As he remarks in a famous and moving passage, some find that the human gesture comes naturally, some do not. To make moral worth, the supreme value achievable by human beings, dependent on such features of character, psychologically determined as they are, would be to make the capacity for moral worth a species of natural advantage; and this is both logically incompatible with the notion of *the moral*, and also in some ultimate sense hideously unfair.

Here it is essential to keep in mind at once two facts about Kant. One is that his work contains the working out to the very end of that thought, a thought which in less thoroughgoing forms marks the greatest difference between moral ideas influenced by Christianity, and those of the ancient world. It is this thought, that moral worth must be separated from any natural advantage whatsoever, which, consistently pursued by Kant, leads to the conclusion that the source of moral thought and action must be located outside the empirically conditioned self. The second fact to be remembered, at the same time, is that Kant's work is in this respect a shattering failure, and the transcendental psychology to which it leads is, where not unintelligible, certainly false. No human characteristic which is relevant to degrees of moral esteem can escape being an empirical characteristic, subject to empirical conditions, psychological history and individual variation, whether it be sensitivity, persistence, imaginativeness, intelligence, good sense; or sympathetic feeling; or strength of will.

Certainly there are very important distinctions between straight-forwardly natural advantages, with the sorts of admiration, love and esteem that apply to these, and those characteristics that elicit some more specifically moral reaction. But one cannot attribute to these distinctions that quite ultimate significance which they may have seemed to possess before one grasped the force of Kant's total, if unintended, *reductio ad absurdum*. In the light of that, we can still do much for these distinctions, but we have to do it in a different way, asking, for in-stance, what the point or significance of moral admiration may be – not just the social significance, but the significance in one's own thought.

Asking that, one may well find reason for thinking that no very adequate conception of moral admiration and its objects will be found in stressing, for instance, characteristics specially associated with monied or academic persons. One might say, reworking in more empirical form Kant's Rousseauesque moral republic, that some more democratic conception should be preferred; and among the relevant sorts of characteristic, the capacity for creative emotional response has the advantage of being, if not equally, at least broadly, distributed.

2 Attitudes, Beliefs and Reasons[1]
Roger Scruton

1 What is the nature of a moral belief? I shall compare two answers to this question, and I shall call these answers, not without precedent, 'emotivism' and 'naturalism'.

According to naturalism, moral beliefs are beliefs. To judge something to be good is to believe that it possesses certain 'natural' features. These features are often said to be relational: a thing has moral value if it relates in some specified way to a human want, need, harm or benefit.

According to emotivism, on the other hand, moral beliefs are attitudes. To judge something to be morally good is to have or take up a certain attitude towards it.

It follows that for naturalism moral reasons are reasons for believing and therefore include truth-conditions. For emotivism they are 'justifying reasons', advanced in support of some attitude or feeling.

I will try to show that Moore's argument against naturalism can be put to use,[2] and that emotivism, although buried for many years beneath abandoned notions in philosophical psychology and the theory of meaning, can be restored to its former plausibility. For emotivism can predict, on the basis of its analysis of moral belief, the actual structure of moral language, whereas naturalism – while superficially more promising – fails to do so.

PART I EMOTIONS, ATTITUDES AND BELIEFS

2 What is an attitude? This question has been strangely neglected in the past both by emotivists and their opponents.

[1] All of the following have made useful criticisms of previous versions of this paper, and I am grateful to them for numerous suggestions: Dr J. E. J. Altham, Mr I. McFetridge, Dr M. K. Tanner, Professor Bernard Williams, Dr S. W. Blackburn and Dr M. J. Budd. I am especially indebted to Dr John Casey, without whose detailed suggestions and criticisms it would have been impossible for me to develop my argument in anything like its present form.

[2] *Principia Ethica* (Cambridge, 1903), ch. 1.

C

In the sense in which there is a contrast between them, attitudes and beliefs are both mental states. For my purposes it is not necessary to draw any distinction between dispositional and categorical states; an analysis of beliefs and attitudes in terms of dispositions will not contradict the view that they are mental states. A feature of both beliefs and attitudes is that they can be *arrived at*, and likewise *given up*. This distinguishes them from traits of character, which can be altered only exceptionally. In general, a man is in a position to give up some of his mental states but not others, and there is no clear division between the two kinds of states.

Attitudes involve objects. Hence a question as to someone's attitude must always take the form 'What is X's attitude to Y?' This question may be answered by citing any one of the following: X's beliefs about Y; his feelings or emotions, the object of which is Y; his wishes, desires, hopes and intentions in respect of Y; any reaction such as irritation which Y might inspire in him; and finally his attitudes to Y. As examples of some of these, consider the following answers to the question, 'What is John's attitude to the Jews?'

(1) He believes them to be shrewd and mercenary (belief).

(2) He feels guilty about their sufferings (feelings, emotions).

(3) He wishes to destroy them, and certainly intends to do all he can to harm them (desires, wishes, intentions).

(4) He is fascinated by them, and drawn towards them (passion,[1] interest).

(5) He despises and disapproves of them (attitudes).

If it is appropriate to refer to so many different mental states in answer to the original question, then either the term 'attitude' covers them all, or else they can each form *part* of an attitude. The first view seems implausible; it is only in limited circumstances that beliefs, desires and so on can be mentioned in reply to the question, 'What is X's attitude to Y?' Answers in terms of these mental states require a context; we wish to know *how* any given belief or desire defines an attitude. Such states must therefore be related to attitudes as parts to the whole. How is this possible? I propose the following two conditions, each necessary, together sufficient for a state's being an attitude:

(*a*) Attitudes are expressed in directed behaviour; that is, be-

---

[1] What I mean by the term 'passion' will become clearer in Section 4.

haviour of a consistent kind directed towards some object or class of objects.

(*b*) Attitudes are answerable to rational considerations. Not only might they be justified or unjustified, but a man must be in a position to abandon them purely on account of a change in his beliefs. Attitudes are *founded* on belief, and a man can give up any attitude to the extent that he can give up the beliefs on which it is founded (he may, of course, find it impossible to do this: he may be compelled to believe against all the evidence that his wife is chaste and honourable). To give up an attitude in the sense required, it is not sufficient that a man should be *caused* by a change of belief eventually to abandon it, or to set himself to abandon it. For beliefs can influence *any* mental state, from traits of character to sensations, in this manner (for example a man may set himself to be more intelligent and mature, on the basis of the belief that these qualities are lacking in himself; or a Buddhist may set himself to ignore his bodily sensations, on the basis of a belief about the relation between soul and body, and as a result he may cease to feel pain where once he did feel it). It must be possible, therefore, to identify beliefs such that, were the subject to abandon them, then there would be no *question* of his abandoning the attitude as well.[1]

These two conditions – (*a*) and (*b*) – exclude the following mental states: noticing, attending, perceiving, etc.; sensations, mental images and 'mere reactions' (such as being startled, or sent into an involuntary tremor). Behaviour characteristic of sensations is not, as a rule,

[1] There is a use of the term 'attitude' in which it denotes a purely behavioural concept, and with this we are not concerned. The logical relation between this use and the one we are discussing is clear; it refers to directed behaviour alone, provided this behaviour be *characteristic* of a mental state. It is in this sense that we speak of aggressive, friendly, attentive and hostile attitudes. We could attribute such attitudes to someone without wishing to say anything definite about his mental state (though certain things we might have said about his mental state will be excluded by our making a judgement of his behavioural attitude). There is also a technical use of the term, as in the expression 'propositional attitude', where only the *second* condition is relevant: the condition of rationality.

It might also be pointed out that, to some extent, my definition of 'attitude' is stipulative. For example, given the right kind of object, condition (*a*) tends to collapse into condition (*b*) – if I ask for someone's attitude to, say, an abstract problem, then a sufficient answer would be the specification of a belief. It should be clear from the above that the kind of attitudes we have to deal with do not have objects for which this collapse of the two conditions occurs.

directed, nor are sensations founded on beliefs in the manner described. Mental images and mere reactions fail to answer to the first condition – they are not directed on to objects in the world. If they are related to the world it is as 'mere response' to a stimulus. They are not responses in the way anger is a response to an insult, or pride a response to the success of a favourite child.[1] Attitudes are responses in this latter sense – in other words they are responses which involve understanding (or misunderstanding) of their objects. 'Understanding' is a *consequence* of the satisfaction of (*a*) and (*b*).

Noticing, perceiving, and so on, may be essential to having an attitude; if I were never able to notice or perceive a Negro, I would find it very difficult to find any direct expression of my attitude to Negroes. However, these states are not correctly described as entering the attitude itself: although they have objects, there is no directed behaviour characteristic of them. And they are certainly not answerable to belief in the way required. On both these counts *seeing* is to be sharply distinguished from one notion of *seeing as*: the criteria for whether someone sees an object under an aspect may bear a marked resemblance to the criteria for saying that he has an attitude to it. There are some uses of the expression 'seeing X as a Y' in which it applies to precisely the kind of 'understanding' of X which is involved in an attitude. The notion of 'seeing under an aspect' cannot be limited to purely perceptual judgements; it applies equally to responses of an emotional kind. Failure to observe this vagueness in the notion of 'seeing as' has been in part responsible for the idea that there is a moral (or, for that matter, aesthetic) sense.

We can now explain why so many different mental states can be cited in answer to our original question. An emotion can be included in an attitude, for emotions are both expressed in directed behaviour and answerable (except in certain special cases) to a changed belief. Often emotions do not occur singly, but in groups, in such a way as to sustain each other. It is in this form that they best satisfy the two conditions we have given. Consequently an answer to the question, 'What is X's attitude to Y?', in terms of one emotion only is seldom adequate; for the question concerns X's overall attitude and it is unlikely that this can be explained in terms of some simple feeling. This becomes clearer as we turn our attention to beliefs.

[1] See G. E. M. Anscombe, *Intention* (Oxford, Blackwell, 1957), section 15.

Many of the criteria for believing are behavioural. Beliefs of a general kind can therefore occur so that their expression consists of behaviour answering to condition (*a*) (beliefs inevitably accord with condition (*b*)). For example, a typical manifestation of the belief that Jews are shrewd and mercenary might be suspicion, reluctance to engage in financial dealings, a desire to avoid being under any obligation and so on. Together these might amount to a consistent and durable pattern of behaviour directed in the appropriate way towards Jews. But it is misleading to say without qualification that beliefs are attitudes. The same belief *could* be manifested in totally different actions. One has not given an answer to the question, 'What is John's attitude to the Jews', by citing these beliefs of his, except in so far as it is taken for granted that the normal way in which human beings manifest such beliefs is in behaviour of a certain kind. Hence, although it sometimes looks as if a complete answer can be given to this question in terms of beliefs, this is largely because what is needed to *give* a complete answer – namely the appropriate behaviour towards some identifiable object – can be inferred from these beliefs, together with a knowledge of human nature.

The case of emotion is not parallel; for while it may often seem implausible to characterize someone's attitude in terms of one emotion, it is not out of the question that a complex emotional state *can* be cited as a complete answer. Thus, 'He hates them' seems inadequate, whereas 'He hates, envies and resents them' does not. A set of beliefs, on the other hand, no matter how complex, can only inform us of someone's attitude in the context of some expectation as to how he will behave.

It cannot be denied that beliefs enter into attitudes in an important way. The behaviour we have just described as characteristic of John's belief that Jews are shrewd and mercenary could not occur without the belief. None the less it is behaviour which goes beyond the belief in important ways. Intentions are similar, in this respect, to beliefs. They answer to condition (*b*): for example, a man must believe that success is not out of the question before he can intend to embark on any project. Intentions presuppose belief and can be taken up and abandoned purely on the basis of a changed belief. But if intentions answer to condition (*a*) this is because they can be taken as the *sign* of an attitude. If I intend to destroy the Jews, then it is to be supposed that I hate them beyond measure. Thus we can imagine mental states which *are* attitudes and which include intentions. The behaviour characteristic of such states also gives criteria for the presence of intentions. Thus the case is exactly parallel to that of belief. Generalizing, we may say that just as, in the example above, John could not be said to behave in the way described *without* having the appropriate belief, so might some attitudes both go beyond desires, wishes and intentions, and equally include sufficient criteria for the ascription of those desires, wishes and intentions.

We have accounted for the answers to our question which cite beliefs, intentions, desires, wishes (and presumably hopes), without conceding that any of these states can be attitudes in themselves. What we have shown, however, is that they might each enter in an important way into those states which *are* correctly described as attitudes. Emotions, passions and attitudes, on the other hand, *do* satisfy the two conditions of directed behaviour and rationality. Why is it, then, that only such states as approval and contempt are generally *called* attitudes?

The answer to this question will become clearer in following sections. Briefly, although emotions and passions can satisfy condition (*a*), they are less rational than approval. They are, as Spinoza said, more 'passive'.[1] There is a difference merely of degree between the three kinds of state: desires, wishes, intentions and beliefs enter into them all in varying degrees. Attitudes are states in which the elements of belief and intention can be most clearly distinguished; in emotions desires and wishes tend to exist in the context of relatively few beliefs and of perhaps no definite intentions.

These four elements do not exhaust the content of emotions and attitudes; it would be impossible to subtract them without remainder from the states of which they form a part. However, I wish to concentrate for the moment on the element of belief. What remains to an emotion or attitude when the belief has been 'subtracted' I will call its 'reactive content', and will use this phrase to cover not only tremors, blushes and inner turmoil, but also the desires, wishes and intentions (again without their characteristic beliefs) which might surround and provide a context for these passive symptoms.

The three kinds of state we are considering might be arranged in an ascending hierarchy, according to the degree of belief contained in

[1] See S. N. Hampshire, *The Freedom of the Individual* (London, 1965), pp. 78 ff.; I owe much, in the following, to Hampshire's account of the distinction between active and passive mental states.

them. Belief itself could then be added to this hierarchy as a kind of fourth state to which they are asymptotically related:

(*a*) Passions, such as the characteristic forms of irritation, rage and desire.

(*b*) Emotions, such as the characteristic forms of sadness (where sadness has an object), jealousy and pride.

(*c*) Attitudes, such as approval and contempt.

(*d*) Beliefs, about a particular thing or type of thing.

Although the element of belief in an attitude can vary, it does not follow that some attitudes are merely beliefs. On the contrary, unless condition (*a*) is satisfied (and belief alone is never sufficient to ensure that it will be), then a mental state could not be called an attitude. This first condition is vital. Our primary interest in asking for a statement of someone's attitude is in his directed behaviour. Often we want to know simply whether he is *for* or *against* something (in a context where 'Why?' questions are appropriate – that is, where condition (*b*) is satisfied). This is brought out by examining a special case of the use of the term 'attitude' to refer to a mental state. This is the sense in which X has an attitude to Y as a Z. The term Z serves then to specify some end *in virtue of which* X might be for or against Y. Z serves both to limit the considerations which X could give as a reason for his behaviour, and to isolate from the totality of X's behaviour towards Y some coherent and directed subsection. For example: 'What is John's attitude to James as chief clerk?'; or 'What is John's attitude to James as an applicant for the job?' The answer might be: 'He is against him on grounds of laziness'. This example serves to bring out another important point: that one can have an *overall* attitude to an object, the components of which are further attitudes directed towards certain features or states of the object.

3 Emotions, attitudes and similar mental states are often said to include beliefs.[1] Hobbes, for example, defines fear as 'aversion, with opinion of hurt from the object',[2] and it is a common view that the belief that

---

[1] See, for example, E. Bedford, *Proceedings of the Aristotelian Society* (1956–7), and also Philippa Foot, 'Moral beliefs', *Proceedings of the Aristotelian Society* (1958–9), where the example of pride is discussed.

[2] *Leviathan*, I. 6.

an object is harmful is essential to fear. Likewise, it seems that a man cannot be *proud* of something without certain beliefs about it; he should believe, for example, that the object of his pride is connected in some manner with himself. Those beliefs which are logically involved in a mental state are always about its object. They are also beliefs of a wide nature; this is to be expected, since our normal way of grouping mental states into kinds (under such concepts as fear, pride, love, aversion and wanting) leaves room for many fine distinctions between states classified together. To characterize a state as fear is only to *begin* a full description of it, and states in other ways completely different may also be classed as fear. So that, if there is a belief in common to all cases of fear, it cannot be very specific – indeed, it may be so general as to take a disjunctive form. This is perhaps the case for fear: rather than saying that fear involves the opinion of hurt from an object, we should perhaps say that it involves the opinion of hurt or disagreeableness (for example). For many states this disjunctive belief is the only one possible to formulate.

I propose to refer to this element of belief included in a mental state as its intentionality. My use of this word will depart from recent practice, although there will be a connection sufficient to justify borrowing the term. For Brentano and his followers, intentionality consists in, or derives from, the fact that all mental states are *directed* in some manner on to objects, and hence involve thoughts relating to those objects. However, there is a distinction between the thought *of* something, and the thought *that* something. If there is a sense in which mental states are essentially directed, then they will all involve the thought *of* an object. We might analyse the notion of 'thinking of' in terms of *entertaining* some proposition about the object; in which case we will have arrived at a conclusion congenial to the followers of Brentano, namely that a proposition (or 'intentional object') is involved in every mental state.

But it is by no means clear that all mental states – even if there is some sense in which they are all directed – involve the thought *that* something is the case. The paradigm of 'thinking that' is believing – a propositional attitude distinct from entertaining. And there seems to be a division among mental states between those which involve an element of belief (such as emotions and attitudes) and those (such as sensations and mental images) which do not.

One of the difficulties which arise in discussing Brentano's notion of intentionality lies in the concept of 'directedness'. It is unclear what is meant by saying that all mental states are essentially directed. I have referred to attitudes and emotions as expressed in 'directed behaviour'. By this I understand a consistent *activity*. The behaviour centres on an object which, as a result, is distinguished from any other objects which the behaviour might encounter. The behaviour also fulfils a certain pattern, and it is this pattern which allows us to speak of it as consistent.[1] A given thing is an object, therefore, purely on account of the importance which some directed activity accords to it. Perhaps, then, this is what is meant by the theory that mental states are directed; that mental states satisfy the first of our two conditions for being an attitude. But, if we accept this account, then we must deny that 'directedness' is a property of all mental states: for sensations and mental images are not directed.

If we *do* take the notion of 'directedness' in such a way, however, then we find that there is a close connection between directedness and intentionality. Directed states seem to include the thought that something is true of their object. In other words, states which answer to our first condition will, through that very fact, answer to the second. Perhaps, then, the two conditions are not logically independent.

This hypothesis is supported by the following consideration. A mental state, so long as it is directed, can include beliefs about its object *whatever* the nature of its object and *whatever* the relation between the object and the state. This seems to suggest that the presence of a belief about some identifiable thing might be part of what it is for a state to have an object. Consider the following:

(1) An object might be a thing (as when I fear a certain dog). Or it might be a state of affairs (as when I want there to be more respect paid to the elderly). Or it might be both (as when I fear a certain dog in fearing that it will jump on me).

(2) The object of a mental state might be the sort of thing that could cause it, as when it is an *event* which precedes the state by some fraction of time (an example would be the man who is surprised at the sudden appearance of a face in the window: the event

---

[1] There are limiting cases where there is no consistent activity properly speaking, but only a *tendency* towards such activity – as when I feel sudden anger at someone but, seeing his helpless submission, immediately cease to feel angry. Also: pangs of grief, even momentary contempt or disapproval.

which causes his surprise is also the object of his surprise). On the other hand, the object might be removed from the state in such a way as to make the hypothesis of a causal relation improbable or even impossible. The object might lie in the distant past (as when I am enraged at the Nazi atrocities), or in the future (as when I feel trepidation at tomorrow's meeting with X). This does not rule out the possibility of an analysis of the relation between an emotion and its object in terms of a causal relation between the emotion and the *thought* of its object. But it does suggest that an analysis in terms of a causal relation between the emotion and the object *itself* must be fallacious. For the cause of any state must be an event or process; it cannot be a particular thing; and it must precede the state by some interval of time. But the object of a mental state can be a particular thing; and it is not necessary that it should bear any one temporal relation to the state.

(3) An object might be related to the state as a possible satis-faction of it – as when I want a glass of wine. Here my obtaining the glass of wine will – it is thought – put an end to my state of wanting; if it does not put an end to it, then this *could* be held to show that I did not, after all, want a glass of wine, or that I did not want *only* a glass of wine. Normally, however, it would not show this, since it seems to be a conceptual truth that I know immediately the ob-ject of my desire, and to introduce the possibility that I might be in error is to introduce an extension of the concept of 'wanting'.[1] Or again an object might be related to the state as its 'origin' – as when I fear or am repelled by something. Here the disappearance of the object will lead, it is thought, to the disappearance of the state. If I am afraid of tomorrow's meeting with X then I must believe that, were I to discover that there will be no such meeting, I would cease to be afraid (here what I call the 'origin' of the state cannot be its cause).

Finally, there are states for which the object is typically neither origin nor satisfaction – love, for example. I can love someone without thinking that my love will be quelled by possessing him, or that it would disappear with his ceasing to exist. If we try to identify beliefs which are necessarily connected with states of this kind we encoun-ter great difficulties. Very often the only beliefs that we can suggest

---

[1] See Wittgenstein, *Blue Book* (Oxford, Blackwell, 1958), pp. 21–2.

take a complex disjunctive form. For example, that I love someone seems to entail that I believe him to possess some one of a list of qualities only one of which *need* characterize the object of my love. In the case of states such as love whose object is neither origin nor satisfaction, there is no easily identifiable belief involved in the state.

Now, although these distinctions are of the first importance, none of them seems to affect this fundamental truth: that if a belief is included in a mental state then this belief concerns its object. If I fear a dog, then it is the *dog* that I believe to be harmful. If I want a glass of wine, then it is the glass of wine which I believe to be agreeable or beneficial. And if I am proud of my son, it is my son whom I believe to cast some credit on me. This certainly seems to suggest that there is a close connection between intentionality (in the sense of belief) and the *directing* of a mental state. In the next section I will discuss how this is so.

In talking of the intentionality of an emotion I am referring to any belief which might be *logically* connected with it: that is, any belief which must occur in every instance of the emotion. Much confusion is introduced into philosophical psychology by the arbitrary division of mental states into kinds, and by the deduction of false logical connections from this. For example, a particular case of fear might rest on a complex variety of beliefs. The removal of any one of these beliefs would then remove the subject's feeling. And here we might want to say that all these beliefs are part of his total state. Accordingly, adopting a standard criterion of state-identity, they are logically involved in this state. At the same time, we might want to characterize his total state as one of fear. Why then are these beliefs not essential to his fear?

We must remember that it is possible to identify his state as one of fear without identifying all the separate beliefs on which *this* fear might depend; only the general belief – that some object is harmful, or disagreeable – needs to be identified. But since this belief is present in *every* case of fear, as a matter of logic, then we cannot talk of fear except where there is this belief. If it is useful to refer to *kinds* of mental state, then we must allow that fear is one such kind. No component of an individual state which is not essential to its being classified as fear, can be logically *involved* in fear. But we could always invent or discover some other classification for which this belief *was* essential.

4 I wish to discuss the intentionality of emotions and attitudes in terms of the third person. This will avoid complications about knowledge of one's own mental state. Let us take the case of pride; the term 'pride' has a wide usage, but it is acceptable as the name of an emotion.

A man cannot be proud of something unless he believes that it has some connection with himself. The admirable qualities of the object of his pride must somehow reflect credit on himself. A man can be proud of something which he has made, or in which he participates, or which belongs to him. The relevant belief is therefore of the widest scope. It enables us to see, none the less, why I can easily understand a man who is proud of his own son, and not quite so easily understand a man who is proud of his neighbour's son. A man is not proud of an object simply because he swells his chest, flushes and looks magnificent in its presence. There must be some connection between this behaviour and the object, and the connection must not be extrinsic. The behaviour must be directed; the man must be proud of the object itself (in the case of verbal behaviour, the directedness of an emotion consists in a readiness on the part of the subject to give certain descriptions of the object of his emotion). This directing of an emotion or attitude on to its object will include gestures and utterances which, in so far as they show a man to be making the required connection will *thereby* reveal that he has certain beliefs about the object. The criteria for saying that X's proud behaviour is directed towards Y will *include* criteria for saying that X believes that an appropriate connection exists between himself and Y. We cannot imagine any expression of X's pride in Y which would not also be an expression of X's belief that Y casts credit on himself.

Generalizing, we may say that in any attitude or emotion there is a belief (its intentionality), and a reactive content or reaction based on this belief, where the behaviour characteristic of the reaction is at the same time characteristic of the belief. For the purpose of the present argument we need to separate these two elements.

It will be at once objected that we cannot talk of two elements until we can separately identify them, and that this seems conceptually impossible. The emotion involves a belief simply because the reaction includes criteria for believing; hence it is impossible to identify the reaction without at the same time identifying a belief. Emotions and attitudes seem to be *modes of believing* certain propositions about their objects.

However, emotions are also ways of *taking* what is believed. We speak of emotions as though it were possible to refer to the belief or to the reaction alone. However difficult it may be to describe an emotional reaction without the attendant belief, it is still possible to identify the belief independently of any particular reaction: a man can believe something to be harmful without thereby fearing it. So there is 'something more' to fear than the belief mentioned, and it is this 'something more' which I refer to by the term 'reaction'. A parallel would be the following: nothing can be green without being extended, evidence for saying that something is green is necessarily evidence for saying that it is extended. None the less, we can talk about greenness without *ipso facto* talking of extension, for we can 'abstract' extension from it. An object might equally be extended by being red, brown or colourless, for example. Likewise, we can talk about reactions without referring to beliefs, for the belief can remain constant while the reaction itself varies over an enormous range. Thus the man in a state of panic, and the man who shows a calm resignation at the approach of death, might each share the belief that they confront something truly harmful. We might want to say that the difference between them is one of *vision* – of how they *see* death; but, at least in some cases, such a difference of vision can be analysed entirely in terms of a difference in reaction. The criteria for saying that someone sees death in a certain way might not be anything like criteria for saying that he believes something to be true of it, but instead special cases of criteria for saying that he has a certain reaction to it, founded on some known belief.

It follows from this that attitudes and emotions can be rationally supported in two ways.[1] The beliefs included in them might be shown to be true; and the reaction accompanying those beliefs might be justified according to canons of practical reasoning. For an example of the latter, consider what I might say in trying to convince someone that it is wrong to be so afraid, or even to be afraid at all, in an admittedly dangerous situation, since the danger is slight, or there is nothing to lose, or everything depends on not being afraid.

The amount, and even the quality, of a given reaction might vary within definite limits without it being wrong to call the emotion, say, fear. And the reaction may be so slight that the belief becomes the

---

[1] See T. Penelhum, 'Pleasure and falsity', in S. N. Hampshire (Ed.), *The Philosophy of Mind* (New York, 1966), p. 248.

dominant part, and yet we could still talk of fear. By extension, the word 'fear' is often used to refer to beliefs alone, when the proposition believed refers to something harmful, dangerous or disagreeable. For example: 'I fear that he might be seeing that woman again'. In this case, although it is true that there is something I fear, I do not *feel* fear of anything.

Here we have the basis for Hume's distinction between calm and turbulent passions. It might be correct to call a state fear when, on the one hand, it consists almost exclusively in a belief that something is dangerous, or when on the other hand, it contains a panic-stricken response to the danger. Hume himself makes the point that calm passions approximate to beliefs when he says that a calm passion is commonly 'so soft and gentle that we are apt to confound it with an idea'.[1]

The hierarchy of mental states referred to at the end of Section 2 can usefully be compared with Hume's distinction. Those states which would in general be called attitudes tend to be 'calmer' than emotions, and emotions, in their turn, calmer than passions. But it is seldom that any psychological predicate will be used to denote a state whose position in the hierarchy is fixed: pride, like fear and even love, can occur in a variety of calm and turbulent forms.

The extreme end of the scale – what I have called 'passions' – is a rather enigmatic category. In this category occur those states whose relation to an object is so indefinite that they only doubtfully include a belief about it – irritation, anger, hostility, perhaps even love. The objects of these states are typically neither their origin nor their satisfaction. A passion is a mental state inclusive enough to involve no belief that can be easily identified; hence it can serve as a model of a reaction in which no belief is involved at all. It is for this reason that philosophers such as Hobbes, who have tried to give an account of the emotions in terms of certain fundamental and recurring elements, have tended to describe each emotion in terms of one of these passions combined with complex differentia of belief and intention. For Hobbes the 'simple passions' were appetite, desire, love, aversion, hate, joy and grief ('grief' being what we could call, I think, 'depression').

---

[1] Hume, *A Treatise of Human Nature*, quoted by Mary Warnock in 'The justification of emotions', *Proceedings of the Aristotelian Society*, supplementary volume (1967). The connection between Hume's distinction and the degree of rationality of an emotion has already been made in Hampshire, *The Freedom of the Individual*, pp. 84–5.

These feelings are indeed ones for which the element of intentionality remains vague or non-existent.[1]

Among 'primitive passions' are certain states said to be only contingently connected with their objects – rage and depression, for example, are 'object-hungry' emotions and can exist as dispositions in the absence of any specific object. Since I am treating mental states only in terms of their hierarchy with respect to belief, it is irrelevant that these object-hungry states should be classed with love and hostility (which cannot exist without an object). The difference between the two kinds of state would be far more apparent were they to be ordered according to the degree of wanting, wishing or intending that they each include. However, it is worth noting one thing: that depression and rage, which are in my sense 'undirected' (or only contingently so), are also totally lacking in intentionality. Love and hostility, on the other hand, seem to be intentional; there must be *some* belief involved in each, though to give the general disjunctive kind to which this belief belongs will prove no easy matter. Depression and rage should not, then, be included in the scale of attitudes. However, there is an important distinction between them and the states definitely excluded, in that they can *colour* attitudes. They can do this because, being 'object-hungry', they possess a permanent disposition to satisfy our two conditions.

We are now in a position to return to our original topic, for we can present a clear idea of one thing that an emotivist and a naturalist must disagree about. The emotivist is claiming that moral beliefs do not lie at the belief end of the hierarchy but are sufficiently close to

---

[1] For Hobbes, the primitive passions tended to reduce to two only: aversion and appetite. Like many other philosophers he tended to distinguish all attitudes as modes of two fundamental reactions – for and against. This tendency is apparent in Aquinas, in Hume and, of course, in Stevenson and his followers. It is also present in Brentano, in a particularly interesting manner. Brentano speaks of the category of the 'emotions' (that is, mental states which go beyond perception and belief) as given by the two 'intentional relations' of love and hate. For Brentano an attitude to some object consists of three such intentional relations: (1) *Vorstellungen*, or ideas. This has a traditionally empiricist meaning, standing for both sense-impressions and what we would call concepts, propositions, etc. Roughly speaking, a *Vorstellung* is anything that can come before the mind, anything that can be, in some wide sense, *entertained*. (2) Judgement – the recognition or rejection according to the canons of truth and falsity of what is entertained. That is, intentionality in my sense. (3) The emotional reaction built on and including this judgement – some mode of love or hate towards the appropriate object (*The Origin of the Knowledge of Right and Wrong*, translated by Cecil Hague (London, 1902 ed.), pp. 13–15).

emotions to enable us to speak of them as attitudes, containing an element of reaction along with the beliefs which constitute their intentionality. One sure way for the emotivist to make his point is by claiming that moral attitudes contain desires and intentions, along with belief. This, as I hope to show, is the case.

5 It is useful at this point to distinguish a few of the possible ways in which the term 'object' might be used in philosophical psychology. This will provide the vocabulary in which to continue our investigation of attitudes.

(1) Real or 'material' object. The real object is the object towards which a man's emotion or attitude is in fact directed. If John is afraid, and something exists of which he is afraid, and that thing is a goat, then the real object of his fear (*what* he is afraid of) is a goat, whatever he might believe it to be.

(2) Notional object. The notional object is given by the description under which the subject sees the real object of his emotion – it is the real object (which may be nothing) as he believes it to be. Nothing about his beliefs entails that there must *be* a real object, nor, if there is such an object, that it is necessary for it to satisfy the description under which he sees it. The emotion might be founded on error (it is for this reason that philosophers who talk of a logical, or non-contingent, relation between an emotion and its object must be referring to the notional, and not to the real object, although this is not always made clear).[1] For example, John might be afraid of the goat because he believes it to be the devil come to carry him off. The description of the goat which he will be prepared to give here *explains* his fear, since it produces a notional object which is characterized as a special case of the formal object of fear.

(3) Formal object. The formal object of an emotion is a *kind* of thing, given by the description under which the notional object must fall if it is to be the notional object of that emotion. It is defined, in other words, by the intentionality of the emotion. For example, the formal object of fear is whatever is harmful (or disagreeable).

---

[1] In fact, if there is such a 'non-contingent' connection it would be misleading to talk of it as uniting the emotion and the notional *object*. The only plausible way of stating the thesis would be in terms of a 'non-contingent' relation between the emotion and the beliefs which *give* the notional object.

(4) Intentional object. Intentional objects are propositions and hence enter into mental states in so far as these states include beliefs. These 'objects' are the reified forms of the thoughts on which mental states depend. I am not concerned with this kind of object; they are the 'real' objects of propositional attitudes, and not of attitudes in the sense we are considering. The term 'intentional object' has often been used indifferently to cover both propositions and *notional* objects. One reason for this might be that, if there is a notional object of an emotion, then there must be an intentional object exactly corresponding to it. For notional objects are given by beliefs, and for every belief that a man has there is an intentional object which is the proposition believed. Since beliefs give rise to intensional contexts in logic this is probably also one of the most important reasons why philosophers have tried to discover criteria for mental states in terms of the intensionality of the language which refers to them.

We must now make a distinction of the first importance: between those attitudes and emotions which are universal, and those which are not. That is, between those which involve an element of consistency, and those which do not.

Among the former, let us take *despite*. If I despise a man, it must be on account of some quality such that I would despise anyone who was similar in that respect. If I claim to despise Smith I must believe that there is some quality of Smith towards which my emotion is directed (the quality can be characterized so specifically that, as a matter of fact, only Smith does possess it). If I do not believe that there is, or that there must be, such a feature, then either I do not understand what it is to despise someone, or else I am being insincere; unless – as could happen – I have wrongly identified in myself some other state of mind, such as jealousy.

Love, on the other hand, does not seem to be universal. Although I might be regarded as odd in saying that I love Smith when I cannot say what it is about Smith that I love, I could not be accused of linguistic error. It might still be true that I love Smith, and that I know that I love him.

Some mental states, therefore, are directed towards things as particulars, and some are directed towards things as tokens or instantiations of some type or property. We can know that X loves Y without identifying any quality of Y on the basis of which X loves him. There is no

D

need to give any particular description under which the notional object of X's love falls, unless we refer to the one description which *must* be true of it if it is to be the notional object of X's love (the description which identifies the formal object of love). On the other hand we cannot say that X despises Y unless it is possible to refer to some quality of Y towards which X's emotion is directed. The notional object of despite is given by a description in universal terms which might be satisfied by any one of an indefinite number of objects. And it is only a contingent matter that a man should despise something under this description; the description serves, therefore, to isolate some type or property towards which his emotion is in fact directed, unlike the formal object description which identifies the emotion he feels.

We can now see that a mental state is most plausibly called an attitude if it contains some universal element. Mental states directed on to particulars do not in general exhibit the coherence and rationality required for attitudes. Particular states can be, none the less, contingently universal; it is often in this form that they enter into attitudes. For example, I might hate Negroes, and as a result hate Jim, who is a Negro (assuming that hatred, like love, is particular). However, the fact that Jim satisfies this description in universal terms (. . . is a Negro) is not part of my hating him but rather my *reason* for hating him. The mere fact of my having such a reason makes my hatred less like a mere feeling and more like an attitude. Since the connection between the universal description and the hatred is contingent I may not know that I hate Jim *because* I hate all Negroes – I may not know why I hate him. But the chances are that I do know why, and this will force me to impose on my feeling a greater measure of the rationality characteristic of attitudes.

Universal states, on the other hand, are usually called attitudes. Should any thing be the object of such a state, then there is of necessity a reason for its being so; to this extent the requirements of consistency and rationality are bound to be satisfied. Thus most of those states which can be shown to be universal will normally be referred to as attitudes rather than emotions, and will tend to occur only at the upper end of the belief-hierarchy. Guilt and shame are among the few universal states which are habitually referred to as emotions, and this largely because of their prominent reactive content. Most of those states which are normally called emotions – love, hatred, anger, depression – are particular in respect of their objects.

It has already been pointed out, by Pitcher, that moral approval is universal.[1] Pitcher wrongly uses this fact as part of an argument to show that approval and disapproval are not really attitudes at all. But there is no reason why there could not be attitudes (in the sense of mental states involving some element of reaction as well as belief) which are universal. There is no reason why there should not be attitudes the notional object of which is a thing *qua* instance of a kind. And if there are specifically moral attitudes they will, as Pitcher shows, be universal in precisely this way.

6 It has been argued that moral beliefs cannot be attitudes, since attitudes and emotions are often identified by reference to moral beliefs, or at least to value judgements of some kind.[2] But if the belief that something is good enters into the intentionality of a given feeling, does this not suggest that it is really a belief about some matter of fact? Take, for example, pride. To feel pride it is not only necessary that a man should believe himself connected with the object of his pride – he must also believe that it has some value. One cannot be proud of something one believes to be worthless. How is it, then, that evaluation is a matter of taking up an attitude, when it seems often to be a necessary element of the belief on which an attitude is based? The same problem occurs, in an even more acute form, with the moral emotions themselves: how can I feel ashamed of something, or guilty about something, unless I believe it to be wrong?

This objection has been urged against any account of morality in terms of desires, for example. Wanting something seems already to involve seeing it under what Miss Anscombe has called a 'desirability characterization';[3] it involves believing that the object has some property which makes it *desirable*. But 'desirable' is a normative term, and to believe or judge something to be desirable is to assign a value to it.

In short, it is objected that a man can only be said to have a given attitude if he sees the object of that attitude under a certain description. And often this description involves evaluative terms. So how can we

---

[1] G. Pitcher, 'On approval', *Philosophical Review* (April 1958).

[2] This point has been made in one form or another by Pitcher, op. cit.; by A. E. Ewing, *Second Thoughts in Moral Philosophy* (London, 1959), pp. 20–1; and by Hampshire, *The Freedom of the Individual*, pp. 78–9.

[3] G. E. M. Anscombe, *Intention*, section 37.

analyse a moral belief in terms of an attitude when attitudes are normally identified by reference to moral beliefs?

Let us turn our attention for a moment to the 'affective terms' – terms such as 'moving', 'exciting', 'depressing', which are used to characterize some object in terms of a possible response to it. It might be said that if I am moved by something, then I see it as, say, beautiful, or touching, or profound, or of human significance, or, simply, as moving. That is, I see it under some one of a group of descriptions, and my ability to produce one of these descriptions of the object of my feeling is a criterion of my having the feeling itself. Thus my feeling might seem to collapse into the belief that the object is moving, or that it has some property on the basis of which I can correctly judge it to be moving, because of some logical relation between that property and 'movingness'. And, since 'moving' is a normative term, to believe, judge or recognize that a thing is moving (all of which involve the belief that it is moving) is to make an evaluation of it.

Now it cannot be denied that by the use of affective terms we do succeed in talking of emotions entirely as though these were a matter of belief: for every emotion we suppose a 'property' of its object. In which case to have the emotion is simply to find that property in the object. The man who is excited by roundabouts would be said to *find them exciting*. And we constantly say such things as 'he finds it depressing', 'he thinks everything is boring', expressions which are equally characteristic of the language of belief. But this argument can get nowhere without begging the question against emotivism. When it is said that a man who approves of something must bring it under the description 'something good', no point against emotivism has been proved until it is shown that this *is* a genuine description. But that is just what the emotivist is disputing. For he wishes to say that to see something as good (or moving) is a matter of having the required mental attitude (approval, or emotion) towards that thing.[1] Hence he cannot say, as the naturalist *can* say, that the belief that a thing is

[1] I do not wish to overemphasize the similarities either between 'good' and other normative terms, or between the attitude of approval and such responses as 'being moved', 'depressed', etc. One marked difference – a difference reflected in the logic of 'good' and 'moving' – lies in the fact that I cannot approve of something without believing that the object of my approval is appropriate (in a sense to be explained); whereas I can – in certain cases – be moved by something which I do not believe to be genuinely moving. This suggests that the relation between 'being moved by X' and 'finding X moving' is more complicated than I have supposed, although in all probability such cases are secondary.

creditable is as much part of the intentionality of pride as the belief that it is connected with oneself. For his claim is that the criteria for saying that someone believes a thing to be creditable are given at least partly by the *reactive*, and not solely by the intentional, content of the emotion. But the emotivist *can* say that believing a thing to be creditable is just as essential to the concept of pride as believing it to be connected with oneself. Just as an emotion cannot be called pride without the appropriate factual belief, so it cannot be called pride without an appropriate reaction to that belief.

Hence it is no objection to the emotivist that he cannot identify certain attitudes independently of moral beliefs – on the contrary, he is bound by his own theory to acknowledge that this is impossible. There is no circularity, since the emotivist says that to have a moral belief is to have an attitude. To believe something to be good *is* to approve of it.

We can see how the notion of 'seeing under a description' or 'seeing as' serves to obscure this point. For not only does it take for granted that the sentence 'X is good' is used as a *description*. It also puts us in mind of an important fact with which emotivism is not yet equipped to deal: a central expression of the moral attitudes is verbal. This connection with verbal behaviour is a function of the rationality of moral attitudes, and any analysis which overlooks the complexities of their verbal expression must fail. To express such an attitude verbally is to give certain as-it-were descriptions of its object. And the *simplest* way of dealing with these 'descriptions' is to regard the utterance of, for example, 'This is good', as the expression of a belief, and the 'description' 'is good' as property-ascribing.

But that would be a mistake: the giving of these descriptions can equally be taken as the verbal expression of an attitude, and, as we shall see, to defend a moral judgement is to defend an attitude and not a belief.

Thus, Miss Anscombe[1] holds that 'to say "I merely want this" without any (desirability) characterization is to deprive the word of sense'. This is intended to show that we cannot describe a man as *wanting* something, unless we can show that he is willing to bring it under certain descriptions. However, Miss Anscombe does not make clear whether it can be known independently of what a man *said* that

[1] *Intention*, section 37.

he was seeing an object under some 'desirability characterization'. It would seem, prima facie, that we could know this. A man who endlessly groped after some saucer of mud would thereby show, at least to some extent, that he found the saucer of mud desirable. The argument would not show that *we* must know what a man believes about an object before we can decide whether he wants it. It would show rather that *he* must be prepared – if he is really to express his desire in saying 'I want X' – to produce various 'descriptions' of X. So the argument states a condition on when I can sincerely say of myself that I want something, and its connection with the logic of 'He wants X' remains dubious. The reference to desirability characterizations seems to come down to this: if a man is to count as wanting something, and if he is to do this simply on the basis of what he says, then his verbal behaviour must be a criterion of wanting. And it will be such a criterion if he brings the object of his desire under certain 'descriptions' of the kind to which Miss Anscombe refers. As far as the logic of desirability goes, this conclusion is neutral as between emotivism and naturalism.

When it is said that to find something moving, interesting and so on, involves seeing it under a description, we should make clear in what sense we are using the term 'description'. To see something under a description may be simply to have an attitude towards it. 'Seeing as', which tends to be assimilated to perception, recognition and hence belief, is in fact a wide notion on the basis of which it is impossible to make the needed distinction between belief and attitude. It refers to any *way of taking* an object – I see an object *as* what it means to me. And what it means to me is not to be given in terms of beliefs alone; my vision of an object is a complicated mixture of reaction and belief. The central criterion for seeing something under a description, in these cases where it is said that one *must* see it under a description in order to have the required 'belief', refers to some reaction or to some specific pattern of behaviour.

7 I will refer to the moral attitudes as 'moral approval' and 'moral disapproval'. In order to support emotivism we must show that moral approval is not totally exhausted by its intentionality. I will devote the present section to discussing what conditions an attitude must satisfy if it is to be considered moral. I will argue that there are three fundamental conditions, and these will show that a reactive element is essential to any moral attitude. I shall try to show that a man who has a moral attitude not only believes, but also wants and intends certain things.

(1) *Universality*. Moral attitudes must be universal.[1] If they were not universal, the *commitment* generally thought to be essential to the notion of morality would be lost. Moral attitudes always aim beyond the present instance to some property or state of affairs as such.

(2) *Overridingness*. Moral commitment is not secured by universality alone. Moral attitudes have a particular sort of authority over a man, and an attitude could be universal without having any such power. There is great plausibility, therefore, in the view which Hare puts forward,[2] that if we are to explain the notion of the moral we must add to universality 'prescriptivity', or 'accepting as a command'. However, it is rightly objected to Hare's analysis that, illuminating as it has proved, it cannot properly account for 'akrasia' or weakness of the will. The authority of a moral principle can still be manifested when a man disobeys it. I shall employ the term 'overridingness' to refer to this authority – moral principles override the counsels of prudence and self interest. By this I do not mean that moral principles are more successful in motivating action than the desires which conflict with them; this is obviously not true. I mean that, whenever a man believes that he ought to do something he will, as it were, *submit* to this belief in some one of a variety of ways. There are many of these ways in which a man may show attachment to a moral principle, and simple obedience is only one of them. The power of a moral principle is both more persistent and more elusive than the power of a command. To accept a command is to make the decision to do whatever is commanded; whereas to accept a moral principle might simply be to feel guilt about one's own incontinence.

We must construe overridingness on the analogy of wanting rather than of deciding. To adopt an overriding attitude is not to decide to embark on any course of action, but rather, as Kant said, to will that action as law. But of course the authority of a moral principle cannot be explained merely in terms of a desire: or, at least, if it can, then it must be explained by referring to desires of a very special kind – namely overriding desires – and this helps not at all with our analysis.

[1] See G. E. Hughes, 'Moral condemnation', in A. I. Melden (Ed.), *Essays in Moral Philosophy* (Seattle, 1958). Hughes gives an excellent account of the universality of condemnation.

[2] R. M. Hare, *Language of Morals* (Oxford, 1952), *passim*.

Since there has been much discussion of this subject, and since it is no part of my present purpose to give a complete account of moral approval, I shall content myself with a few remarks only.

One criterion for a man's having an overriding attitude in favour of Xs is that he should favour the existence of Xs regardless of any other attitudes which might conflict with this aim. It is also a criterion, though not a sufficient condition, that he should *desire* always to favour the existence of Xs in this way. Another very important criterion, about which much discussion has centred, is that he should feel guilt whenever he lapses from this ideal. 'Guilt' is here taken as a general concept covering all manner of self-inflicted punishment. In this sense the term covers a wide variety of feelings, only some of which we should normally refer to as guilt – for example, it seems to cover such reactions as remorse, wishing a punishment on oneself, and shame. There is, of course, a great similarity among these feelings; they all seem to include some intention to try to act otherwise in future. But there are also important differences. Guilt, for example, seems to be a more 'private' feeling than shame – this is brought out by the fact that, whereas I can feel ashamed of *another's* behaviour, I can only feel guilt at my *own*. Guilt is the expression of a recriminating conscience, whereas shame is less reflective, consisting above all in the desire to hide oneself from the eyes of others. Indeed, a stern Protestant morality might abjure the sense of shame, insisting that the guilty man must show himself in his sin, and thereby gain proper consciousness of it through the universal disapprobation. It seems, therefore, that some of the emotions normally classed under 'guilt' might be 'outward-looking', concerned with the public aspect of one's fault, while others may be 'inward-looking', concerned with the nature of the fault and one's own unworthiness in the eyes of conscience. These separate emotions have distinct, though related, expressions; a striking example is to be found in Masaccio's painting of the expulsion of Adam and Eve from Paradise in the Brancacci chapel. In Adam we can see the beginnings of self-knowledge; he covers his face with his hands, inwardly attending to the sin he has committed; at the same time he steps forward with determination away from Paradise. By contrast, Eve wails helplessly, attempting to hide her body, and thrown into confusion by her sudden shame.

Doubtless other criteria could be given for the property I have called 'overridingness'; one can submit to a moral principle in almost as many ways as one can submit to the authority of another man. But in general the criteria tend to group about two poles – action on the one hand and feelings of self-reproach on the other. These two criteria have been discussed as conditions governing when a judgement is to count as moral. It would be less controversial, as we shall see, to relate them to moral attitudes.

That overridingness is a necessary condition is shown by the fact that someone who neither acts according to his principles, nor feels any emotion when he does not do so, is said to be insincere.

(3) *Normativity.* Overridingness and universality are not sufficient, for they do not capture the social aspect of moral attitudes. We need a further condition. Pitcher, for example,[1] says that I cannot be said to approve of something unless I believe that others ought to approve of it as well (he uses this as a special case of the argument criticized in the previous section – the argument which claims that the moral attitudes must be identified by reference to moral beliefs). Although an emotivist cannot agree with this formulation, he must none the less take seriously the fact that a man's moral attitudes refer beyond himself; they include a desire for a conformity of attitude. A man cannot be said to disapprove of theft if he is indifferent to the fact that thieves are generally admired. I propose to call this further condition 'normativity', and under this head I will refer, in fact, to two separate, but related, conditions which the moral attitude must fulfil.

(*a*) Moral attitudes include a desire for a *conformity* of attitudes. If I approve of something, then I must want others to approve of it also. This desire, like the desire expressed in the condition of 'overridingness' has a peculiarly 'moral' character. I might, for example, show a disposition to blame, or react against, those who do not share my moral attitudes.

(*b*) More generally, moral attitudes are concerned with proposing laws to which everyone (or everyone who in any way matters as a social being)[2] must conform, in specifiable circumstances.

[1] 'On approval', *Philosophical Review* (April 1958).
[2] The notion of 'willing as law for all mankind' (Kant's formulation of the logical basis of his categorical imperative), which I am trying to recapture here, must not be made too rigorous. Otherwise we could arbitrarily denounce the attitudes of various primitive peoples as not moral. A tribe might not make a moral *distinction* between its members and those of another tribe. It might not regard the latter as objects of moral judgement at all.

Again, a normative attitude will tend to involve reactions in favour of those who accord with certain requirements and against those who do not. These reactions resemble emotions familiar in non-moral contexts, but in fact they belong primarily to the moral sphere. They may also be so attenuated as to acquire a quasi-legal expression: they will then consist purely in the attempt to impose sanctions on offenders and reward those who conform, perhaps with very little overtly emotional response at all. It is not necessary, however, that moral feelings should express themselves in this legalistic manner; in many central cases we find the emotional response playing the largest part. A man cannot count as having a moral attitude unless it can be shown that he has *some* tendency to respond unfavourably towards those who do not act in accordance with it. He must be disposed to feel some reproach, anger or disappointment, and these reactions must not be the result merely of a belief that what was done was in some way harmful to *himself*. He must reproach a man purely because he falls short of some standard of behaviour. In general, therefore, a moral attitude will include a desire to influence people and persuade them to conformity to one's own moral views. This explains the *persuasive* nature of moral judgements, as discussed by Stevenson.[1] Unless someone's attitude has this public, persuasive aspect, it could not be called moral.

This serves to clarify the distinction between despite and dis-approval. Although despite is universal, it is not overriding: it does not commit the person who despises to the attempt to remove or change the feature which occasions his despite. On the contrary, he may take pleasure in exercising his contempt, even when he is himself the object of it, and may therefore desire more opportunities for its expression. Nor is despite normative: if I despise cowardice, I am not thereby committed to any desire that others should despise what I do, nor am I committed to wishing that all cowards should become brave men. On the other hand, if I disapprove of a man because of his cowardice, then I must want him to be otherwise, and I must also want him to want to be otherwise, and I must be against cowardice in general.

The two conditions involved in the notion of normativity correspond to two different ways in which I can desire others to conform to my

---

[1] 'The emotive meaning of ethical terms', in W. Sellars and J. Hospers (Eds.), *Readings in Ethical Theory* (New York, 1952).

moral views: (1) I might wish their feelings to be the same as mine; (2) I might wish them to act in accordance with my principles whatever their own feelings. In the former case they will be acting *from* my principles, and in the latter case they will be acting merely *in accordance with* them. A moral principle which counselled tolerance of the moral views of others is best construed as condemning (2). It would certainly be conceptually confused were it to condemn both (1) and (2), for this would be to forbid itself the status of a moral principle. (1) is the more essential condition (corresponding to (a) above). Although we could still call an attitude moral if (2) is not fulfilled, it is not clear that it could be called moral if (2) is fulfilled but not (1).[1]

Normativity is a formal condition, and has no substantive moral content. For example, nothing can be deduced from it about the positive nature of the objects of moral attitudes. A few conclusions about the intentionality of moral attitudes can none the less be drawn, of which I give here two examples.

First, normativity rules out the possibility of making a moral distinction which one believes to be 'arbitrary'. I must desire a general conformity to my moral attitudes; hence it is impossible for me to have a moral code in which I draw distinctions between people which I believe it would be impossible for others to recognize as morally significant. If I am to be rational, I must have a moral code in which there is some chance that my two desires – for conformity to laws in behaviour, and for a community of attitude in favour of these laws – can be fulfilled. I cannot make distinctions between people which I believe will make it certain that, however rational they might be, other men could not come to share my moral views. This conclusion is neutral with respect to any particular moral code – it is still possible that a man may in fact make a moral distinction on absolutely any grounds. But it is not the case that he can make a moral distinction and at the same time believe it to be 'arbitrary' (in the sense of being impossible for all but

---

[1] It is important to see that (2), and consequently the condition (b) above, are secondary conditions. There are many attitudes which we would want to call normative (that are concerned with some notion of what it is right or correct to feel or do) where the desire for conformity in behaviour cannot play a significant part. These are the attitudes generally grouped under the concept of taste – aesthetic attitudes and preferences of a normative kind. These attitudes are universal (although this has been questioned, wrongly I think, in the case of aesthetics), but they are not overriding, and therefore lack the sense of guilt and recrimination which is the distinguishing mark of moral feelings.

a certain group of people, or all but himself, to recognize as relevant). Thus the condition of normativity does not rule out any particular ways of making moral distinctions. None the less, it avoids the paradoxes which result from accounting for the social nature of morality in terms of universality alone. For it does not allow that a man can make just any distinction, irrespective of his (factual) beliefs; he *can* make any distinction, but he cannot believe that the distinctions he makes are 'arbitrary' in the above sense. For most moral distinctions normally made – for example, those of class, race, tribe and age group – it is very easy to see how the accusation of arbitrariness can be rebutted. Other distinctions – those of colour (where colour is not taken as a sign of race), physical size, and so on – are less easy to defend, and can perhaps only carry moral weight for someone with false beliefs about what such distinctions entail.

It also follows from the condition of normativity that the moral attitudes, despite their dependence on universal characterizations of their objects, are essentially expressed towards people. Only in this way can they fulfil their normative function. Although we approve of states of affairs, actions and so on, we manifest our approval through praising, blaming, rewarding and punishing human beings. Hence our disapproval of a state of affairs will extend to those whom we think responsible for it. As a result, we cannot have a moral attitude to something while believing it to be beyond human control.

These three conditions – universality, overridingness and normativity – will entail many such conclusions for the intentional content of moral attitudes; some of these I will refer to later in this paper. However, they also entail that the moral attitudes *must* have a reactive content. Sincerely willing as a law for oneself and others is not to be elucidated in terms of belief alone.

There is an asymmetry worth mentioning between moral approval and moral disapproval. The latter seems more directly tied to emotion than the former. The most common manifestation of disapproval towards an action or quality is blame, or the imposition of a sanction (in one's own case these are substituted by guilt and penitence). Moral approval seldom finds such a direct expression: to approve of an action is in general to acquiesce in its being done. The attitude of approval seems to reduce, therefore, to simple permission. For this reason, it is sometimes thought that approval is not like an emotion at all. Of course, this would not amount to a refutation of the claim that approval is an attitude, nor would it be a reason for saying that approval is really a belief.

In any case, the asymmetry is really only apparent. For although approval seldom leads to active *praise*, it cannot be analysed without referring to the moral emotions appropriate to disapproval. For what is central to approval is indignation against the man who does not do what he ought. The moral approval of X entails the moral disapproval of not-X. This moral disapproval is to be analysed in terms of actions and feelings, and therefore it involves a reactive element. Since disapproval has this reactive character, then approval also must be a genuine attitude, and not a disguised belief.[1]

I have talked of the three criteria for moral attitudes as necessary conditions. No one of them is sufficient, and it is even doubtful that they are sufficient when taken together. It might also be doubted whether they are really necessary. For I have spoken of overridingness and normativity in behavioural terms, whereas it would seem that a man can often reveal a moral attitude in what he says, for instance by calm deliberation about a course of action. Sometimes it might be more correct to say of such a man that he is proposing, rather than adopting, a moral attitude. But this is not always so. I will argue later that the ways in which a man might manifest a moral attitude in what he says *do* conform to these three criteria. Moral reasoning is an expression of universality, normativity and overridingness, being a secondary (verbal) criterion for when someone is taking up an attitude containing these three features.

There is still much to be said about the intentionality of moral attitudes. But whatever is said about intentionality will not affect the emotivist position provided that the conditions just enumerated show that the moral attitudes contain a reactive element. And they *do* show this, for they entail that to believe anything to be good includes *wanting* other men to favour it. Moral attitudes include desires.

There is one qualification which must be made: I have not dealt with the attitudes expressed in *ideals*. These seem to be distinct from

---

[1] I do not suggest that disapproval must *always* manifest itself in proper indignation. If I disapprove of cowardice, then it is not necessary that I feel indignant at every coward; some instances of cowardice might leave me cold, and some might be too far removed to engage my emotions at all. However, there must be *some* situations in which I would feel indignant at cowardice, and all cowards must *tend* to awaken my indignation, however remote from me.

the moral attitudes as described above, although closely related. Here we must say that often the element of wanting is replaced by a *wish*, in the light of certain acknowledged improbabilities. Hence, an ideal may included beliefs and intentions different from those present for a common moral attitude: it might not include the belief that its object is totally under human control, although it must include the belief that it is the *kind of thing* which could be under such control. Nor will it always include the desire simply to act in accordance with the ideal; a man with an ideal must be content with approximations. Ideals are moral attitudes, none the less; they are universal, overriding (though it is not the desire to act in conformity with them which overrides) and normative (although it is not the total concurrence of all men that is willed).

<h3 style="text-align:center">PART II CRITERIA, REASONS AND OBJECTIVITY</h3>

8 A naturalist can agree with everything said in the previous section. He can agree that there are 'moral' attitudes and that they are to be analysed in the way I have suggested. But he will claim that it is not moral *attitudes* which are expressed in moral judgement. The belief that X is good might be distinct from the 'moral approval' of X. At most, the naturalist will say, such a belief will belong to the intentionality of approval. Hence, it is a contingent fact if men always morally approve of that which they believe to be good (assuming that the attitude which I have analysed is really to be called approval – which of course the naturalist would deny; he would prefer to call it by some other name).

We must therefore pursue our discussion at a deeper level. It is necessary to decide whether 'X is morally good' expresses in its standard use a belief or a moral attitude. To this end, I will treat naturalism and emotivism as alternate hypotheses, each with its own predictions about the logic of moral lanaguage; these predictions can then be compared with the facts of linguistic usage.

If the statement that X is morally good expresses a belief, then the rules governing the use of the expression 'X is good' must refer to the truth-conditions of this belief. Their being answerable to truth-conditions, and identified by reference to these conditions, is what distinguishes beliefs from all other mental states. It follows that, if statements of the form 'X is good' express beliefs, then there will be criteria for their truth. On the other hand, if statements of this form express attitudes, then they will not have criteria; such statements will answer only to necessary conditions, conditions governing the *kind* of thing to which they are applied. Thus naturalism predicts that there will be criteria for the truth of moral judgements; emotivism predicts that there will be none, and many of the now familiar arguments in favour of one or the other theory can be seen as attempts to refute either of these predictions.

By a 'criterion for X's being A (in this case good, right or some other moral predicate)' I mean: 'feature F such that the fact that X has F is necessarily a reason for calling it A'. This, I take it, is what Wittgenstein had in mind when he used the term 'criterion'. A criterion marks out a conventional relation between statements such that a man who accepts one statement ('X has F') and denies that he has a reason for asserting the other ('X is A') – while believing that he has no further reason for *denying* that X has A – has misunderstood the concept of A-ness. Hence the presence of F is necessarily a reason for calling something A, and the presence in X of F and other features similarly related to the concept of A-ness could be logically sufficient for its being A. If a statement expresses a belief then it will be expected that the criteria for correctly making that statement will refer to the truth-conditions of this belief. Hence they will be criteria in the Wittgensteinian sense; they will be reasons which state a logical connection between the statement and its grounds. Wittgenstein also thought that criteria must be such that their presence in anything is detectable. For Wittgenstein, therefore, the notion of a criterion served to close the gap, in the case of descriptive utterances, between epistemology and logic.

In view of this it is not surprising that moral philosophers have made so much use of the terms 'criterion of merit' and 'criterion of value', and have laid so much stress on the nature of moral *reasoning* (or the question what it *is* for a reason to support a moral judgement). Superficially, the emotivist's prediction – that there are no *criteria* of merit, no reasons which I *must* accept as a matter of logic if I am to make a moral judgement – seems to be the right one. Naturalists have therefore tried to produce arguments to show that moral reasoning has a structure approaching that of the deductive ideal. However, in their most common form, these arguments pay insufficient attention to the varieties of relation between a judgement and the reasons which support it. What these arguments say about moral reasoning is in fact quite compatible with emotivism. For although naturalism and emotivism each entail a separate thesis about the relation between moral judgements and moral reasons, the arguments I shall discuss do not show either to be wrong.

These arguments are to be found, in summary form, in G. J. Warnock's *Contemporary Moral Philosophy*.[1] Warnock, however, in discussing whether there are 'criteria of merit' uses the term 'criterion' in such a way that 'criterion of' means 'reason for'. In the following I shall use the term 'criterion' only in the Wittgensteinian sense.

Warnock reaches the following tentative conclusion: 'that, notwithstanding the general "anti-naturalist" doctrine, there are certain kinds of facts or features which are necessarily criteria of moral evaluation'; and that 'this implies that moral arguments might in principle be demonstrative, logically cogent'.[2] The use of the expression 'necessarily criteria' shows that Warnock is here using 'criterion' to mean 'reason'. None the less, it is evident that he is raising the issue of whether there are criteria in the Wittgensteinian sense, and that he means to assert that there are such criteria, and hence that some form of naturalism is defensible (this is brought out by his making a connection between the existence of criteria and the demonstrability of moral argument).

The question here is whether moral reasons must simply belong to a certain *kind* or species, or whether there are facts which are necessarily reasons, i.e. whether there are facts within the area of 'moral reasons' which are criteria. If what is meant is that there is a *kind* of fact or feature to which all facts or features which are 'criteria' (i.e. reasons) must necessarily belong, then the implication – that moral arguments might in principle be demonstrative – does not hold. For the implication depends on there being *criteria* – that is, features of the object (not just *kinds* of feature) which necessarily give us a reason for calling it good. This is a view which Warnock *does* state (pp. 67–9), but for which his only argument seems to be the following: 'The *relevance* of considerations as to the welfare of human beings cannot, in the context of moral debate, be denied.' But, again, the phrase 'considerations as to the welfare of human beings' serves no further than to define an area into which moral reasoning must fall. It does not tell us which of these considerations must in itself be a reason, nor why any

[1] (London, 1967). [2] Ibid., p. 69.

such reason should support rather than count against any particular judgement. For it is unclear *which* considerations as to *whose* welfare are to be considered 'relevant'; nor in what this relevance consists. And this, the emotivist will retort, is due solely to the following: that to say anything more precise is to utter a moral precept, not a conceptual truth.

Briefly, then, Warnock wishes to say that considerations of human welfare are necessarily relevant to moral judgement, 'we must be prepared to acknowledge these as reasons if we are to count as considering the matter in hand "from the moral point of view"' (p. 68). But, as we have seen, the statement of this theory wavers between two contrasting versions. I shall call both of these Naturalism, even though the weaker form is not really Naturalism (in my sense) at all. The two versions are:

(A) *Strong Naturalism.* 'Good', as used in moral judgements, is necessarily connected with certain features of whatever is judged to be good. There are criteria for something's being good, just as there are criteria for something's being human, alive or useful. Note that the possibility of strong naturalism is not affected by any theory to the effect that 'good' is an incomplete term, that one can never say of something that it is good *simpliciter*, but only that it is good, as being of a certain kind. For the 'kind' in question can still define criteria according to which the word 'good' must be used when applied to things of this kind. And if there are such criteria then they are conceptually connected with goodness as of this kind. Anyone who recognizes the presence of these criteria in something (of a certain kind) and yet denies that he has a reason for calling it good, either does not understand the concept of goodness or does not understand what it is to be a thing of this kind. Hence there is no 'choice' of moral standards[1] and the distinction between descriptive and evaluative uses of language breaks down.

(B) *Weak Naturalism.* 'Good' is connected with reasons of a certain *kind* (reasons which refer to features in a certain area). That is, anything proposed as a morally relevant consideration must refer to features of a certain kind. But no *particular* feature is necessarily a reason for calling something good. Hence there are no features which count as criteria, and we have 'choice' of our standards within defined limits.

Let us take the theory in its weak form: if someone is to reason

[1] Hare, *Language of Morals.*

E

morally he must bring forward reasons of a certain *kind* (moral reasons are often supposed to refer to human welfare, wants, needs and so on). This is a thesis about moral reasoning, what it is for a process of reasoning to count as moral. It is supposed to be a necessary condition that the conclusion of such reasoning be based upon considerations of a certain kind. The first thing to notice is that this theory is quite compatible with emotivism as an analysis of moral judgement. Emotivists might very well be prepared to say that moral judgement and moral reasoning are logically independent, and that if there are canons of correct or appropriate reasoning in support of a moral judgement it is not necessary for a man to be aware of them in order to make, accept or act upon such a judgement. Thus philosophers have tended to confuse two quite distinct kinds of weak naturalism:

(1) The view that there is a necessary connection between moral judgement and moral reasoning, so that it is part of the notion of a moral principle that it should be based upon reasons of a certain kind. If a man is to count as having a moral principle, he must show that he believes that there are reasons of a certain kind which support it.

(2) The view that moral reasoning and moral principles are logically independent, although moral reasons must none the less, if they are to be moral, be of a certain kind. If a man is to support his principle at all – if he is to argue in a way consistent with his principle's being a moral one, i.e. if his arguments really are to support his principle as a *moral* principle – he must have recourse to reasons of a certain kind. However, it is not part of the notion of a moral principle that a man *should* support his principle in such a way, or even that he should believe such support to be possible. Hence a man's use of the term 'good' need not be connected with reasons of this kind in order to count as a moral use.

9 Thus (2) asserts that moral *argument* must take a certain form, whereas (1) asserts that moral argument is an essential part of morality. Neither of these theories defines what the relation between moral reasons and moral principles must be: all that either of them requires is that moral reasons should in fact *support* the principles for which they are adduced as reasons. It is not clear whether there is some criterial connection which will allow a deductive decision procedure. So that even if (1)

were established, strong (that is to say, genuine) naturalism would not have been proved. It is not an argument against emotivism that moral reasons are necessarily involved in moral principles (although this might be held to make emotivism implausible) unless that means that moral reasons are *necessarily* reasons. But this does not follow. None the less, I will argue for the moment as though (1) were less congenial to the emotivist than (2), and as though the truth of (1), although compatible with weak naturalism, tended to support something stronger. Later I will return to the distinction between (1) and (2) in order to show that (1) is not only compatible with emotivism, but in fact entailed by it. The distinction between weak and strong naturalism will then be seen to be much more significant than it may appear at this stage.

(2) would be incompatible with any deductive decision procedure for the following reason: it asserts that a man can hold or accept a moral principle and therefore fully *understand* a moral principle, without its being the case that he can support it with reasons of any kind. Hence such reasons cannot be logically connected with the moral principle. If they *were* so connected they would enter into a proper grasp of the meaning of the principle. I do not say that this is a conclusive argument, but it is the sort of consideration which might lead the emotivist to deny that there can be criteria of moral value. If ethical words have emotive meaning[1] then to understand what they mean is to take up an attitude of the kind outlined in Section 7 towards the things to which one applies them. Emotivism is not damaged, therefore, by the view that moral *reasoning* must take a certain form. It would have to be shown that understanding a moral principle involves having a grasp of reasons which might justify it. For in that case it might plausibly be said that understanding a moral principle cannot be elucidated solely in terms of its connection with an attitude. To accept (2), on the other hand, is to reject this argument, and to reject naturalism as an account of moral principles. Naturalism requires that moral reasons be criteria; hence a man must know what reasons would support his moral judgement before he can know what belief his judgement expresses, i.e. before he can understand it.

We must now consider the arguments against (2) and in favour of strong naturalism. These arguments are directed against *any* view which

---

[1] This notion I will explain in the next section.

tries to give an account of what it is to understand a moral principle without referring to reasons which might be given in support of it. One such argument might be: 'We would not understand a man who said that clapping was wrong'. Or, more cogently, 'We would only understand a man who said that clapping was wrong if he were ready to support this judgement – however misguidedly – with certain reasons' (say there was always a danger of clapping leading to inadvertent deaths: in the Talmud is recounted the story of Lemech who, clapping in an access of grief, struck his son's head between his palms and thereby slew the boy, who was of a tender age). That is, we could only understand him if we could see what *beliefs* he was expressing in his judgement. We could not understand such a man, it is supposed, precisely because his moral judgement (so-called) is not connected with considerations of human benefit and harm, welfare, wants, needs, etc.

Now, perhaps it is true to say that we do not understand someone whose supposed moral utterances are not connected with *some* such notion as benefit, harm, want or welfare. We can agree with Warnock that 'though in a sense one might say that absolutely any feature of (The Martians') environment might be regarded by them as a criterion of merit or desirability, this is not to say that we could always understand it being so regarded; it is rather to concede that we have no understanding of hypothetical Martians'. But none the less *this* does not refute the anti-naturalist argument, which need only claim that we should be able to understand from the Martians' behaviour that some given feature of their environment *is* being used as a 'criterion of merit'. And Warnock, in setting up the example, seems implicitly to have admitted that this might be so. At least we need further arguments to show the contrary. The fact that we do not understand the Martians, and hence do not, in a sense, understand their evaluations – in the sense that we do not understand, for example, their feelings, their attitudes, their form of life – is not to the point. We can understand what a man says without understanding him in saying it.[1] I can understand that a man means to say that clapping is morally wrong, even though, as a result, I cease to understand the first thing about him. The naturalist must show, therefore, that we do not understand the Martians' *utterances* on the grounds that they seem to treat as criteria of merit features which could not possibly be so. In that case we cannot be

[1] See Anscombe, *Intention*, section 18.

sure that they employ criteria of *merit* at all; their language contains an incomprehensible element.

10 If we are to meet this argument, we must reconsider the idea of emotive meaning. The notion of an emotive meaning has suffered in the past at the hands of those defending it. For example, Stevenson's emotivism is inseparably bound up with his causal theory of meaning, and many of the criticisms that have since been made of emotivism have really been criticisms of the causal theory of meaning. Recently, however, J. O. Urmson has made a notable attempt to discuss emotivism in the context of a more plausible account of meaning.[1]

If we were to attempt a detailed discussion of emotive meaning it would be necessary to begin with Urmson's treatment, for it is by far the most interesting and far-sighted that has yet been produced. For the purposes of the present argument, however, it is only necessary to give a brief sketch of a substitute for Stevenson's causal theory of meaning;[2] in producing this substitute it will be more convenient to keep within the terms which have traditionally been used. Urmson attempts to replace far more of Stevenson's theory than seems to me strictly necessary for the purpose of defending what remains. He wishes to abandon the notion that a statement can have an emotive meaning if it is used to express an attitude, producing instead an analysis of evaluative statements in terms of the illocutionary act of commendation. A statement is evaluative if in making it one is *commending* a certain attitude. For the purpose of the present argument there is no need to make such a radical departure from Stevenson's vocabulary and I shall try to restore the theory of emotivism in something like its original form. This has the advantage of making the contrast with naturalism easier to envisage; the type of meaning which a sentence has is defined by the mental state (belief or attitude) which it expresses.[3]

If an emotive meaning is a matter of what a word evokes, or what

[1] This occurs in his admirable book, *The Emotive Theory of Ethics* (London, 1968).

[2] An account of the causal theory is to be found in *Ethics and Language* (New Haven, 1944).

[3] It must be added that I will be departing from Stevenson's theory in one important point: Stevenson says that besides expressing an attitude, an evaluative statement must *evoke* a corresponding attitude in the hearer. As can be seen from the argument in Section 7, this is to confuse the fact that the moral attitudes are normative, and hence characteristically expressed in the context of a desire for agreement, and a consequent attempt at persuasion, with a further element in the meaning of the language which expresses them.

feeling accompanies its utterance, then any word can have an emotive meaning: Stevenson's mistake was not primarily that of identifying an illocutionary with a perlocutionary act, as Urmson claims, but rather that of giving a false account of what kind of connection between an attitude and a word would be necessary for one to say that the expressive function of the word is a part of its meaning. Prescriptivism did not – in its classical form, as expounded by Hare – rely on any particular theory of meaning. It simply tried to get by with the assertion that certain kinds of utterance might 'entail' commands. Neither theory made it very clear that, in analysing the meaning of an utterance, one is setting limits to when a man can be said to understand the utterance. Once we have acknowledged this, most of the familiar objections can be overcome.[1]

To understand a sentence is to know how to use it correctly. 'Correctly' here does not necessarily mean 'to say something true'. There is a distinction between factual and linguistic correctness. It could be the case that the majority of a man's belief-expressing (descriptive) judgements should be false. And some particular sentences he might *always* use to say something false (for example, 'She is a witch'). But it could not be the case that *all* his descriptive judgements are false. In order to give sense to the idea of someone's *making* judgements about the world, some of these judgements must sometimes be correct. There is no particular judgement which needs to be right on any occasion. For some judgements, none the less, it is very implausible to suppose that one could understand them and regularly make mistakes. Suppose, for example, that a man always said something false in saying 'This is a cow'. Then, either he does not understand the sentence (for example, he does not understand what a cow is), or else he is so little able to discern what surrounds him that his uttering the sentence must be taken as an accident. For if he could never tell when there was a cow before him, then this must be because he is unable to recognize the presence of those features which are criteria for something's being a cow. But if he is unable to recognize these, it is at once doubtful that he can recognize *anything* – in which case it is impossible to know how he could be taught language at all, or how any public check could be kept on his use of descriptive terms. His experience, so radically different from our own, would isolate him in

---

[1] These objections can be found in Ewing, *Second Thoughts in Moral Philosophy*, ch. I.

a private world, and in such a case the temptation is to say that he could have no language to express his beliefs at all.

Despite this, it is quite possible for a normal person to go wrong in one of his beliefs while correctly using the sentence which expresses it. For he might be able to show in some other way that he connects his assertion with the truth-conditions of the appropriate belief. For example, if I said 'This is a cow', and showed care to step aside at the point where it might be, commented on the length of its horns, wondered whether it had been recently milked – if I manifest, in short, a full understanding of the criteria for the truth of this assertion, and a genuine belief in its truth – then I would also show that I meant what I said in a standard sense, even when what I said was false.

If a sentence is descriptive (is standardly used to express a belief) then a man only counts as using the sentence correctly if, when sincerely asserting it, he holds the belief in question. The criteria for assertion are complicated, and I shall pass over the problem of defining them; also there is more to the notion of expression than this bare minimum. What more there is, however, does not concern us here. For what is important is that we can give a parallel condition for when a sentence standardly expresses an attitude. A sentence expresses an attitude if a man must *have* the attitude whenever he uses the sentence assertorically. Otherwise, if he is sincere, we must say that he does not understand the meaning of the sentence. There are further conditions for when a sentence expresses a mental state; for we have not yet shown what it is for a sentence to assert or put forward a belief or attitude. These conditions will presumably refer to the intentions with which the sentence must be used.[1]

We must be careful not to limit the notion of moral judgement to the class of action-guiding principles (such as 'It is wrong to despise your enemies'). As Warnock points out, prescriptivism is overfed with examples of this kind. So, on the face of it, is naturalism: the adducing of considerations relating to human benefit and harm is characteristic of argument in favour of a course of action ('Hate your enemy, do not despise him. Then may all his triumphs be your triumphs'). It is less plausible to say that one is committed to such

---

[1] See H. P. Grice, 'Meaning', *Philosophical Review* (July 1957). It should be noted that my account of the relation between understanding the meaning of a sentence and certain mental states applies only to sincere assertions. Insincere assertions (e.g. lies) must be explained as derivative.

reasoning in making judgements of virtue ('Courage is a good thing in a man') even though it may be possible to argue in this way about virtues ('Without courage a man achieves nothing').

Let us suppose, then, that a man accepts a moral judgement only if he cares in a certain way about the object of the judgement. It must be the real object of one of his moral attitudes (as these were sketched in Section 7). So that his judgement that this object has a moral value will be a moral judgement because it expresses a moral attitude.

This does not entail that a man cannot show that he has a moral attitude to something purely by advancing *reasons* of a morally relevant sort in its favour. And the type of reasoning referred to in the thesis of weak naturalism – the adducing of considerations relating to human benefit, harm, want and need – is closely connected with the moral attitudes. For reasoning in such a way can exhibit an attitude for which the *central* criteria are given by the notion of *holding a moral principle* or *believing something to be right* and not by the notion of arguing in *support* of such a principle.

Emotivism asserts that moral principles have emotive force, and that this is their distinguishing logical feature. Moral predicates thus have a special kind of meaning which breaks the connection between the 'criteria' according to which their application might be justified and the meaning which they have. In moral language there is a gap between logic and epistemology of a kind which Wittgenstein argued did not exist in descriptive language. Therefore 'criteria' here cannot have the sense which Wittgenstein gave the term, and any reasoning in support of a moral principle can only be moral in so far as it tends, or is held, to support the attitude on which a principle is based. Consider, then, the case of an action-guiding principle. Any support of this principle must appeal to the kind of reason which justifies acting in a certain way. To justify the action is to justify an attitude in favour of it.

It can be seen at once that to support a moral conclusion by reasons which refer to human wants, needs and benefits shows a grasp of moral concepts, in a way that appeals to self-interest do not. First, to give such support to a principle is to bring forward acknowledged *reasons for acting*; hence it is to presuppose that the principle has the force of an overriding attitude. It is to show understanding of the fact that acceptance of the principle consists, primarily, in doing what it enjoins.

Secondly, in bringing forward reasons of this kind a man exhibits a concern for general standards of behaviour, and thus presupposes that the principle has the force of a *normative* attitude. For he gives reasons which, not being based on self-interest, are held as valid for everyone. His reasons refer to what all men could be supposed to want as an accepted standard of behaviour for themselves and their fellows. It follows that some principle of impartiality will be a dominant characteristic of moral reasoning: a man certainly expresses a normative attitude in producing reasons which he believes to be reasons for acting for men in general.

This explains why there is such a similarity between the reasons given in support of a moral principle and those given in support of a command. Attitudes, like emotions, have an active and a passive side: they are equally motives which govern a man's actions, and responses which he feels.[1] Hence it is not surprising that moral judgements tend to divide into two kinds – action-guiding principles and judgements of virtue. Reasoning in support of the former resembles the justification of a command, since it consists in justification of a motive for action. Reasoning in favour of judgements of virtue is more like the justification of a feeling or response, and hence shows analogies to aesthetic reasoning. Both, however, are instances of practical reason and both can be seen as supporting a special kind of attitude.

The truth in the weak version of naturalism is then this: reasoning according to the canons of human benefit, harm, etc., is the verbal expression of a moral attitude. Is it possible, then, to manifest a moral belief by reasoning alone? In a sense it is. The casuist who produces a carefully worked out code of behaviour, complete with its rationale, can be said to share the moral beliefs expressed in that code if the reasons he gives really *are* moral; that is, if these reasons take for granted that the principles he puts forward are overriding and normative. But suppose that he never shows any tendency to act in accordance with the code, and never worries about the disobedience of other people? This would present us with a conflict of criteria: for only in what he says, not in what he does, would the man be attributing to certain principles an overriding and normative force. However, actions are in general more revealing than words. We would normally say of such a man that he assents to a moral scheme intellectually without really adopting it (this brings out a contrast between attitudes and beliefs –

[1] See R. S. Peters, 'Emotions and the category of passivity', *Proceedings of the Aristotelian Society* (1961–2).

it is difficult to imagine how a man could assent to a belief intellectually, and yet not adopt it; this is because there is no reactive content to belief which could constitute this further mode of assent). We might also notice that a man who proposes a moral scheme without acting in accordance with it can more plausibly be said to accept it when he expounds it with imagination. This is another source of contrast with belief: what we require of a man who proposes a system of morality is that he shows an understanding of what it is to *adopt* and *act in accordance* with it. He should manifest an understanding of the worldview and the feelings and responses which would be expressed in his moral scheme. This certainly suggests that a reason is moral because it supports an attitude.

11 Thus the weak form of naturalism can be construed as a truth about moral reasoning, even *granted* an emotivist theory of ethics. Furthermore, a weak form of naturalism could be put forward as a theory about the *content* of moral principles, without prejudice to the tenets of emotivism. Because the moral attitudes can be directed on to all sorts of contrasting and incompatible things, there arises a notion of justification, analogous to the justification of feelings and actions, and hence a notion of moral reasoning. However, the intentionality of the moral attitude will limit its possible objects.[1]

A man can only be said to approve of something, it might be argued, if he has certain beliefs about it, and these beliefs could be of the kind which a weak naturalism would require – that the thing in question is in some way beneficial. However much the intentionality of the moral attitudes might limit the range of their possible objects, this cannot refute the view that it is on account of his having these attitudes and not on account of his ability to support them with reasons that a man takes up 'the moral point of view'. The intentionality of an emotion or attitude may fix its formal object, and hence the area in which its actual object must occur or be believed to occur. It cannot fix what the real or notional object is to be on any particular occasion. Thus the epistemological question still remains – towards which of all the possible

[1] On this point see Philippa Foot, 'Moral beliefs', *Proceedings of the Aristotelian Society* (1958–9); also 'Moral arguments', *Mind*, vol. LXVII, No. 268 (October 1958). I do not suggest that Mrs Foot would in any way regard her conclusions as compatible with emotivism. Such a suggestion would be profoundly alien to her way of thinking, which proposes as its ideal the establishment of a strong form of naturalism, wherein 'good' is connected with criteria in the Wittgensteinian sense.

objects might a man be *justified* in feeling this emotion? The notion of intentionality would seem to leave the question of criteria untouched. It can only provide an argument against emotivism if the notional object of a moral attitude must be described in moral terms – e.g. if one can only feel approval towards something if one believes it to be good. But this is a position which, as I said in Section 6, has never been properly defended.

Naturalists and their opponents have often argued at cross-purposes here. In particular, one very common argument for a naturalist position is expressed as follows: we could not (logically) believe that stupidity was a criterion of merit in a man. We could not praise a man's stupidity (at least, not under that description). But this argument only sets a limit to what *could* be a reason for calling someone good, and can thus quite easily be construed as a thesis about the intentionality of moral praise or approval. In which case, should it be proved, the emotivist need only agree. He too can deny that we understand the Martians in their sup- posed evaluations for the reason that they do not *make* evaluations.

12 It follows from the above that weak and strong naturalism are of totally different status, and that the latter cannot be regarded as a stringent version of the former. For the introduction of criteria, which are other than mere necessary conditions for the ascription of a moral predicate,[1] converts moral judgements from expressions of attitude to expressions of belief. The important question is whether *strong* naturalism is true. The epistemological problem – how do we derive a moral conclusion from matters of fact? – cannot be settled without deciding between strong naturalism on the one hand and theories like emotivism on the other. Arguments in the abstract about the 'content of morality' cannot settle it.

We can now see that a thesis such as (2) entails that the 'Naturalistic Fallacy' is a genuine philosophical error. According to (2), under- standing a moral principle does not involve any knowledge of what

[1] The term 'moral predicate' must go without an explanation for the moment. A moral predicate is some predicate like 'good', 'bad', 'right' or 'wrong' which is standardly used to make a moral judgement. Moral judgements can also be made by the use of such terms as 'ought' and 'duty' – and moral judgements made in these terms will equally lack criteria. It might also be thought that terms which name virtues and vices – 'honest', 'treacherous', etc. – have a claim to be called moral predicates. I will discuss this point in the final section.

would count as a reason for its truth (a reason for accepting it). Hence the moral use of 'good' is not connected to criteria in the Wittgensteinian sense; it can be understood without understanding what the reasons for an ethical judgement might be, or what reasons *could* be given for it. This contrasts with condition-governed, or descriptive predicates. A philosophical problem about a descriptive predicate is a problem about the criteria for its application – whether these criteria can be clearly stated as necessary and sufficient conditions, whether there is a family resemblance between them, and so on. A philosophical problem about 'good' is a problem about how the meaning of this predicate can be analysed *without* referring to criteria for its application.

Thus we could formulate the naturalistic fallacy as follows: it is the fallacy of supposing that moral predicates have criteria, in Wittgenstein's sense, when in fact they do not have criteria, and when it can always be meaningfully said of any proposed criterion that it does not give a reason for calling something good. Consequently any prescription of the form, 'You must always allow that courage is a reason for calling a man good', has a moral and not a logical force. Therefore strong naturalism commits the naturalistic fallacy, should the theory that there are no criteria for moral evaluation be true.

Now it does seem to be possible for there to be ultimate disagreements in ethics. Two people could disagree with each other about the application of any ethical term and consistently refuse to accept any reasons which might have resolved their dispute. The strength of Moore's argument lies simply in this: there never seems to be a point at which it becomes *logically odd* to deny that the presence of some feature is a reason for a thing's being good. Invariably, if there *is* a mistake, it has the character of moral error. Moore's argument serves therefore to confirm, in the absence of any evidence to the contrary, the emotivist's prediction as to the nature of moral reasons.

This brings us to another point where it is useful to discuss *Principia Ethica*. Whereas the analogy between 'good' and 'beneficial' is of little epistemological significance (given the absence of criteria in the case of 'good'), there is a striking analogy between 'good' and 'yellow'. Colour predicates are *simple* in that no criteria are used in applying them – either a man sees that a book is yellow or else he does not. Similarly ethical predicates, according to Moore's argument against the naturalist, have no criteria for their application – a man either sees the wrongness of an action or else he does not.

The absence of criteria in the case of perceptually simple predicates does not entail the absence of truth-conditions. Although no criteria are used to establish the truth of 'This is yellow', this does not show that the sentence 'X is yellow' expresses something other than a belief. Intuitionism can be seen as a kind of limiting case of naturalism, in which the theory that moral beliefs are beliefs and not attitudes is reconciled with the absence of criteria for moral judgement.[1] If it can be shown that the resemblance between moral and colour predicates holds good in precisely those respects that enable us to say of the latter that they are used to express beliefs, then emotivism is destroyed.

Before pursuing this analogy, it is worth mentioning one important objection to it: that it falls before the fact of ethical supervenience. If moral predicates are truly to capture the formal conditions which are intrinsic to the moral attitudes then they must satisfy the requirement of universality. Thus it is no accident that a man can meaningfully ascribe moral value only to a *kind* of thing (where the kind is given by some *other* predicate than 'good'). To be more precise, if a man applies such a predicate to a particular, it is on account of its being a token or instance of a certain type or property. I can only judge an action to be wrong if it belongs to a kind which I believe to be wrong. Ethical predicates are supervenient on natural characteristics.

Thus the analogy with colour judgements is incomplete. Goodness belongs to a thing only because of some property of it. The same could not be said for colours; ethical 'properties', unlike colours, are properties of types. But there may still be analogies between our attribution of colours to particulars, and our ascription of ethical predicates to types. These will suggest that the intuitionist thesis is less absurd than it has sometimes been held to be. One parallel between the perception of colours and the ascription of goodness is that they each have their characteristic form of blindness: colour- and moral-blindness. The parallel between these is well known; sometimes it has been supposed complete.[2] But it is not complete, and this is of great significance. For I can talk someone out of his moral-blindness, get him to see as good something which he previously thought to be indifferent or even bad. But I cannot talk someone out of his colour-blindness in the same way, even though I can force him to admit that he is *wrong* in his colour judgements.

[1] See p. 81.
[2] See, for example, S. Zink, *The Concepts of Ethics* (London, 1962), pp. 27 ff.

The analogy is best approached through one of the standard objections to intuitionism, given by Warnock as follows:

> to say that daffodils are yellow is to attribute a 'character' to daffodils; to say that aesthetic enjoyment is good is to attribute a 'character' to aesthetic enjoyment (according to intuitionism); but we detect the character of daffodils by looking at them: how do we detect that other character in aesthetic enjoyment? If disputes should arise, in what way might they be resolved? If I wonder whether some moral proposition is really true, how should I investigate the question, where should I look for reassurance? There are, it appears, moral facts; how, then, are moral facts established? To such questions as these the theory offers, in effect, no answer at all.[1]

In this passage Warnock has implicitly limited the attribution of 'characters' to types: he has thus somewhat unjustly supposed that if ethical intuition is to be epistemologically like colour perception it must consist in looking at individual instances of a kind in order to see what ethical 'character' the members of that kind have. But intuition must be different from this sort of looking, since it is concerned with the perusal of a *type* of action or character, and seeing whether, *as a type*, it is good, bad or indifferent.[2] And certainly there *is* such a process of moral persual, not wholly unlike visual 'looking'.

The main force of Warnock's objection resides, then, in the second question – how do we settle disputes? Let us ask this question of 'yellow': if someone persists in saying that a daffodil which he sees is green, what do we say? There is no logical mistake of which he can be convicted, other than that of thinking something to be green which is yellow. Likewise if thesis (2) is true, there is no feature we can point to, such that a man who persists in the belief that murder is right whenever one can get away with it will be forced to withdraw his judgement or be convicted of misunderstanding the term 'right'. What then do we say about someone who disagrees with us? Hutcheson thought that this question had substantially the *same* answer in the cases of moral and colour judgements:

But whether our moral Sense be subject to such a Disorder as to

---

[1] *Contemporary Moral Philosophy*, pp. 14–15.

[2] This point vitiates Mill's argument against the existence of a moral sense, on the basis of the 'generality' of moral principles (Utilitarianism, Section I).

have different Perceptions, from the same apprehended Affections in an Agent, at different times, as the Eye may have of the Colours of an altered Object, it is not easy to determine: Perhaps it will be hard to find any Instances of such a Change. What Reason could correct, if it fell into such a disorder, I know not: except suggesting to its remembrance its former Approbations, and representing the general Sense of Mankind. But this does not prove Ideas of Virtue and Vice to be previous to a Sense, more than a like Correction of the Ideas of Colour in a Person under the Jaundice, proves that Colours are perceived by Reason, previously to Sense.[1]

Hutcheson here talks of a general sense of mankind, without seeming to notice that, in the case of moral judgements, it is possible to doubt that there is such a thing. It might be the case, none the less, that if ethical judgements are to be objective there must be 'agreement in judgements'. Our faith in the objectivity of morals is certainly undermined when we discover that there is no such agreement. At the same time, the logic of moral predicates seems to presuppose objectivity, as Moore pointed out; and to argue *for* objectivity and against criteria seems to lead, as it led Moore, to intuitionism.

But can we secure objectivity for morals on the basis of a matter of fact agreement as we can for simple perceptual judgements? If not, what is the relevance of 'agreement in judgements' to ethical objectivity? Let us return to the analogy with colours.

In the case of colours, disputes are settled by appeal to standard examples. If a man sees a standard as red, yet sees some particular instance of redness as green, then there is nothing that can be done in the way of argument to change his way of seeing things. He will admit that he is wrong, but he cannot change his perceptions. The reason why we can operate here with standard examples, and a notion of objectivity, is that, in general, people who agree about the application of a colour predicate to the standard will also agree about the further application of the predicate in all apart from borderline cases. A simple perceptual judgement has a truth-condition[2] just because there is agreement among those who make the most, and the most consistent, per-

---

[1] Illustrations, in L. A. Selby-Bigge, *British Moralists* (Oxford, 1897), vol. 1, p. 416.
[2] The only simple statement of the truth-condition appropriate to the belief that X is yellow is the statement that X is yellow. This is what is meant by calling yellow a 'simple' quality.

ceptual discriminations, and because there is no possible *argument* which could make them perceive things differently.

Therefore, if the analogy is to be sufficient for the objectivity of moral judgements, we must be able to refer to standard examples. A man's response to these standards will then be a measure of his capacity to agree without collusion in the moral view of his fellows. If we could show that there are such standard examples, then it would be plausible to suggest that, although moral judgements are not made on the basis of criteria, they none the less refer to truth-conditions, and hence express beliefs. This is certainly the common-sense view of morality; it is in this way that the 'language-game' of morality is learned. A child is taught moral language by means of standard examples of good and evil. He thereby acquires a certain pattern of feeling, as a result of which his further application of moral terms will be in agreement with the application of those terms by other members of his community. The agreement which shows him to be a moral being is not the product of a common perceptual capacity. It consists in his sharing in a community of attitudes.

The analogy, then, is the following: the individual capacity to discover the objective truth in judgements of colour and of morals (supposing there *is* to be an objective truth) could only be measured against the things he judges, by examining his conformity to standards; it could not be discovered by considering his ability to bring forward reasons for his views. Seeing for oneself that an action is right is a matter of feeling about it in the right way, and the individual capacity to feel rightly must be judged with reference to standards fixed, not only in a given society or culture, but among all men as such. The difference lies in the fact that the individual capacity is a capacity for feeling, in the sense of having emotions and attitudes of a certain sort, whereas with *colours* it is a capacity for the right sensory impressions. Hence, in the case of morals, the standards cannot be universal, or at least can only be so accidentally.

But if this is the case then the demand for objectivity cannot be satisfied. In other words, there can be no truth-condition for a moral judgement. The fact that colours are objective properties is dependent on the fact that it is not within a man's normal powers to alter his sense-impressions; nor is it within anyone else's power to alter them by argument, nor do they vary from person to person or from day to day. None of this is true of emotions or attitudes. A man need never be compelled to admit that he is wrong in a moral judgement. For he can understand moral language and simply disagree *morally* with others about its application. The world – that which is objectively there – may not be a logical construction out of sense-impressions, but at least our sensory capacities, when measured against it, are being equally measured against those of other men. There is, therefore, some intimate connection between our sensory states and what is objectively the case. The world cannot make room for emotion in the same way and, however much we pour emotion on to the facts, to borrow Wittgenstein's metaphor, it will always flow off them.[1]

Nor would it affect this point were there to be a widespread agreement in moral attitudes. The very fact that it is logically possible to bring *reasons* against such an attitude, and be led to abandon it on the strength of these reasons, is sufficient to undermine the objectivity which the intuitionists are searching for. If a Messiah should come among us tomorrow and change our moral views, he would not have changed the things we judge, but only our way of judging them.

13 In defending the insights of Moore and the Intuitionists, we have adopted a position which is fully emotivist. But what has just been said immediately gives rise to two objections. First, has not emotivism undermined the notion of ethical objectivity? Yet is it not an obvious fact that moral judgements cannot be *held* as though they were subjective? Do they not presuppose their own objectivity? And is not this the reason why moral language adopts a subject-predicate form, and is not susceptible, for example, to any reduction in terms of imperatives? Secondly, how do we explain our sense that radical disagreement in moral judgements seems to undermine the objectivity of morals?

We must now produce a notion which will serve the same purposes as the idea of objectivity, and yet which will maintain the connection between ethical predicates and attitudes. I shall suggest a way in which a seeming objectivity might be indefinitely sustained in moral discourse, despite intersubjective disagreement. I wish to propose a view of moral 'objectivity' as indefinitely suspended subjectivity.

Although a man cannot choose to have the emotions and attitudes he has, he is none the less in a position to change them, and he is

[1] 'Lecture on ethics' *Philosophical Review* (January 1965).

F

answerable for them to the extent that we can persuade him by rational argument to give up the beliefs on which they depend, or modify them in the light of an improved conception of what they entail. Thus people have tried to look for a notion of objectivity in the *giving of reasons*, not seeing that these reasons might not be connected in the way required for objectivity with the judgements they support. As it is, standards of reasoning which provide a conclusive decision procedure are standards which embody values, and are not prior to them.

But there is a strong temptation to suppose that moral reasoning, even if it is not a matter of producing criteria, can at least produce reasons of universal validity. One consideration that lends support to this view is that the reasons which justify my doing or approving of something are like those which justify my believing something, in that they must be equally good for anyone else in a similar situation. Thus moral beliefs are not simply a matter of preference. Indeed, emotivism must admit this. Let us again examine the moral attitudes and see how their formal conditions might affect the nature of moral reasons. We have already seen that the moral attitude is universal, and this entails that moral predicates are supervenient. So, if a man manifests a moral attitude towards something, it will be on account of features of it, such that, were those features to occur in something else, he would take up the same attitude. The universality of the moral attitudes entails that moral judgements must be universalizable. It is sometimes thought that universalizability is sufficient to introduce moral 'criteria' or moral reasons, and hence that if moral judgements are universal then no one can assess something morally without using 'criteria of merit'. In other words, the term 'criterion of merit' is often used to refer to the defining property of the *type* towards which goodness is ascribed. But if goodness is a property of types then in saying that an action is good because it is, say, an expression of benevolence, I am not using a *criterion* of goodness; if there are criteria then I need them not for this judgement, but for the ascription of goodness to the characteristic of benevolence.[1] Thus, while critics of *The Language of Morals* have attacked universalizability as a trivial condition of moral reasoning (since, as is rightly said,[2] it is a condition of any reasoning

---

[1] Hare is misleading on this point, particularly in putting forward the view that moral judgements have descriptive as well as prescriptive meaning purely because of their universality. See *Freedom and Reason* (Oxford, 1963), p. 15.

[2] E.g. by D. H. Monro, *Philosophy*, No. 137 (April and July 1961).

whatsoever), it is a far from trivial condition of a moral *attitude*. Taken in this way, universalizability is merely the linguistic reflection of a central feature of moral attitudes, the feature which distinguishes them from mere feelings.

However, although universalizability tells us very little about moral reasoning, it follows from the *normative* character of moral attitudes, that if moral reasoning is to support moral principles then it must produce reasons for anyone to act in accordance with them. It follows that a man can only hold a moral principle as a rational agent. The reasons for this are as follows:

(1) If a man sincerely approves of an action or a state of affairs, then he must believe that it possesses some feature which defines a type of which he also approves. Hence moral principles do not only contain what Hutcheson called 'exciting reasons'; merely in stating them we already give a 'justifying reason' for acting from them. No matter how unthinking a man may be, he cannot count as approving of an action unless he can answer at least one 'Why?'-question. Asked to justify the action, he can always cite the principle (his answer might be 'I approve of that action, or I seek to perform that action, because it is an instance of benevolence'). This is presumably why Hare argued that universalizability can account for the rationality of moral judgement and can provide 'criteria' of moral value.

It is worth noting that this 'Why?'-question will be applicable to any action done from the principle, and *here* it seems to have the same sense as the 'Why?'-question whose applicability Miss Anscombe has argued to be the criterion of an intentional act.[1] That is, acting *from* a moral principle, as opposed to merely acting in accordance with it, will necessarily be intentional, assuming the truth of Miss Anscombe's thesis. So will the punishing of someone who disobeys the principle (thus there is no such thing as unintentional punishment, even though the intended punishment might be applied to a person whom it was not intended to punish).

(2) More important, however, is the following: in the case of a moral attitude (as opposed to an attitude which is *merely* universal) there is no quick way out of the 'Why?'-question. Once it has been raised, I cannot simply reject it, without tending to show myself insincere. For if I have a moral attitude then I am committed to

[1] See *Intention*, section 16.

proposing a law of conduct; as a result I am not at liberty to construe any 'Why?'-question as a query about my merely personal desires; nor am I at liberty to think that it does not matter if such a question could not be answered in a way acceptable to others. For I am supposing that it is possible for the law which I propose to be a law for others as well as for myself. Therefore, I must be disposed to think that there are reasons for acting in the desired way which are generalizable; and to reject the 'Why?'-question is to show that I believe there are no such reasons. In most circumstances, to reject the 'Why?'-question will be to abandon the normative point of view; for it will be to show that one's concern is not with a law of action to which all men should submit, but with a personal desire, for example, or a personal resentment. If it is asked why I am against some course of action, and I cite the principle which this action contravenes, and if it is further asked why I am against actions of that *kind*, then I am not at liberty to reply 'I just am!' without this answer being taken as definitive of what attitude I have; I will be supposed to be expressing anger or resentment at some individual occurrence.

We can see therefore that the principle of universalizability is not trivial: because moral judgements are universalizable, a 'Why?'-question is always in place. And further, because moral judgements are normative, there is no definite point at which this 'Why?'-question can be rejected. Of course, a man's reasons will eventually give out; having stated his fundamental moral position he may find that there is little else he can do in the way of producing reasons in its favour. But he may none the less believe that there are reasons (he may not know what reasons) which would produce an agreement in attitude. At least he cannot believe that it is out of the question that there could be such reasons. Suppose A believes that courage is a virtue, and B asks him 'Why?' Now if A's attitude to courage is a moral attitude, and if he believes that B has understood as much, then he must construe B as asking for a reason why he, B, should favour courage. And if A is really concerned with proposing a law of conduct for others, then he cannot simply say that B's question is out of place; he must believe that either something *could* be said which might bring B to favour courage, or else that B is in some way blind, or else that his own moral attitude is questionable.

This does not mean that a man must always argue in favour of his moral beliefs until they have been proved or disproved. It means simply that he must show an unwillingness to *reject* 'Why?'-questions. Nor does it mean that he must always *try* to argue, or *know how* to argue, in favour of his moral beliefs: it would be sufficient if he thought that, for each of these beliefs, there must *be* an intersubjectively acceptable reason for holding it, even if he does not yet know what it is. Normativity is sufficient, none the less, to make moral attitudes into a species of judgement, and, as I shall argue, it also guarantees that the linguistic expression of moral attitudes will be similar to the linguistic expression of other kinds of judgements, such as beliefs.

The normative nature of the moral attitude entails that moral ends will be more complex, and more amenable to reasoning, than those towards which intentional action is generally directed. For it is not open to a man to answer a 'Why?'-question simply by saying 'That's just what I want'; he is committed to believing that others should share his desire. For example, someone might ask me 'Why did you give money to that man?', and I might answer, 'Because he is a poor tramp'. I am then asked 'Why give money to poor tramps?' I continue to answer until I come down to saying – for example – 'In giving money to that man I was confirming the sentiment of subservience in the underprivileged classes'. Asked why I did such a thing, I could not answer 'That's just what I *want*' without thereby abandoning the moral point of view. I am being asked to give reasons why you should adopt, *as an end*, the desire for subservience among certain classes of people.

(3) The upshot of all this is that it is possible to construe moral reasoning as *a series of successive answers to a single 'Why?'-question*, asked of some course of action or way of life.[1] And it is part of having a moral attitude that one will not simply reject 'Why?'-questions; one will either pursue them to the point of agreement, or else give up in the conviction that one's opponent is mistaken or irrational.

This contrasts with a common view of the nature of moral reasoning. This is the view that the first answer to the 'Why?'-question quotes a principle: 'Actions of this kind are wrong'. After this moral reasoning is supposed to take a totally different form, consisting in the peculiarly *moral* justification of the principle. On the contrary, argument in

---

[1] This is not to limit morality to action-guiding principles, since judgements of virtue also only have sense in so far as they can be shown to enjoin acting and behaving in certain ways. However, these ways will be many and various for any such judgement.

favour of a principle is of the same logical kind as argument from the principle to a particular course of action. The only difference is that a man must necessarily be in possession of the reason which enables him to proceed from the principle to the action, whereas he may only believe that there *are* reasons for the principle itself.

This is a conclusion about the intentionality of moral approval: a man only approves of something if he believes that there are reasons of a certain kind (practical reasons) for acting in accordance with his attitude. It follows logically from someone's having a moral attitude that he believes that there is *some* (indefinite) process of reasoning of a kind which could refer, at some point, to genuine intersubjective agreement. He is committed to this belief as much as he is committed, by the universality of the attitude, to being able to produce the first reason in this chain of justification.

It is worth mentioning here a method of establishing weak naturalism, on the basis of an emotivist theory of ethics. It is sometimes said that anything a man wants to do or obtain is conceived by him as a benefit. To all desires there corresponds the thought of a benefit. This notion of 'benefit' is descriptive, and very inclusive; if I want something for myself, then I must believe that it is a benefit to me in this extremely minimal sense – wanting is intentional in this way.[1] In like manner it might be suggested that if I want something for men in general – and therefore if I have a normative attitude in favour of something – I must believe it to be a benefit to men in general. Therefore I cannot have a moral belief without relating the object which I approve of to considerations of human benefit and harm.

14 We can now show how the emotivist is to account for the apparent objectivity of moral judgements. Let us return for a moment to the distinction drawn earlier[2] between two views of the relation between moral reasons and moral principles. On the first view – (1) – moral reasons are necessarily involved in moral principles, whereas on the second view – (2) – moral principles and moral reasons are totally

---

[1] Cf. the scholastic argument which says that a man can only want something under the aspect of a good (*sub specie boni*). The *bonum* here referred to is a wide notion similar to the minimal sense of 'benefit' which weak naturalism proposes as a moral 'criterion'. It is equally descriptive, or if it is not, then according to the argument of Section 6, an emotivist must deny that it characterizes the intentionality of approval.

[2] On p. 58.

independent; there is no need for a man to believe that there are any reasons for his moral views. We can now see not only that (1) is not equivalent to strong naturalism, but also that the emotivist must accept (1) – or something like it – and reject (2). Up to now I have argued entirely as though (2) is the alternative most congenial to emotivism, but in fact this is not so. For we have seen that a man has a moral attitude only if he believes that there are replies to any 'Why?'-question asked of a judgement or action issuing from that attitude. Moral attitudes include practical reasons; a moral judgement can only be made by someone who believes that there are practical reasons which support it.

Thus moral principles are necessarily connected with moral reasons, even though moral reasons are not necessarily reasons (they are not criteria). Hence, a strong version of the weak naturalist thesis can be defended without giving way to naturalism in its proper form. For an argument against the naturalistic fallacy is valid even on the basis of (1); if there are no moral criteria, then it is still a fallacy to suppose that an argument in favour of deductive canons for moral reasoning can have a conceptual and not a moral force.

In other words, to admit (1) does not commit the emotivist to any particular view about how moral reasons support moral judgements. Nor does it commit him to saying that the *kind of reason* to which 'weak naturalism' refers must be specifiable in a way acceptable to the majority of moral agents. It must simply be that the man who gives a moral reason for his action believes it to be at least to some extent acceptable to others as a reason for acting in such a way. For the emotivist it is also a logical truth that, if a man has a moral principle, he has at least one reason for acting in accordance with it, as well as some readiness to give further reasons as they are required.

This indefinite element of practical reason included in the moral attitudes explains the constant attraction of naturalism, with its insistence that approval is a disguised belief. I can produce reasons for my moral attitudes, and these reasons will only be acceptable if I can show that they have intersubjective validity. When I discuss my moral opinions with another or with myself, it is as if I were engaged in proving them right or wrong. But the sole end of such discussion is to bring about agreement, and the giving of reasons can always come to rest when this is achieved. Hence moral discussion takes for granted that there is an agreement somewhere to be discovered. Once agreement has been reached there is no point in bringing further reasons, any more than there is in the case of colour judgements.

Suppose, then, that two people are engaged in moral discussion in support of opposing moral views. And suppose that one of the disputants should be convinced by the arguments of his opponent. Then, because he has changed his opinion as a result of accepting a *reason*, he would not characterize his conversion as discovering the subjectivity of his original judgement, but rather as discovering it to be false. Therefore, although there can be no decision procedure of the kind appropriate to beliefs, it is still necessary that reference to agreement be preserved. However sharp the initial disagreement, no moral argument can proceed without the assumption of some *underlying* agreement on the basis of which one of the parties could be shown to be in error. A man who argued morally by producing reasons which he knew his opponent could *not* agree with might, in many cases, be considered insincere; he would not be thought to be arguing morally. My conclusion, then, is this: moral argument can come to *rest* in agreement. When there is no agreement, however, argument is always possible – for it can never be proved that there is an ultimate disagreement about what would count as a good *reason* for an attitude. In adducing reasons, therefore, the appearance of agreement can be indefinitely maintained. As a result, we might say that the subjectivity of moral judgements (the fact that, in making them, one is expressing an attitude and not a belief) is 'suspended' in rational discussion. There is 'suspended subjectivity' whenever (*a*) agreement is presupposed, and questions do not need to arise as long as there is agreement; and (*b*) disputes give rise to practical arguments, with the adducing of reasons which can only have strength on the supposition of some further agreement. These reasons are practical – they are of the sort used to justify attitudes, emotions and actions. They are totally different from the Wittgensteinian 'critieria', not being conventionally connected with the judgements they support, but rather referring to motives, or reasons for acting.

Not only moral predicates satisfy these two conditions: suspended subjectivity is characteristic of normative discourse generally. Affective terms also possess this property. You and I might agree that lions are frightening, and this agreement might be manifested in a general similarity of response towards lions. We could, in the context of our shared response, quite readily understand each other while totally disagreeing about the reasons for our mutual opinion. Suppose, however, that you insist that only cowards are frightened of animals. You are suggesting that some other response than fear is the right one. And the reason which you give assumes that we have at least one common attitude – to cowards. There is no end to the possibilities of further agreement to which we might at any stage refer. And always the reasons which are produced are reasons for feeling a certain emotion; they are nothing like 'criteria' for the ascription of a predicate.

PART III THE STRUCTURE OF MORAL LANGUAGE

15 We have completed the examination of the attitude of approval, and compared it with beliefs; and we have discovered that the intentionality of moral approval includes the belief that there are practical reasons underlying any instance of the attitude. On this account approval becomes a species of judgement, analogous to belief, and hence the expression of approval has the appearance of objectivity.

This does not explain, however, why moral language is alike in every respect to the language ('descriptive' or 'property-ascribing' language) which expresses beliefs. It is to Moore's credit that he noticed that moral language did have this property-ascribing structure. And both intuitionism and naturalism successfully predict that this should be the case. It has been thought one of the gravest objections to emotivism that it cannot make this prediction. Moreover, several writers have attempted to produce arguments to show that no language which expresses an attitude *can* behave in the manner of moral language.[1] If this is the case, then emotivism is discredited. The objections may be summarized under two heads:

(A) If the predicate, 'good', expresses an attitude, and if this is part of its meaning, then it must also express the attitude in conditional contexts. For example – P: 'If he is a good man, then he is happy'. Otherwise it would have a different *meaning* in conditional contexts from the meaning it has in assertoric contexts. And this cannot be allowed, since P, together with Q: 'He is a good man', entails R: 'He is happy'. But no entailment relation of this kind could hold if the protasis of P did not mean the same as Q.

[1] See J. R. Searle, 'Meaning and speech-acts', *Philosophical Review* (1962); Bernard Williams, 'Morality and the emotions', in this volume; and P. T. Geach, 'Assertion', *Philosophical Review* (October 1965).

On the other hand, we cannot say that 'good' is used in P to express an attitude. The whole purpose of P might be to *withhold* one's approval, for one might be told 'But he is not happy', in which case it follows again that S: 'He is not good', and it must therefore be possible to hold P and S consistently. Hence P cannot be an expression of approval, since a man who expressed approval of another, and at the same time claimed that he was not good would, on the emotivist view, be inconsistent, or insincere.

This contrasts with:

(*a*) Imperatives, questions, and other sentence-forms which are characteristically used with a force other than that of expressing a belief. These cannot enter the protasis of conditionals at all, and their part in logical operations is highly dubious. Recently the notion of an imperative inference has received many attacks, and at the very least it poses problems not to be met with in inferences involving ethical expressions.

(*b*) Expletives, such as 'blasted', and predicates, such as 'nigger', which do preserve their expressive value in all logical contexts and which therefore seem to be linguistically connected with this expressive value. For example, 'If he is a nigger then he will not be accepted' standardly expresses the speaker's contempt towards Negroes. Or, 'If he has broken his blasted tricycle again he will go without his pocket money', which expresses the speaker's anger over the possible breaking of a tricycle (this development of the argument is due to Bernard Williams).[1]

(B) Judgements of value can be true or false, unlike imperatives or questions. We can also make a distinction between merely believing something to be good and really knowing it to be good (a point used to great effect by Moore and Ewing).

These two objections amount to the very powerful claim that, whatever we say about moral attitudes, the language which is supposed to express them behaves as though it were entirely descriptive and property-ascribing. Moral language seems to have built into it a logic of property-ascription. Therefore, if we wish to base our conclusions about the nature of moral evaluation on the analysis of moral language

[1] 'Morality and the emotions', in this volume. Williams's example has been slightly changed.

alone, we must come back to agreeing with Moore, or with the naturalists, that ethical propositions express beliefs and not attitudes.

First, let us examine predicates such as 'nigger', which the theory I am discussing would hold to be linguistically connected with an attitude. It seems to me that the grounds given for saying that this connection is part of the *meaning* of 'nigger' are grounds for saying precisely the opposite. For the same belief could be conveyed by saying either 'He is a Negro' or 'He is a nigger', and the logic of 'nigger' is alike in every respect to that of 'Negro'; the two predicates have precisely the same criteria for their application. However, because 'nigger' is generally used by people who despise Negroes, we cannot say that the choice between using one or the other word is entirely neutral. It follows that anybody who knew this fact about the word 'nigger', and who still used it instead of 'Negro', would thereby show that he had *chosen* a word generally associated with a certain attitude. Since it must be assumed that this is entirely intentional on his part, he will thus be *expressing* that attitude. Since he is expressing an attitude through choosing a word (as opposed to using a word which is connected by a meaning rule with a certain attitude) then it is evident that this attitude will be expressed in whatever logical context the word occurs.[1] For it does not make any difference to the attitude which such a choice expresses that the word, once it has been chosen, should occur in a conditional or in an assertion. It could perhaps be said that I *conversationally* express a certain attitude in using a word like 'nigger'. Thus we could distinguish cases of expression where the expression is part of the meaning of the words one uses, from cases where it comes about through various extraneous *facts* about the use of those words. This distinction would perhaps correspond to that made by Grice, between conversational implication and logical implication, in the case of descriptive utterances.[2]

In the case of 'blasted', we cannot deny that the expressive content is part of the meaning of the word (there are no criteria for the application of 'blasted', nor are there necessary conditions governing that

---

[1] This does not apply if the word 'nigger' is mentioned rather than used, nor does it apply if it occurs in an intensional context. For example, I am certainly not expressing an attitude in saying 'The word "nigger" is now considered impolite', nor in saying 'If you think of him as a nigger, then that shows how prejudiced you are'.

[2] See H. P. Grice, 'The causal theory of perception', in G. J. Warnock (Ed.), *The Philosophy of Perception* (Oxford, 1967), pp. 90–5.

to which it can be applied). However, in this case, the intentionality of the emotion expressed is nil: it is a 'primitive passion' of anger or irritation. The intentionality of an attitude consists in (*a*) the belief on which it is founded, and (*b*) any belief in the existence of justifying reasons which someone might be committed to by having this attitude. In the case of irritation, however, any belief or propensity to justify is only *contingently* associated with the feeling. It follows that there will be nothing to hypothesize, as it were, in the conditional use of any term (such as 'blasted') which standardly expresses irritation.

Let us take the example of the tricycle: since 'blasted' is used to express a 'non-cognitive' emotion, there is no information contained in 'That's his blasted tricycle' which is not already contained in 'That's his tricycle' (this explains the pointlessness of 'You are blasted' or 'He's not just a man he's a blasted man' – irritation, unlike approval is not a mode of judgement). Because of this, nothing is conditionalized by the occurrence of 'blasted' in the protasis – there is no belief nor any process of justification to serve as the hypothesis posited by the use of 'if'. Hence there can be no explanation of the occurrence of 'blasted' in the protasis at all, except on the basis of the expressive quality which it has. Once again, therefore, it is the *choice* of the word 'blasted', included no matter where, which will express the irritation.

If irritation has no intentional content, then the two sentences 'He is an Englishman' and 'He is a blasted Englishman' must express the same belief. In that case, an inference of the following form should be deductively valid: 'If he is a blasted Englishman, then I will certainly not get on with him; he is an Englishman, therefore I will certainly not get on with him'. It should be valid because the belief expressed in the protasis of the conditional does not go beyond the belief expressed by 'He is an Englishman'. Logical relations of the kind expressed in deductive inferences hold between beliefs, on account of their truth-conditions. The inference 'If *a* then *b*; *c*, therefore *b*' is valid if the truth-conditions of the belief expressed by '*c*' include those of the belief expressed by '*a*'.

A moment's reflection will reveal that the inference in question *is* valid. On the other hand, we can expect that words which express attitudes with a complex intentional content will be able to play a part of their own in deductive inferences. 'Good' will differ from 'blasted' in a way which will reflect the fact that approval is more intentional than irritation. Thus, 'He is a good man' and 'He is a man' cannot be taken as expressions of the same belief. The first expresses the belief that he is a man, together with the beliefs essential to the intentionality of approval. Therefore the inference 'If he is a good man he will be rewarded; he is a man, therefore he will be rewarded' must be invalid. For the intentionality of approval provides further beliefs which could be hypothesized in a conditional ascription of goodness.

If 'good' must capture the indefinite element of justification involved in the moral attitudes, then it is to be expected that the adjective which, when used assertorically, is accompanied by this attitude could be used conditionally without it. But this is not a ground for saying that the attitude-expressing function of moral language is not part of its meaning. For an emotivist can hold consistently all the following propositions:

(1) When used assertorically – e.g. in 'this is good' – the adjective 'good' expresses an attitude; and this is part of its meaning in the sense that someone who did not so use it would not be making a moral judgement, and hence would not understand the notion of moral goodness.

(2) When used conditionally – e.g. in 'If he is a good man then he is a happy man', the adjective 'good' need not be used by someone who has any specific attitude.

(3) The word 'good' is not ambiguous from context to context.

For the argument does not prevent the emotivist from saying that 'good' in its conditional use has precisely the same meaning which it has in its assertoric use. We are still able to say that its meaning is such that *if* used assertorically *then* it must be used by someone who has a certain attitude, and this is the meaning which it has even when it is not used assertorically. For the reasons for saying that 'good' standardly expresses an attitude derive from conditions governing its assertoric use. The argument can only show emotivism to be wrong if it points to some fact about the use of moral language which emotivism cannot predict. But a consideration of the intentional content of approval shows that emotivism can also predict the use of 'good' in conditionals, and can correctly compare this use with that of 'blasted' and of 'nigger'. For when 'good' is used conditionally, it is not the attitude of approval which is hypothesized but the intentional content of that attitude.

16 A strong reason for thinking that objection (A) is conclusive against emotivism is that if it is 'part of the meaning' of ethical terms that they should, when used assertorically, express attitudes, then it must be possible to paraphrase their meaning in order to reveal, *as a component of it*, the attitude expressed. In that case, the expressive element would enter as a component of the meaning even when the term occurred in contexts where it could *not* be expressing an attitude. But this is precisely what an emotivist must avoid, if he is to maintain the distinction between descriptive and evaluative meaning.

One modern attempt to get round objection (A) – that of Urmson – falls into this error. Urmson[1] says that 'good' has the central illocutionary force of expressing an 'evaluation'. This is his way of putting the emotive idea, that 'good' expresses an attitude in its assertoric use. He explains that an illocutionary force is central if 'anyone who assented to the utterance with any illocutionary force could not consistently dissent from it when used with that illocutionary force' (p. 138). He then tries to give a definition of 'good' which will incorporate the central illocutionary force of expressing a 'favourable evaluation' as part of its meaning: 'good' = 'satisfies a description such that no one can correctly dissent from a favourable evaluation (as of some kind or from some point of view) of an object that satisfies the description' (p. 142). But, as an explanation of the meaning of the term 'good', this hinges on the notion of *correctness* and it is not certain what this notion is meant to be. On the most obvious interpretation of the term 'correctly' the definition collapses into a familiar form of intuitionism: good becomes that towards which it is right to take up a pro-attitude. The definition is then circular as an explanation of normative language in terms of attitudes, since it relies on the notion of 'rightness'. Thus the definition becomes 'good' = 'that which ought (on the basis of observable features) to be the object of a favourable evaluation'.[2]

What seems clear is that any attempt to introduce the attitude of approval as 'part of the meaning' of ethical terms leads to too direct a reference to the process of justification which underlies the possibility of treating moral judgements as objective at all. If the reference is as direct as this, then the justification of attitudes exhausts the meaning of moral terms: 'good' simply means 'justified as object of approval'.

[1] *The Emotive Theory of Ethics.*

[2] This definition was defended admirably by Ewing in *Second Thoughts in Moral Philosophy*, on the basis of the property-ascribing nature of moral discourse.

In that case the attitude of approval itself drops out of the meaning rules governing the use of the term 'good', and no clear explanation of the meaning of 'good' can be given without referring to the process of justification as *moral* justification, whatever that may be. But one advantage of emotivism is that it allows the notion of justification to enter as part of the 'cognitive content' of moral language, without requiring that we should be able to give any specification, except in the loosest terms, of what this justification might consist in. In this way it captures what seems to be the salient feature of ethical discourse – that it can operate as an intersubjective and rational language without there being descriptive criteria for the application of moral terms. It can maintain intersubjectivity in the absence of a defined decision procedure. Thus emotivism allows us to give an explanation of the meaning of moral predicates in terms of attitudes, while leaving the problem as to the nature of moral reasons more or less open. Considering the confusion into which practical reasoning is habitually plunged, this is an evident advantage. To take up a view such as Urmson's we are thrown right into the middle of the problem of *validity* in practical reasoning, and the only quick way out is to define the notion of justification in moral terms – in which case the autonomous, property-ascribing nature of moral language is vindicated, and emotivism ceases to be a plausible view.

There remains objection (B). How is it that we can apply predicates like 'true', 'false', 'probable', 'certain', 'known' and 'believed' to moral propositions, if these propositions express attitudes and not beliefs? Once again, it seems that the reference to intersubjective validity must be more centrally connected with the meaning of moral predicates than emotivism allows. Moral propositions have the same form as propositions expressing belief, and we speak of believing and knowing them, wondering whether they are true, coming to the conclusion that they are not true, and so on.[1] All this is essential to moral language, and it is well known that an imperativist analysis, for example, has great difficulty in explaining such facts as these.

This is a genuine difficulty, but it is less devastating than it seems at first sight. I shall show that moral language is very likely to have the features of a property-ascribing language if it is to express the moral attitudes. And I will try to show that the moral attitudes lay down the

---

[1] For a discussion of this point, in relation to the property-ascribing nature of moral language, see J. N. Findlay, *Values and Intentions* (London, 1961), pp. 222–4.

required conditions for moral language, without conceding that these attitudes are any nearer to beliefs than they are to emotions.

17 If, as I have been supposing, moral attitudes contain an element of reaction, and are not exhausted by the beliefs which are essential to them, then they cannot be expressed in a language the predicates of which are criterion-governed.

Any language which is to give voice to the moral attitudes must satisfy the following conditions:

(*a*) It must be possible to connect its assertoric use with the expression of a favourable attitude.

(*b*) It must contain within itself the *intersubjective* reference which the normative basis of the moral attitude requires. Hence there will be advantages if, as Moore believed, the language is property-ascribing.

(*c*) It must also allow a prior division of the objects to which it applies into types, in order to satisfy the universality requirement. It could not, for example, be a language of property-ascription analogous to colour language.

(*d*) It must allow the possibility of an indefinite number of 'Why'-questions asked of any object to which it is applied.

(*e*) It must have central application to human conduct, and the ends human beings wish to achieve.

Each of these conditions reflects one of the criteria for an attitude's being moral. (*a*) corresponds to the fact that approval is a species of favouring. (*b*) corresponds to the normative, social nature of the moral attitudes; (*c*) to their universality and (*d*) to the indefinite possibilities of justification which these last two conditions, taken together with the proposition that human beings are rational agents, entail. (*e*) reflects the fact that moral attitudes are concerned with legislating between different kinds of human conduct.

Now it so happens that there is a language which is both genuinely property-ascribing, and which also satisfies these five conditions. This language differs from the language of morals only in the following way: that its use is governed by criteria, and that (as a result) the connection with attitudes referred to in condition (*a*) is a connection of fact and not of logic. This is the language whose terms have invariably been used for the purpose of formulating moral laws – the language of *utility*. This language contains the predicates 'good', 'right', 'bad' and 'wrong' and the important word 'ought'. Yet all these words have a different sense when used in the language of utility from their sense in moral judgements. Only naturalists have been able to explain why we use the same terms at all in these two separate linguistic activities. But if it so happens that the conditions normally governing the use of these terms (in the language of utility) are precisely those which enable the expression of moral attitudes, then the emotivist will also be able to explain why these terms are used in common between the two language-games. In doing so, he will show why it is that moral language has the appearance of a language of property-ascription. And he will, at the same time, maintain his advantage over the naturalist, since he can grant the structure of moral language while still retaining his valuable explanation of *why* moral criteria cannot be produced.

Suppose I advise someone who is working beside me 'You ought to use *this* hammer', or 'This hammer is better' (better *as* a hammer, or better for your purpose). Let us examine how the logic of these assertions stands up to conditions (*a*) to (*e*) above.

(*a*) Must I be expressing a pro-attitude towards the hammer in question? I think it will be difficult to make out a case for saying that I must as a matter of logic be expressing such an attitude – I may be entirely indifferent to the functions hammers are characteristically used to perform (in a way that I cannot be indifferent to the objects of my moral judgements if I am to be sincere). Besides, the primary meaning rule governing the use of the term 'good' in 'good hammer' will involve reference to a criterion, such that to use the word according to this criterion is to manifest a correct linguistic grasp. This criterion is concerned, broadly speaking, with utility: a good hammer is a hammer which performs well (where performing well is explained in terms of the frequency, completeness, etc., of the required results) the functions which hammers perform. This is a criterion in the Wittgensteinian sense, and it is a criterion that is generalizable over all uses of 'good' in the language of utility: the word 'hammer' must of course be substituted by 'X' for any expression 'Good X' – that is, the attributive character of 'good' ensures that it can be criterion-governed and unambiguous when used in the language of utility.[1] We can also produce

[1] For an explanation of the attributive nature of 'good' see P. T. Geach, 'Good and evil', in Philippa Foot (Ed.), *Theories of Ethics* (Oxford, 1967). Note that not all uses of 'good' are attributive. There are the following distinguishable forms: 'good as an X,'

G

a further, more general use of 'good' in the language of utility, equivalent to 'good for some specific purpose', where the purpose is no longer defined by the nature of the object called good. However, there is strong temptation to say that, although there is no *logical* connection between 'good' (as used in the language of utility) and any favourable attitude, there is still a strong matter of fact connection, such that anybody who called a hammer 'good' but never preferred it to a hammer he judged inferior, would create puzzlement. There is a presupposition of communal interest which underlies the language of utility and conditions our using it at all. Someone who used it without sharing the relevant interests, and without showing any tendency to act according to his judgements (say, he always seemed to want *bad* or useless things), would not show any interest in discussions involving utility judgements, and his judgements when they were uttered would be automatically suspect.

It has been claimed by Duncan-Jones[1] that we tend not to use the term 'good' at all, except of things towards which there is a prior conviction that the functions they perform are *morally* good – the notion of a good *thief*, for example, is paradoxical. Duncan-Jones concludes from this that 'good' is not primarily attributive, since its attributive use depends on a prior evaluation of the things to which it is attributed *as good sorts of thing*. Hence the attributive use would seem to be logically secondary to the moral use of 'good' to express a favourable evaluation of a *kind of thing*, *tout court*.

However, Duncan-Jones's argument is not conclusive. It is still possible that the moral use of 'good' is not primary to, but rather dependent on, its use in the language of utility. For it is not the ability to use 'good' non-attributively that underlies its use in utility judgements. There is no sense in which the moral approval of mechanics, doctors and so on as good things needs to be expressed in precisely these terms before the language of utility can be brought to bear on mechanics and doctors. All that is required might be that the relevant

---

'good X', 'good for (some purpose or some thing)', and 'good' (*simpliciter*). The attributive use is common to most judgements in which 'good' characteristically occurs – judgements of utility and of morality, aesthetics and so on. The use of 'good' in which it cannot be replaced by 'good *as*' or 'good *for*' something, seems to be reserved for the expression of attitudes: it is characteristic of aesthetics, ethics and other activities where a normative attitude seeks to be expressed.

[1] A. Duncan-Jones, 'Good things and good thieves', *Analysis*, vol. 26, No. 4 (March 1966).

attitudes of general approval should *exist* – otherwise the point of utility language would disappear. It might be that the use of utility language presupposes a sufficient pro-attitude towards the things to which it is applied. Thus someone who said 'He is a good thief' while showing disapproval of thieves, might conceivably be said to be putting himself outside the context in which his utterance would have point. If this is the case, then it is so not because his disapproval of thieves must be expressed in a way which conflicts with the linguistic form of his original judgement (i.e. in some such way as 'Thieves are bad things'), but simply because he disapproves of thieves, whatever form he may choose in which to express this disapproval.

Thus Duncan-Jones's argument could be taken as proving that the language of utility satisfies condition (*a*), because of certain matters of fact which underlie its use. But this could be argued independently, without resorting to a conclusion as strong as that which Duncan-Jones's argument produces. We need not say that there is no point to the language of utility outside the context of certain attitudes; it is enough to point out that a judgement of utility is characteristically a sufficient ground for taking up a favourable attitude – provided, of course, that one has the purposes to which the judgement refers. So that a man who makes a judgement of utility will be taken, in general, as expressing a favourable attitude towards (as recommending) whatever he judges. And this is true, even though his judgement does not itself express a favourable attitude, but rather a belief about some matter of fact.

(*b*) Condition (*b*) is satisfied in two ways. First, the presence of a criterion governing the attributive use of 'good' (and, consequently, the use of 'ought-judgements' to correspond with this use) ensures that the language of 'good' should be property-ascribing. For in saying that something is good one is attributing a (relational) property to it: that of fulfilling to a high degree certain purposes. Hence a reference to intersubjective agreement is included on an elementary logical level: anybody who agreed that the purpose of hammers was to drive nails into wood, and who agreed that a given hammer drove nails more deeply, more reliably, etc., than another, and yet who denied that it was therefore a better hammer than the other, would be guilty of a linguistic error. He could be shown to have contradicted himself (if he was using 'good' as a predicate of utility).

But the reference to intersubjective agreement comes also at a deeper level, and this is very important, since it shows exactly in what way the suspended subjectivity of ethical judgements might be captured by the language of utility. For if 'good X' is to have a recognized use according to the criterion given, it must be possible to specify some purpose for which Xs are standardly used which will qualify as *the* purpose of Xs. Hence there must be intersubjective agreement over the functions of given items. If this agreement is well founded then often the function of an object may become part of its definition – as in 'knife', 'mechanic' and so on. In general, artefacts and human roles are the only objects to which characteristic functions are ascribed. Hence it is usually a matter of course, since artefacts and roles are created with a purpose in view, that the purpose for which they are made will be built into the concept which refers to them. Of other things one can only use the language of utility in the sense of 'good for certain purposes', as in 'good stone', 'good beach', etc.

But because there exists disagreement in purposes between people, it is quite possible for one man to disagree with another over the application of 'good' to knives, and yet still mean the same by this word (still be using it according to the stated criterion). For example, he might only use knives for the purpose of observing his face in their shining blades. Hence he will disagree almost entirely in his application of the word 'good' to knives with someone who used knives for cutting.

Of course the disagreement here is not a real disagreement in use – for the criterion employed by the two parties is precisely the same. It is simply that one man calls a knife good with respect to one set of purposes, while the other calls it good with respect to the more familiar purposes for which knives are used. And their disagreement could be settled at once, in so far as it is linguistic. However, underlying the superficial linguistic disagreement, there is a genuine disagreement of attitude towards knives. And this disagreement of attitude is reflected in a disparity between the two applications of the predicate 'good'.

Hence the language of utility contains a reference to purposes such that it must be the case – before something can be called good of its kind definitively – that men agree about what purposes things of that kind have. It involves reference to an intersubjective agreement on a level deeper than that which the criterion governing the use of the language requires. Therefore there is already built into such predicates as 'good' – which are undeniably property-ascribing in the language of utility – the reference to the intersubjective agreement in attitudes which is required if 'good' is to function as a moral word. There already exists in the language of utility a logical structure similar to that required for the 'suspended subjectivity' discussed in Sections 13 and 14. If there were no agreement in purposes between people, then it is not the case that utility language would *collapse*; we could still talk of things being good for certain purposes. What we could not say, however, would be such things as, 'This is good *as* a knife', 'This is a good hammer'. Hence there is a subsection of utility language which *does* depend for its use on a reference to intersubjective agreement in attitudes, and it is this subsection that we shall expect to be employed as the language of morals, since it answers to condition (*b*).

(*c*) Because of the connection between certain features of hammers and the functions that hammers characteristically perform, 'good' as applied to hammers is normally used as though it were supervenient on these features – though strictly speaking it is not. That is to say, that which justifies the application of the term 'good' to a hammer will be features which are only as a matter of fact connected with the function of hammers. These features – weight, length of handle, etc. – will function like the 'criteria' (in Warnock's sense) for moral judgements: they will serve to delimit types of thing, such that if a person calls a hammer good it will be because he believes it to belong to a certain type. This is not *always* so – for example, a man may pick up a hammer and, observing its performance, pronounce it quite correctly to be good, without knowing at all *why* it is good. None the less, there will always as a matter of fact be some feature or set of features contingently associated with the function required, and hence there arises a notion of standards which govern the use of utility language. These standards serve to supervise, as it were, the operation of the utility criterion. Thus one man might say 'I call a knife good if it has a shiny blade', whereas another will say 'I call a knife good if it has a sharp blade and a long handle'.[1]

---

[1] There is a distinction between moral rules (rules of thumb) and moral principles (on which such rules depend) which allows this kind of empirical supervenience in the moral case. Here propositions asserting empirical supervenience are supported by principles equally supervenient (only logically so). For example: 'This action is wrong'; 'Why?'; 'Because it is telling a lie'; 'But why is that a reason for saying that it is wrong?'; 'Because telling a lie is (in general) deceiving someone'; etc. . . . until an ultimate principle is stated: 'Because it is really breaking the kind of trust between people that makes happiness possible, and happiness is the only possible good' (for example). It is this ultimate principle which

(*d*) This contingent supervenience of utility characteristic also allows utility language to satisfy condition (*d*). For any property given as the *basis* for an attribution of goodness in the utility sense it can always be asked 'Why?' – e.g. 'Why do you call a knife good just because of its shiny blade?' Here of course the reasoning often does stop with the definition of a purely personal end, but it need not always do so. A man can be called upon to justify the purpose for which he uses knives, so that often a 'Why?'-question asked of an attribution of goodness to knives leads to questions asked of the purpose which this attribution reflects.

Hence, there is a more or less open possibility of 'Why?'-questions in support of any judgement of utility. And the basis for that judgement will generally consist in a reference to properties of which it also makes sense to ask why *they* are a reason for attributing goodness to the thing which possesses them. Here the 'Why?'-question can only be answered by giving practical reasons.

(*e*) It should be obvious that condition (*e*) is satisfied by the language of utility: this language could not exist at all independently of the purposes and aims of human beings, and its primary function is to give a rational means of describing the world in terms of those aims and purposes.

Given that we have this language which satisfies all the requirements specified for the possibility of a moral language, it is not surprising that it should also be used to express moral convictions. This explains why it is that we use 'good' and 'ought' and so on in contexts both of utility and of ethical (or for that matter aesthetic) evaluation – a fact which certainly needs explaining. We use the language as it stands – that is, as a language of property-ascription. For only in preserving its property-ascribing form will the language of utility enable us to capture the indefinite intentional content of the moral attitudes. It is this content which will then be hypothesized in conditionals and so forth.

We need only add the one meaning rule to secure a moral sense for these terms of utility – the rule that in assertions they should give voice to a certain attitude. This is sufficient to change the *manner* in which 'good', for example, will meet conditions (*a*) to (*e*), but it will not affect

---

defines most clearly the moral attitude of the man who supports it; the moral rules are only moral because, being held by the man in question to be of a piece with his principle, they express the same attitude.

the *fact* of its meeting them. And the fact that it still meets them will ensure that moral goodness can be treated as a property without conceptual confusion. The emotivist, then, can explain:

(1) The fact that moral questions and questions of utility are discussed in the same language.

(2) The fact that this language seems to be property-ascribing in both cases.

(3) The fact (pointed out by Moore) that there are no criteria for the application of moral terms – so that any proposed criterion can always be called *morally* into question.

(4) The fact that the central criteria whereby we decide whether a man's judgement is moral concern his actions and feelings.

Naturalism can explain (1) and (2), but is committed to denying (3); yet (3) seems sufficiently clear to cast considerable doubt on the truth of naturalism. Naturalism must also say that (4) refers to a matter of fact connection between attitudes and judgements, and this seems plainly false.

18 We must now make a few remarks on the concepts of truth, knowledge and validity, as applied to ethics. Urmson suggests that we can talk of moral principles being true, and moral arguments being valid, because we have in ethics a notion of *standards* according to which any moral statement can be judged.[1] Thus I can give sense to the question 'Is it true that X is good?' as a request for information concerning whether or not X attains to the standards laid down for the value of things of that kind. Likewise, a valid argument from 'X has natural properties P, Q, R, etc.' to 'X is good' is an argument in which P, Q, R, etc., refer to the standards of goodness for things of that kind.

However, these are not cases of *ethical* applications of the notions of truth and validity at all. As we argued above, ethical properties are necessarily properties of types; therefore it follows that every moral principle will define a standard of goodness. If I approve of benevolence, I will *ipso facto* adopt benevolence as a standard of goodness. Discovering whether something satisfies certain standards is then simply discovering whether or not it belongs to some type of which I approve. This is an entirely factual matter; it is either true or false that an object

---

[1] *The Emotive Theory of Ethics*, ch. 7.

belongs to a certain type. Likewise, we can hardly say that the inference, from 'Objects of type T are good, and this is an object of type T' to 'This object is good', is a paradigm case of *ethical* validity – for it is simply an instance of deduction. It should be clear from previous discussion that if the notions of truth and validity are to apply specifically to ethical judgements it must be on the basis of practical reason and not, as Urmson implies, on the basis of deduction.

This becomes clear as soon as we ask the question 'Is it true that . . .?' of the moral principle itself (or as soon as we ask the question 'Is it valid to move from "This man is benevolent" to "This man is good"?'). The problematic use of 'It is true that . . .', 'X knows that . . .', '. . . is valid', occurs when the gaps are filled by the statement of a moral principle (or standard). Urmson's argument gives no account at all of *this* application of the concepts of truth, knowledge and validity.

What, then, is the difference between knowing and believing a moral principle, and what is it for a moral principle to be true?

As we have said, there is a direct answer to this last question in the case of descriptive language; there is no problem in stating truth-conditions for statements involving predicates whose use is governed by criteria. We need only refer to these criteria. The logical question as to the meaning of descriptive terms is connected with the epistemological problem as to how we know the proposition expressed in their assertoric use to be true. But if emotivism is right, there is an unbridgeable gap between the logical and the epistemological in the case of ethics. The meaning rules of the term 'good' do not give truth-conditions for the assertion that a thing is good. The logical question about what is to count as a correct use of moral terms (linguistically) cannot be connected with the epistemological question as to how I can know something to be good, since the answer to the first question leaves undetermined what is to be said in answer to the second. So, it is objected, to say 'I know X is good' is to make an evaluative judgement once more, and hence the reasons which entitle me to claim knowledge are themselves reasons because of some evaluative principle as to what is to count as a *good* (not just a relevant) reason.

But surely this is not the whole truth. When a man says 'I used to believe that hanging was a good thing, but now I know that it is not', he is surely doing more than giving voice to a change of attitude. He is saying also that his previous attitude was *mistaken*, whereas his present attitude is correct or justified in a way that entitles him to speak of knowledge.

Here once again we seem to encounter a disparity between moral language and the predictions which emotivism can make. In the last section I showed how, on the basis of emotivism, it can be predicted that moral language should be property-ascribing. It remains to show that emotivism can give sufficient sense to the concepts of truth, validity and knowledge (all of which are vital to any property-ascribing language). A man who claims to know that something is good must not only believe it to be so – he must also believe that there are adequate grounds for his assertion. The question is: what sense can we attribute to the notion of 'adequate grounds' or 'justification' in this context? In what does the justification of a moral belief consist?

As I have made clear, the theory of emotivism entails that no 'justification' can show a moral judgement to be objectively true. Even if the notion of truth can be applied to ethics it cannot carry the implication of objectivity. If it did carry this implication then we would require truth-conditions to support the ascription of truth for moral judgements, and these are not forthcoming. The application of such concepts as truth and justification must again imply suspended subjectivity and not objectivity. A moral judgement *cannot* be objectively true, but it can stand up to the test of moral argument, either because people agree about it, or because it can be supported on the basis of *other* propositions over which they *could* agree.

It is clear, therefore, that for the emotivist, concepts such as justification, validity and truth must all be deprived of their objective reference in ethical contexts. They too must possess suspended subjectivity.

Likewise, if knowledge is justified true belief, it makes *sense* to say that people sometimes know moral propositions. But since there are no criteria for the truth of a moral judgement, and none for its being justified, there can be no criteria for saying that a man knows any given moral proposition. The statement that a man knows a moral proposition must also possess suspended subjectivity. For there is no decision procedure. This lack of a test for objective truth is combined with the perpetual possibility of conflict of attitudes, together with further disagreement about what might count as a good reason in support of any moral attitude. Therefore, although it is possible to believe that a moral principle is true, and believe that it is justified, and although it is possible to have reasons for believing that what one believes to be justification really is justification (and so on, indefinitely), it is impossible to *know* that a moral judgement really *is* justified, for there are no criteria whereby this could be decided. In other words, although it is possible to claim that one knows a moral proposition, it is not possible to know that one knows. Although, therefore, there is a point to concepts such as knowledge, validity and justification in this area, one cannot be certain that one's application of them is correct. So that, if there is sense to these concepts, it must be derived from their use in other language-games. We have already seen that this might be so: moral language can be usefully construed as secondary to the language of utility. This is an area where the least that can be said is that no entailment holds between 'X knows that *p*' and 'X knows that he knows that *p*'. But this inference has never appeared valid to more than a few.

19 There is a problem which I have so far not mentioned, but which might be thought to be the most important problem in ethics: under what conditions is an attitude shown to be justified?

Naturalism tries to avoid this question, by saying that it is no part of ethics. For ethical language is used to refer to the facts which justify a moral attitude. *How* these facts justify the attitude, and why people have these attitudes to the facts, is another matter. For emotivism, on the other hand, the problem of justification becomes a problem for ethics itself. To justify the moral attitude is to justify the statement which expresses it.

What emotivism has to say about this question is very simple, but before discussing the point, it is worth mentioning the possibility of an intermediate position between emotivism and naturalism, a position for which this problem of justification might seem to be less urgent. It might be thought that moral language could be used in-determinately, either to express a belief, or to express the attitude which this belief is supposed to justify. If we examine uses of 'good' which do not *definitely* belong to the language of utility, and which do not *definitely* belong to the language of morals, then it often seems that they hover in this indeterminate way between the two – 'good as a doctor', for example. When I say that someone is a good doctor it is not totally certain whether this is to be assimilated to the belief-expressing paradigm – as in 'good for certain purposes', where the use of 'good' is governed by a criterion – or whether it is to be assimilated to attitude-expressing statements – such as the moral principles exemplified by 'X is a good kind of thing'.

However, the view that 'good' expresses both a belief and an attitude is not defensible. For this view must say one or other of the following:

(1) 'Good' is used *either* in expressing a belief *or* in expressing an attitude. In which case it is governed by two logically independent meaning-rules and has, therefore, the two separate but related senses we have discussed.

(2) 'Good' is used correctly in giving voice to a belief and an attitude *together*. But if this is so, to identify the attitude as a moral attitude is to identify it *as* containing that belief. Under this description, therefore, the belief will quite simply collapse into the intentionality of moral approval. The theory will simply be emotivism in the form we have defended it.

So this view is not a possible alternative. Let us return then to the problem of practical reasoning: 'How can an attitude be justified?' For a naturalist this problem becomes 'How can we justify "approving" of what is good?' (where 'approval' is analysed in the way suggested in Section 7). For the emotivist, who is perhaps more honest in this matter, the problem is 'How can we know anything to be good?' Quite plainly, there is only one answer that an emotivist can give – although we can give sense to our *claims* to know moral propositions, we can never *know* them. There cannot be an objectively valid answer to the question. Any answer we give must possess suspended subjectivity and therefore will not, in the relevant sense, be an answer. If the question is asking for an objective statement of how we can know that anything is good, then it is nonsense. For the naturalist likewise it is difficult to see what sense could be given to the question: for how can we refer to justification when we have already stated – in giving the facts of the case – what is right? On the other hand it seems that there ought to be sense to this question. For the naturalist must allow that it is a purely contingent matter that, believing something to be good, I also think that I have a reason for favouring it. Whereas this is not possible for emotivism. If I think that something is good, then this entails that I have a reason for favouring it. If you ask for truth-conditions which will allow us to tell when my reason is a good reason, then your demand is without sense: you have not understood the difference between reasons for acting and reasons for believing. It is simply a *matter of fact* if human beings have attitudes to certain states of affairs, and hence it is a matter of fact if these states of affairs can provide people with reasons for acting in a certain way. This is the point from which ethics must start, not the point at which it must arrive. This, in Wittgenstein's phrase, is what is 'given'.

A reading of early emotivists often leaves the impression that to account for morality in terms of attitudes is incurably naïve. But a proper consideration of what an attitude can involve will show that emotivism need be neither naïve nor pernicious. A normative attitude is not the kind of thing which is expressed by 'Booh!' or 'Hurrah!'; rather, it will involve a whole pattern of thought and feeling. It may have its own peculiar verbal expression – and I have tried to show how this is possible. But it will be revealed also in other aspects of linguistic activity. This is partly responsible for the naturalist's insistence that some criterion-governed judgements are also moral. For a man can 'choose' (to borrow Hare's metaphor) many of the terms in which he describes his world, and his choice will often reflect a moral viewpoint. It may be that my use of terms which denote virtues and vices ('honest', 'treacherous', 'benevolent' and so on) will always reflect my underlying moral point of view. The fact that I make *these* classifications is an expression, or at least a symptom, of my moral feelings. Thus, although describing a man's character in terms of virtues and vices is a linguistic activity governed by truth-conditions, it will often have the appearance of moral judgement. For a moral attitude may be reflected in the choice of terms which the description employs.

Likewise, moral beliefs will be reflected in other spheres of human activity. A man's aesthetic preferences, his human relationships, and even his feelings about what must be true, all reflect the form of life which I have described as moral.

3 Moral Realism
S. W. Blackburn

I

Granted that it is correct to reply to a moral utterance by saying 'That's true' or 'That's not true', the question remains of what sort of assessment is indicated by these responses. Dummett, with whose paper this emphasis is associated, also says that a statement is false if a state of affairs obtains such that a man asserting the statement and envisaging that state of affairs as a possibility would be held to have spoken misleadingly.[1] But there are ways and ways of speaking misleadingly, of which speaking falsely is only one; and indeed not always one, as when you say something false knowing that the hearer will misinterpret it as something true. Even apart from the possibility of misleading someone only as to my beliefs or my authority, still I can mislead someone *about the truth of the subject under discussion* when a state of affairs exists, and I envisage it as a possibility (and indeed more than a possibility), and I say nothing but the truth. I would do this for example if I told an interested child that some elephants are at least twice as large as some fleas. Worse than that, in what way does a man speak misleadingly if he sincerely judges a thing to be good, envisaging the possibility that he may be wrong, according to standards of which we are aware and with which we disagree? We hold his judgement false, but I don't think we would hold him to have spoken misleadingly, unless we just meant: what he said would mislead anyone who believed it as to the truth about whether the thing is good. But then the relevant assessment of misleadingness is itself to be understood in terms of truth.

Nevertheless, perhaps some other candidate for the correspondence relation than one constructed from misleadingness exists. It is the purpose of this paper to argue that there are features of the claim that a moral judgement is true which prevent this being taken as the claim that it corresponds in any way with a state of affairs. It follows that an attribution of truth to such a judgement must involve a different

[1] M. Dummett, 'Truth', *Proceedings of the Aristotelian Society* (1958–9), p. 150.

sort of assessment, and it is a secondary purpose of the paper to ask what that might be, and whether it should be thought surprising that we have a form of utterance with this form of assessment. I shall call the view that the truth of moral utterances is to consist in their correspondence with some fact or state of affairs 'moral realism'; it is this view which I shall argue is false. Another way of characterizing realism, adopted by Dummett,[1] would be as the belief that for any moral proposition there must be something in virtue of which either it or its negation is true. This certainly points to the same view: the advantage in stressing that it is the existence or non-existence of a state of affairs which determines truth or falsity, according to the realist, is that it is precisely the disparity between the logical conditions upon the existence of states of affairs, and those upon moral truth, which is to be urged in what follows.

There exist already two well-known arguments for the falsity of moral realism. Both take one feature of assent to a moral proposition, and claim that this is not a feature of belief that some state of affairs obtains; whence it follows that assent to a moral proposition – which may be expressed as belief that it is true – is not belief that some state of affairs obtains, and thence that the truth of a moral proposition does not consist in the existence of any state of affairs. The features which these arguments seize upon concern respectively our attitudes and our actions.

The first argument, then, emphasizes the connection between real assent to a moral proposition and the possession of a certain attitude to its subject. At its strongest, it can be stated as follows. Belief that a thing is good entails possession of a certain attitude towards it. No belief that a thing enters into a state of affairs entails the possession of any attitude towards it. Therefore, belief that a thing is good is not belief that it enters into a state of affairs, and moral propositions must be distinguished from propositions with realistic truth conditions.

The trouble with this argument lies in the second premiss. For it is not at all evident that no belief that a thing enters into a state of affairs – no belief, that is, with realistic truth conditions – can entail[2] the possession of an attitude towards its subject. Consider, for example, the belief that a person X is *in possession of the truth* about some matter.

[1] M. Dummett, 'Truth', *Proceedings of the Aristotelian Society* (1958–9), p. 157.

[2] I am using 'entails' throughout in the logical sense, so that P entails Q strictly implies that P strictly implies Q.

This is clearly a factual belief. But if I come to hold this belief about X, doesn't it follow that my attitude towards X alters? I become prepared to defer to X's opinion on the matter, or commend his views to other people whom I wish to inform, and each of these is quite naturally construed as possession of an attitude towards X. Again, consider the way in which one's attitude to a statement must change according to whether one believes it to be true. Finally, there are beliefs such as the belief that something is alive which may also entail the possession of an attitude, even if all that can be said about the attitude is that it is one which one feels towards things that are alive, but not towards other things. Now these examples may produce a certain impatience. All that they could prove, it may be thought, is that the notion of an attitude can be used to cover such things as a belief that something is alive, or true. Seen this way, Wittgenstein's remark, 'My attitude towards him is an attitude towards a soul. I am not of the opinion that he has a soul',[1] tells us more about attitudes than about the judgement that people have souls. Now this can only be part of the truth, for it fails to explain why Wittgenstein's remark is a good deal more intelligible than, say, 'My attitude towards the room is an attitude towards a room with a bottle in it. I am not of the opinion that there is a bottle in it', but even if this was all that my examples indicated, it is enough to topple the anti-realist argument that we are considering. For if it is correct to say that real assent to the proposition that a thing is alive, or true, entails that my attitude towards it is an attitude towards a live thing, or a true proposition, then even if real assent to the proposition that a thing is good entails that my attitude towards it is an attitude towards a good thing – namely one of approval – still goodness may be as much a property of a thing as life or truth.

To this it will be replied that there are features of moral approval which are not shared by my other examples of 'attitudes', which enable it to be identified independently of statement of a moral belief. These features concern the necessary consequences for our choices and actions of holding a moral position. So the second argument we are to consider hopes to find, in the connection between moral belief and the will, a proof that moral realism is false. In so doing it would hope to find a practical aspect of moral approval which will distinguish it from other examples of attitudes, and so reinstate the first argument. I shall briefly describe two difficulties into which this line of thought

[1] Wittgenstein, *Philosophical Investigations* (Oxford, Blackwell, 1958), Part II, ¶ iv.

runs, not in order to show that it cannot be correct, but in order to show that the obstacles in the way of its proper statement are sufficiently great for a new line of attack on moral realism to be not entirely otiose.

The position is, then, that the anti-realist is to describe a connection between moral belief and the will in such a way that it is clear that moral belief necessarily has connections which no realistic belief need have. The first trap is that of simply giving a false description of the connection, making it, for example, logically impossible to do something which one believes to be wrong, or logically impossible to will something which one believes to be bad. When it is realized that these things are possible, various things may be said about the situations in which they happen, which fall into the second trap, that of failing to identify a connection which will perform what the argument requires. For example, if the claim is made that necessarily (other things being equal) an action done contrary to a moral belief produces remorse, or guilt, then unless remorse or guilt can be identified as something further than attitudes felt towards actions which the person believes himself to have performed and which he believes to have been wrong, nothing to the purpose has been achieved. It would be like proving that the belief that a proposition is true cannot be a realistic belief, because it has this connection with the will: that upon considering a past action of stating the negation of a proposition believed true one must feel the attitude ϕ, where ϕ is that attitude felt towards the past production of falsehood.

A better approach might be to try to identify this connection by considering the place which a moral belief holds in practical reasoning. The best statement of this for the purpose of the argument would, I think, go something like this. Consider the situation in which a person X is wondering whether to do A or to do B. Suppose a person Y tells him that A is the right thing to do. Suppose that X believes Y. Then it is logically necessary that this belief is *relevant to his decision*. On the other hand, there can be no realistic belief of which this is necessary, for, as Hume saw, the relevance of belief that some state of affairs obtains to a decision is always contingent upon the existence of a desire whose fulfilment that state of affairs affects. Now this argument, as its antiquity suggests, is not easy to assess, and I shall not say by any means everything that ought to be said about it. But the central difficulty is clear. To say that a belief is relevant to a decision is, analytically, to say that it *ought to be taken into account if the decision is to be the right one*. So the first premiss of the argument says that it is logically necessary that the belief (that A is the right thing to do) ought to be taken into account if X's decision is to be the right one. Now this may be logically necessary, but only as it is logically necessary that the belief that A is the cheapest thing to do ought to be taken into account if the decision is to be the cheapest one. In short, the production of this argument only serves as a prelude to an explanation of the analyticity above, for otherwise it merely underlines connections between moral concepts. So until such an explanation is produced this approach cannot be said to have produced the required connection between morality and the will.

II

There are, then, obstacles in the way of disproving moral realism by considering assent to a moral proposition. What I now want to do is to present an argument against moral realism which starts directly from the notion of the truth of a moral proposition. The form of the argument is this. I shall first describe two properties of moral truth, and then try to show how, jointly, they provide an insuperable difficulty for a realistic theory. The argument is not original[1] but so far as I know it has never received a clear or detailed presentation in print.

The first property is that of supervenience. It is widely held that moral properties are supervenient or consequential upon naturalistic ones. The general notion of supervenience is capable of various slightly different expressions. We can take firstly:

(S₁) A property M is supervenient upon properties $N_1 \ldots N_n$ if M is not identical with any of $N_1 \ldots N_n$, nor with any truth function of them, and it is logically impossible that a thing which is M should cease to be M without changing in respect of some member of $N_1 \ldots N_n$.

This is equivalent to saying that a thing ceasing to be M strictly implies that it has changed in respect of some member of $N_1 \ldots N_n$. So a contraposed version says that a thing remaining the same in respect of all members of $N_1 \ldots N_n$ strictly implies that it does not cease to be M. However, the notion of supervenience which we want in ethics should be slightly stronger than this, for moral properties are capable

---

[1] It was given to me in conversation by Dr C. Lewy.

H

of degree, and we should, if we believe in the supervenience of moral properties, also hold that a thing cannot come to possess them, or come to possess them in a greater or lesser degree than hitherto, without changing some of its naturalistic properties. So a better version is:

> (S) A property M is supervenient upon properties $N_1 \ldots N_n$ if M is not identical with any of $N_1 \ldots N_n$ nor with any truth function of them, and it is logically impossible that a thing should become M, or cease to be M, or become more or less M than before, without changing in respect of some member of $N_1 \ldots N_n$.

Again, a contraposed version says that a thing remaining the same in respect of all members of $N_1 \ldots N_n$ strictly implies that it remains the same in point of possession, lack of possession, or degree, of M-ness.

(S) defines a notion of a supervenience of a property applying to one thing over a period of time. But we also believe that if two things are the same in their naturalistic properties, then it follows that they are identical in their moral properties, i.e. have the same moral worth. This notion of supervenience can be defined:

> (S_2) A property M is supervenient$_2$ upon properties $N_1 \ldots N_n$ if M is not identical with any of $N_1 \ldots N_n$, nor with any truth function of them, and it is logically impossible that two things should each possess the same properties from the set $N_1 \ldots N_n$ to the same degree, without both failing to possess M, or both possessing M, to the same degree.

For our purposes we need not distinguish between supervenience and supervenience$_2$. It is difficult to think of a property which might be supervenient upon some others in the sense of (S), but not supervenient$_2$ upon those others in the sense of (S_2), and I can think of no argument which might be used to show that moral properties are supervenient upon naturalistic ones in one sense but not the other. So from this point, when I talk of supervenience, I shall take it to include both notions, and the claim that moral properties are supervenient upon naturalistic ones embraces both the claim that they are supervenient in the sense of (S), and in the sense of (S_2). It should be noted that (S) and (S_2) define supervenience in terms of logical impossibility, and it is a logical claim about the interrelations of sets of properties that is being made. It may, for example, be a physical impossibility that two materials should be identical in their crystalline properties but one strong and the other not, or a biological impossibility that two twins should come from the same ovum, and one be a zebra and the other not. But neither of these impossibilities indicates supervenience in the sense which I have defined, for neither is a logical claim. Similarly, if it was only a moral impossibility that two things should be identical in naturalistic properties but different in moral worth, then moral worth would not be supervenient upon naturalistic properties in my sense. One thing, then, which must be established in defending this part of the argument, is that if somebody claimed, say, that an action was absolutely identical in every respect with another, except that it was much worse, or that a feature of character like courage had changed in no way in its nature, relations, consequences, yet was of much less value than formerly, it would be a logical and not merely a moral mistake that had been made.

The other feature of moral truth which is needed to support the argument is even more commonly believed in than its supervenience. It is that the possession of moral worth is not entailed by the possession of any set of naturalistic properties whatsoever, in any degree whatsoever. This lack of entailment has often been claimed, and often disputed, and often confused with other claims, such as that moral properties are not identical with naturalistic ones, or that moral properties have no criteria in a Wittgensteinian sense. So the precise claim that is being made is this:

(E) There is no moral proposition whose truth is entailed by any proposition ascribing naturalistic properties to its subject.

This is not the claim that moral properties are not identical with any naturalistic ones. For although such an identity would ensure an entailment both from naturalistic to moral propositions, and vice versa, to suppose that the existence of the entailment would ensure the identity is simply to indulge in wishful thinking. There are counter-examples to the thesis that Fa only entails Ga if F is identical with G or some conjunct of which G is a member, which have never been satisfactorily explained away, and it cannot be confidently assumed at the outset that this would not be one of them. Of course Moore's concern in *Principia Ethica* was to disprove the thesis that there is an identity, not the thesis that there is an entailment.

Secondly, (E) is not the claim that there are no naturalistic properties which are *necessarily reasons* for an ascription of a moral property. To say that P is necessarily a reason for Q is[1] to say that, necessarily, coming to know P ought to increase one's confidence in Q. Now suppose that there exist naturalistic properties such that necessarily coming to know that a thing possesses such a property ought to increase one's confidence that it is good. It would by no means follow that (E) is false. For it does not follow that any statement that a thing possesses one of these properties can be given which is a conclusive reason for the thing being good, in the sense that, having come to know that statement, whatever else one learns about the thing in question, one is right to be certain that it is good. Whereas if an entailment exists, that is precisely what can be done, for if P entails Q, then the conjunction of P with any proposition whatsoever entails Q. This sort of consideration should be familiar from other areas of philosophy. For example, it is very plausible to suppose that some statements about what seems to be the case to some observers are necessarily reasons for supposing certain things to be true of the external world. That is, it is plausibly supposed to be necessary, and not contingent (for what could it be contingent upon?) that something's seeming to be yellow under appropriate conditions to an apparently normal person is a reason for supposing it to be yellow. But few people are prepared to believe that such statements about what seems to be the case can entail that something is the case. A better example comes from consideration of induction. It is very plausible to suppose that, necessarily, upon coming to know of the existence of certain past regularities one ought to increase one's confidence in certain appropriately related predictions. Yet there is no entailment between the evidence and the prediction. Now it is no part of my purpose to claim that these positions about perception and induction are correct in affirming that some things are necessarily reasons for others while no entailment can be produced. But the evident plausibility of supposing this is sufficient to show that claims about lack of entailment must be very sharply separated from claims about lack of a necessary reasoning relationship, and that it cannot be safely assumed that argument against the latter claim will transfer to the former. *A fortiori*, one must keep the claim that, necessarily, reasons for moral judgements must come from certain areas (facts concerning human interests, for example) entirely distinct from the claim that there is an entailment from some propositions describing things in those areas, to a moral proposition.

[1] With minor complications.

Thirdly, (E) is not the denial that there exist criteria, in a Wittgensteinian sense, for the ascription of moral properties. What is meant by saying that P is a criterion, in a Wittgensteinian sense, for Q is, of course, not at all clear. It certainly doesn't mean just that P is necessarily a reason for Q, for there are cases where it is plausible to suppose that one proposition is necessarily a reason for another, yet extremely unnatural to call it a criterion, in any sense, for the other. Nor would anyone who believes in the necessary reasoning relationship want to express it in this way. I have already given one example where this is true, in pointing out that perhaps certain facts about the past necessarily provide a reason for certain predictions; for surely nobody would want to express this by saying that perhaps some facts about the past are criteria, in a Wittgensteinian sense, for the truth of certain predictions. Again, for at least most values of P and Q, P is necessarily a reason for the conjunction P&Q. Yet surely P is not therefore a criterion, in any sense, for the truth of P&Q. Or, to take a familiar case, just as some philosophers claim that someone's exhibiting certain behaviour is necessarily a reason for supposing that he is in pain, so learning of some unobserved person that he was in pain at a certain time may be necessarily a reason for supposing that he exhibited certain behaviour at or around that time, but it is obviously not a Wittgensteinian criterion of exhibiting that behaviour.[1]

Perhaps some condition limiting the type of fact with which P and Q are respectively concerned can be added to the condition that P is necessarily a reason for Q to give an acceptable sense of 'criterion'. The result would be a conjunctive definition: 'P is a criterion of Q if and only if P is necessarily a reason for Q and knowing the sort of fact which P describes is the only way of knowing propositions like Q' would be a plausible attempt, and one which would give the result that if P described a naturalistic fact, and Q was a moral proposition, and P was necessarily a reason for Q, then P would be a criterion of Q. But then the question of whether there are naturalistic criteria for moral propositions would in effect be the question of whether there are neces-

---

[1] Strictly speaking the propositions that might be thought necessary are not of the form 'coming to know P ought to increase one's confidence in Q', but rather 'If the situation is (in some respects) normal, coming to know P ought to increase one's confidence in Q'. For example, it could at best be 'If there is no reason to suppose that he is pretending or abnormal, then coming to know that he exhibited certain behaviour ought to increase one's confidence that he was in pain', which could be supposed necessary.

sary reasoning relationships, and, as we saw, this question must not be confused with that of the truth of (E).

These preliminary remarks serve only to distinguish (E) from other claims which a naturalist might wish to dispute: the important point is that (E) denies the existence of an entailment, not of a 'logical connection' of a weaker sort, nor of logical constraint on the areas from which morally relevant considerations must be adduced. This much said, I shall postpone further discussion of (E) and (S) until I have described the difficulty which they provide for moral realism. For it will turn out that a principle in some respects weaker than (E) can serve as a basis for the argument, so that although (E), being a familiar claim to moral philosophers, may provide the clearest starting point, the anti-realist might rest his position on something less controversial.

What, then, is the difficulty for realism which the lack of entailment described in (E) and the supervenience described in (S) and (S₂) jointly promise? Suppose that we ask a moral realist to describe his position, showing it to be compatible with the lack of entailment and supervenience. He has to say that the truth of a moral proposition consists in the existence of a state of affairs, which it reports; that the existence of this state of affairs is not entailed by the existence of other, naturalistic facts; yet that the continuation of these facts entails that the moral state of affairs continues as it is. Now this may at first sight seem harmless enough, and perhaps it is not actually inconsistent, but it is very mysterious. To make the peculiarity of the view evident we can put it like this. Imagine a thing A which has a certain set of naturalistic properties and relations. A also has a certain degree of moral worth, say, it is very good. This, according to the realist, reports the existence of a state of affairs: A's goodness. Now the existence of this state of affairs is not entailed by A being as it is in all naturalistic respects. This means, since all the propositions involved are entirely contingent, that the existence of this state of affairs is not strictly implied by A being as it is in all naturalistic respects. That is, it is logically possible that A should be as it is in all naturalistic respects, yet this further state of affairs not exist. But if *that*'s a logical possibility, *why* isn't it a logical possibility that A should stay as it is in all naturalistic respects, and this further state of affairs cease to exist? If it's a logical possibility that A should be as it is in all naturalistic respects, and not be good, why isn't it a logical possibility that A should stay as it is in all naturalistic respects, when it was once good, and cease to be good?

The existence of the naturalistic facts doesn't guarantee, logically, the moral state of affairs, so why should their continuation give a logical guarantee of the continued existence of the moral state of affairs? Again, these questions can be put in terms of (S_2), giving the puzzle for the realist that if A has some naturalistic properties, and is also good, but its goodness is a distinct further fact not following from its naturalistic features, and B has those features as well, then it is to follow that B also is good. And this is a puzzle for the realist because there is no reason at all, on his theory, why this should follow. If the goodness is, as it were, an *ex gratia* payment to A, one to which it is not as a matter of logic entitled in virtue of being as it is in all naturalistic respects, then it should be consistent to suppose that although given to A, it was not given to B, which merely shares the naturalistic features which do not entail the goodness.

It may not, at first sight, be clear why these problems are particularly acute for the realist. If joint supervenience and lack of entailment are problematic for any theory, then it is no objection to realism that it finds them particularly hard to explain. But the situation is not like that. For although the correspondence theory of truth, of which moral realism is an instance, is often thought to be entirely vacuous, it does in fact offer a distinct picture of the truth of propositions: each proposition may be construed as asserting that a certain state of affairs (namely, that in whose existence or non-existence its truth or falsity consists) exists. And, however grave for some purposes is the circularity introduced in the parenthesis, this has the definite consequence that the truth of propositions should be subject to just the logical constraints which govern the existence of states of affairs. But this is exactly what does not happen with moral truth, where we are asked to make intelligible the notion of a state of affairs subject to the constraint that its existence does not follow from the naturalistic facts being as they are. Now while I cannot see that there is an inconsistency in holding this, it is not philosophically very inviting. Supervenience becomes, for the realist, an opaque, isolated, logical fact, for which no explanation can be proffered.

We can now see why a weaker claim than (E) will support the argument equally well. (E) asserts that *no* proposition ascribing a degree of worth to a thing is entailed by any naturalistic proposition, however complicated. But all we need for the argument is that there are *some* propositions ascribing worth to things which are not entailed by any naturalistic proposition, however complicated. For if there are some such moral propositions they nevertheless still ascribe properties which are supervenient upon the naturalistic facts, and their supervenience is again an objectionable peculiarity for the realist. Of course, if we weaken the premiss in this way, it is theoretically open to a realist to say that some moral truths are entailed by naturalistic facts, and his realism is a theory about these, and others are not, and his realism does not apply to these. But in that case the position has the disadvantage of simply postulating a large, but hitherto unsuspected, dichotomy in moral truths, and then leaving one half, the interesting half, of this dichotomy, completely unexplained. Since this is not very attractive, the argument is just as strong if we use as one premiss, instead of (E):

(E′) There are some moral propositions which are true, but whose truth is not entailed by any naturalistic facts about their subject.

This is quite a significant strengthening of the argument, for using this premiss we need not defend ourselves against the view that in some cases 'is' does entail 'ought'. All we hold, in adopting (E′) is that in some cases it does not, yet that the ought proposition can be a moral truth all the same. Thus J. R. Searle's well-known argument[1] that in some cases there are purely naturalistic criteria for undertaking an obligation, and that sometimes it can follow from an obligation having been undertaken that, other things being equal, it ought to be fulfilled; this argument, even if it convinces us that there is an entailment and that the 'ought' in the conclusion is a moral 'ought', so that someone who considers the fact that he promised to do A irrelevant to the decision whether to do A or not A is illogical rather than immoral, is beside the point. For there is no prospect at all of extending these considerations to cover all moral truths. Searle's argument, as he himself notices, can cover only moral propositions which are true because of certain *institutional* facts. When an action is truly described in the terms appropriate to an institutionalized activity ('He was clean bowled'), it would seem to follow that consequences which the rules of that activity prescribe ought to be brought about ('He ought to stop batting'). But of course no morality is going to suppose that all moral

---

[1] J. R. Searle, 'How to derive "ought" from "is"', *Philosophical Review* (1964).

truths are, in this way, institutional. For a start that would make it impossible to raise a moral question about the existence of the institution, and in any case there are obviously features of human life whose lack of desirability is not a matter of the rules of institutions.

Does the position sometimes called 'neo-naturalism', associated with the work of Mrs Foot, advance reasons for denying (E′)? I do not think so. A central claim of this view is that necessarily certain qualities – courage, justice, temperance – are qualities by which men come to act well: because they are needed in anything other than an accidental fulfilment of any desire or need whatsoever, anyone, whatever his moral nature, has to prize them. It seems to me that there can be no need to deny this sort of claim in defending (E′). For how can this view, even when allied with the view that human harm and injury are necessarily bad and human benefit necessarily good, be used to demonstrate every moral truth? Consider, for example, the view that a state of satisfaction is only a good thing if its object is somehow appropriate, so that it adds nothing to the worth of a state of affairs if, say, somebody achieves content or satisfaction by contemplating or creating something totally unfitting. This is an important moral view, underlying many people's discontent with Utilitarianism. And of course many people would reply that it is illiberal and false, that although it is a pity that people should contemplate or create unfitting things, it is nevertheless better, given that they do, that they should be satisfied with them than not. Now is it likely that, even allowing Mrs Foot's claim that certain things are necessarily good, we shall find naturalistic facts entailing that one of these views is true and the other false? I cannot see that it is. Of course, someone might argue as follows: necessarily human benefit is good, necessarily satisfaction is a benefit, so it follows from the fact that someone has achieved some satisfaction that, whatever its object, something good has come about. But this is a very weak way of trying to show the anti-utilitarian to be illogical rather than immoral,[1] for he is of course denying that it is even true, let alone necessary, that all cases of satisfaction are, in any morally relevant sense, a benefit to their possessors. Satisfaction at inappropriate objects is, according to him, something that should not be wished upon anyone, even if the only alternative is dissatisfaction at those same objects.

Another line would deny that the notions of truth or falsity are

[1] G. E. Moore, *Principia Ethica*, ch. VI.

applicable in these cases, where no entailment exists. It would thus be possible to deny (E′) by denying that there exist any further moral truths beyond those which are entailed by naturalistic facts. So neither the proposition that satisfaction is good only if its object is appropriate, nor its negation, is true or false, and the dispute between the utilitarian and his opponent is not to be construed as a dispute about moral truth. But this is not only *ad hoc*, it is itself a serious departure from realism. For one consequence of realism is that the law of the excluded middle applies: either the state of affairs in which the goodness of unfitting satisfaction consists exists or it doesn't. In the former case the proposition that such satisfaction is good is true, and in the latter case false. The point is that the correspondence theory seems to allow no third alternative, and quite obviously the picture of moral truth that the realist presents would make the description of such an alternative a most unenviable task.

It seems then that (E′) is reasonably secure, at least so far as recent argument which might certainly seem to be in opposition to it is concerned. The question now remains whether the other premiss, that moral worth is supervenient upon naturalistic properties, is indisputable. I doubt very much whether anybody would feel entirely happy about disputing it, so even if there is no very good argument for it which a realist need accept, it may be quite proper to accept it as an axiom of meta-ethics. However, what can be done is to show how certain natural ways of explaining the feature of supervenience are not open to the realist, so that it is an objectionable fact for him, but not for others. We can also show that if, faced with this, he does try to deny the necessity of supervenience, this can only be at the cost of making moral truths unimportant. It has often been realized that moral realism runs this danger; what I wish to do is to show how the adoption of one escape route from the argument ends in its succumbing to the danger.

A natural way of explaining the supervenience of moral properties would, for an anti-realist, be something like this. There can be no question that we often choose, admire, commend, desire, objects because of their naturalistic properties. Now it is not possible to hold an attitude to a thing because of its possessing certain properties and, at the same time, not hold that attitude to a thing which is believed to have the same properties. The non-existence of the attitude in the second case shows that it is not because of the shared properties that I hold it in the first case. Now moral attitudes are to be held towards things because of their naturalistic properties. Therefore it is not possible to hold a moral attitude to one thing, believe a second to be exactly alike, yet at the same time not hold the attitude to the other. Anybody who appears to do this is convicted of misidentifying a caprice as a moral opinion.

This line of thought is insufficient for the realist. We saw earlier that he need not refrain from talking about moral attitudes: it is just that he thinks this a less clear alternative to talking about moral beliefs. But if we rephrase the preceding paragraph in terms of moral belief, it is obviously insufficient to explain supervenience. For we obtain: we hold moral beliefs about things because of their naturalistic properties; it is not possible to hold a belief about one thing because it satisfies some condition, and, at the same time, not hold that belief about another thing which is believed to satisfy the same condition. Therefore, it is not possible to hold a moral belief about a thing, believe a second to be exactly alike in all naturalistic respects, yet at the same time not hold the belief about the other thing. But this doesn't explain supervenience at all: it merely shows the realist putting conditions upon what can be *believed* to be the truth, not upon what *is* the truth. Our belief, he is saying, has to be consistent across naturalistic similarities – but this is no explanation of why, on his theory, the truth has to be. Furthermore, once we have grasped the inadequacy of his picture to account for supervenience, we may doubt his right to help himself to conditions upon belief which mean that beliefs are to be constrained as though supervenience were true. Why, that is, should a realistic theory accept that things believed to be naturalistically alike cannot be believed to be of distinct worth? Surely the condition on belief is that it should be true, and the trouble with inconsistency is that it is false: but the realist, as we have seen, offers no explanation of why this sort of inconsistency in moral belief should yield falsehood.

Finally, suppose the realist takes the apparent consequence of his position seriously, and denies supervenience. Then he holds that it is possible that the worth, say, of a feature of human life, such as courage, should alter although its intrinsic nature, its consequences, relation to our desires and so forth, remain the same. The only conclusion is that it is possible that the worth of courage should be irrelevant to our interest in it, attitudes towards it, preparedness to urge it on our children or to criticize or commend someone for possessing it. For when moral truth is that pure there *can* be no reason for being interested in it – nothing hangs upon the worth of courage changing if its relation to everything perceptible remains the same, and no reason could possibly be given for being interested in this fact.

Moral realism, then, is false. The purpose of the next section is to introduce the consequences of this for the logic of moral discourse. For it is natural to suppose that the falsity of realism entails the falsity of any propositional account of moral discourse. For this reason many people might suppose that the results of Section II could better be expressed as a disproof of the thesis that moral utterances express propositions, or of the thesis that goodness is an attribute. But this is too hasty. If propositions are what can be true, false, believed, hypothesized, premisses of arguments, enter into entailment relations, then it is not at all attractive to suppose that 'Courage is an intrinsically good thing' expresses no proposition, even if the only natural theory about the truth of that proposition is certainly false.

III

The argument of Section I showed that it is easy to overestimate the amount that has been gained if we talk in terms of moral attitudes rather than moral beliefs. However, in the last section, I claimed that an anti-realistic theory does have a distinct advantage in being alone consistent with supervenience and lack of entailment, and I sketched a way in which a theory based on attitudes might account for the former phenomenon. However, this was just a sketch, and we must now see whether it could be successful by describing the connection that an anti-realist must draw between moral attitudes and moral predicates. The problem is this. It is easy to think that the meaning of moral predicates has been given if it is said that they are used in sentences which, when uttered assertively, express the speaker's attitude to the subject of the discourse. At any rate, *if* this is true, and *if* a suitable account of the attitude is given,[1] it is easy to think that all that is needed to give an analysis of moral discourse has been done. However, it has been pointed out by J. R. Searle[2] and others that this is not so. For such a description of the use of moral sentences leaves us completely in the dark as to what

---

[1] This is a problem to which this paper makes no contribution. For an investigation of it, see Roger Scruton, 'Attitudes, beliefs and reasons', in this volume.

[2] 'Meaning and speech-acts', *Philosophical Review* (1962), pp. 423 ff.

happens when such sentences are used not assertively, but in less direct contexts. For example, suppose we are told that the sentence 'Courage is an intrinsically good thing' is standardly used so that in asserting it a speaker is expressing his attitude, namely approval, to courage. This does not, it is argued, enable us to construe: 'If courage is an intrinsically good thing, then organized games should be a part of school curricula', or 'No statement of the naturalistic properties of courage entails that courage is an intrinsically good thing', since in neither of these is any moral value attributed to courage, and no attitude to it is expressed. So the problem, for an anti-realist, is that of showing how the original insight as to what is done when a moral proposition is asserted also gives him an explanation of what is done when the sentence expressing it occurs in such contexts.

There are, I think, two natural ways for the anti-realist to attempt to meet this challenge, and it can be shown that neither of them will do. The first is to suppose that in an indirect context[1] some proposition about an attitude is being hypothesized, said to be entailed, or otherwise involved. Now this is clearly unnatural, because the anti-realist is not claiming that in a direct context, when asserted straightforwardly, moral sentences express propositions about attitudes. This would be to hold a realistic theory, if the proposition expressed was supposed to be simply one claiming the existence of certain attitudes, or to fail to give a theory of moral discourse at all. If, for example, the view was that in asserting that courage is intrinsically good one is asserting that an attitude of approval to courage is *appropriate*, then this, although true, is unhelpful. For the judgement that approval is appropriate is a moral judgement, and giving it as a synonym for the original removes no problems of analysis or epistemology which the original causes. So if an anti-realist tried to answer Searle's point by saying that what is hypothesized is 'If an attitude of approval to courage is appropriate, then . . .', no ground is gained at all, for still nothing has been done to explain how moral judgements can occur in indirect contexts. The same point applies to more complicated versions. Urmson, discussing only judgements of something as good of a kind or from a point of view, suggests that 'good' means 'satisfies a description such that no one can correctly dissent from a favourable evaluation (as of some kind or from

---

[1] I do not, fortunately, need to embark on the analysis of the notion of an indirect context. For the purpose of the argument it is just taken to embrace those contexts in which the moral proposition is expressed, but not asserted.

some point of view) of an object that satisfies that description'.[1] But if this was extended to try to give a theory of moral judgement, precisely the same objection would apply: to say that nobody can correctly dissent from a favourable evaluation of a good thing is true but completely unhelpful.

The other thing that an anti-realist might try to do is to suppose that in an indirect context a naturalistic proposition is being hypothesized, said to be entailed, or otherwise involved. *Which* naturalistic proposition would, I take it, be determined by the moral views of the person who utters the sentence expressing the hypothetical, or other compound proposition. Thus take:

(H) If courage is an intrinsically good thing then organized games should be a part of school curricula.

This would be a sentence which is interpreted on a particular occasion of utterance by our knowing the moral standards of the man uttering it, and supposing that he is hypothesizing that courage has the naturalistic properties which he would give as reasons for its being intrinsically good. Again, there is difficulty in reconciling this view of indirect contexts with the view that it is not a naturalistic proposition which is asserted when it is said that courage is a good thing. For if you and I, with different standards, each assert (H) we have hypothesized different things, but then, unless in asserting that courage is intrinsically good we assert different things, at least one of us is construed as hypothesizing something other than what he asserts, which makes it difficult to see how *modus ponendo ponens* is valid when used on moral propositions. Also some hypotheticals will become tautologous when they have a moral antecedent and naturalistic consequent, namely those in which the naturalistic consequent gives the facts which the speaker would use as his standards for the truth of the moral antecedent. Thus 'If courage is intrinsically good, then it is a quality by which men must act to achieve happiness' might be tautologous as uttered by me. But it doesn't look much like a tautology, for disagreement with it seems to be disagreement with a substantive moral claim, a claim about the necessary conditions of intrinsic worth of a quality, rather than the sort of disagreement about the use of words which disagreement with a tautology usually involves. In short, if an anti-

[1] J. O. Urmson, *The Emotive Theory of Ethics* (London, 1968), p. 142.

realist takes this view of indirect contexts he is opening himself to the classical, Moorean objection to naturalism, and the apparent sophistication of the position renders it no less vulnerable.

The trouble with both these attempts to escape from Searle's argument is that they try to answer the question *what* is being hypothesized, said to be entailed, etc.; and we have a definite view of how to set about questions of this sort. We try to give an *analysis* of the moral proposition, and this turns out to be either incorrect or unhelpful. Instead I propose to consider the total sentence expressing the hypothetical, or entailment, and to give a theory of what these say and why we have these locutions to say it. The nature of the theory can best be presented via an example. Consider:

(I) No statement of the naturalistic properties of courage entails that it is an intrinsically good thing.

Here is a sentence in which the proposition that courage is an intrinsically good thing is expressed but not asserted, so what can an anti-realist theory, based on the way in which an attitude is expressed when a moral proposition is asserted, say about it? The answer is given if we extend Frege's theory of such contexts to sentences which express attitudes. Frege thought that sentences occur in contexts in which they refer to propositions which they normally express. I suggest that in (I) we refer to an attitude: an attitude is the subject of the proposition expressed by (I), and it is quite easy to see what is said about that attitude. For according to an anti-realist (I) is not asserting the logical independence of the existence of two states of affairs, the moral and the naturalistic. It is an expression of a fact about the moral attitude of approval towards courage, and says that nobody who fails to approve of courage while knowing all that there is to be known about it cannot be convicted of a logical mistake. This is a claim about the nature of the moral attitude, and the statement (I) is what I shall call a 'propositional reflection' of this claim. By a 'propositional reflection' I mean roughly any statement which, while appearing to make a factual claim about states of affairs, their interrelations and their logic, is actually making claims about attitudes, *although* none of the propositions involved in the statement is to be analysed into one whose subject is an attitude. I am afraid that this is probably quite obscure, and I shall not, in this paper, make the notion nearly as clear as I think it could be made, but further examples of the use of the notion should help.

If we turn again to the anti-realistic explanation of (S), given on pages 114-15, we can see that it shares with the explanation of (I) the feature that an attitude – the attitude of moral approval – is said to have certain properties, and this by itself is the truth of which (S) is, in the above sense, a propositional reflection. Thus, the moral attitude is said to be necessarily held because of the naturalistic properties of its objects, and the statement of supervenience, made in terms of which differences entail which others, is a realistic-appearing way of putting the view that difference in moral attitude to two things must, logically, be justified by difference in beliefs about them. So the theory, if it works for other examples of indirect contexts, does give an account of the relation between moral predicates and moral attitudes which allows the anti-realist explanation of supervenience to be successful.

The idea fares well when we consider hypotheticals again. A hypothetical, such as (H), although it appears to be making a claim that one state of affairs exists if another does, must be taken as a propositional reflection of a claim about attitudes. This claim is that an attitude of approval to courage in itself involves an attitude of approval to organized games as part of the curriculum in every school. It does not, of course, involve this as a matter of logic, but then neither is (H) true as a matter of logic. To show that one attitude does involve the other it is necessary to show that organized games are intimately connected with the production of the quality of courage and lack other disadvantages. This is precisely what would have to be shown to verify the original hypothetical, (H). If we attack the claim that one attitude involves the other ('Surely not – organized games at school promote cruelty and cowardice'), we produce just the propositions which are reasons against the original hypothetical. Clearly with moral as with natural discourse there is a variety of grounds on which an 'if . . . then . . .' proposition might be held, but this elasticity is preserved by varieties of involvement. Consider, for example, logically necessary propositions using moral antecedents: 'If you ought to divide the pound evenly between ten people, then you ought to give them two shillings each'.[1] This is necessarily true. The analysandum which refers to attitudes must therefore be necessarily true also. And 'Approval of dividing the pound evenly between ten people involves approval of giving them two shillings each' can easily be given a sense

[1] An example suggested by Mr Tom Baldwin, who most helpfully criticized an earlier version on this point.

in which it expresses a necessary truth – namely, that one attitude cannot be *consistently* held without the other. This logical constraint upon consistency in attitude must not, of course, be thought to derive in any way from the logical interrelations of moral propositions which it analyses. It is rather explained by pointing out that it is logically impossible to divide a pound evenly between ten people without giving each of them two shillings, so for this type of example the analysis can show in a genuinely explanatory way how the hypothetical refers to attitudes and expresses their relations.

The validity of *modus ponendo ponens* as a rule of inference is preserved by this treatment of moral hypotheticals. The question, for the anti-realist, is that of how his account of the hypothetical is to cohere with his account of straightforward assertion in such a way that 'P and if P then Q' entails Q, where P is a moral proposition. The theory tells us that anybody asserting 'P and if P then Q' where P attributes worth to a thing *expresses* his attitude to that thing, and *asserts* that that attitude involves a further attitude or belief. There is, when that has been done, a logical inconsistency in not holding the further attitude or belief. It is this logical inconsistency which is expressed by saying that *modus ponendo ponens* is valid: its validity is a reflection of possible logical inconsistency in attitudes and beliefs.

A moral proposition can be the antecedent of an hypothetical of which the consequent is not a moral proposition. Here the claim of which this form is a propositional reflection is that the attitude involves a belief, not another attitude. 'If courage is an intrinsically good thing then it is a quality by which a man must act to achieve happiness' is a reflection of the view that an attitude of approval to courage in itself involves belief that courage is a quality by which a man must act to achieve happiness. This is a statement of one's moral standards: only someone with a specific moral position will hold that the attitude involves that belief, and this reflects perfectly well the point that I made earlier, that such an hypothetical is a statement of a standard, and if attacked is attacked as such and not, for example, as a sort of contradiction or empirical falsehood.

It may be thought at this point that too much weight is put upon the word 'involves'. For how can an attitude involve a belief (or a belief an attitude) in such a way? We recognize that people can hold the moral attitude without the belief and vice versa: what other involvement is there? To say that the attitude of approval to courage

I

involves the belief that courage is a quality by which a man must act to achieve happiness is, as I said, to express a moral standard, to make a moral claim. The subtle thing is that the subject of the claim is now the attitude of approval of courage, and it is said that this *ought* to involve the belief that courage involves happiness. It is important to see that there is nothing in the least troublesome about this being a moral proposition: the object was not to show that such standard-giving hypotheticals are not moral propositions, but to show how they could be so. And they are quite straightforward moral propositions expressing the way in which attitudes ought to vary with beliefs.

This analysis has the further property that it enables us to deal with expressions of moral fallibility, in my opinion the hardest context of all for an anti-realist to understand. Consider 'I strongly believe that X is a good man, but I may be wrong'. Here we express an attitude to X, but then what happens? For a realist, we simply state the possibility that our belief does not accord with the facts, but what can an anti-realist say about it? It is easy to say that here I express an attitude to my moral attitude to X, and of course I do, but the question is whether this second-order attitude can be described consistently with anti-realism. For if we have to describe the second-order attitude just as 'belief in the possibility that the attitude of approval to X is unjustified', then we are in no better position than those who rest their analysis on attitudes being 'appropriate'. But let us consider what we envisage when we admit that we may be wrong in a moral belief. We envisage that we could, at some future date, want to change our attitude to the subject of the belief, not because that has changed, but because we realize that we have made a mistake. The mistake could be of one of two kinds. Taking the example of 'X is a good man', we can envisage that we may have been mistaken about X: he isn't really kind, he only likes to appear so, and so forth. Or I can envisage a mistake in my standards. I think that a man's being kind is a reason for thinking that he is a good man. That is, I think that the belief that a man is kind ought to tend to create an attitude of approval towards him. This, as I explained above, is another moral belief, whose subject is the variation of an attitude with a belief. But I may be mistaken here, too: I can envisage, at least as a bare possibility, that some argument, or someone, or some event, should come along and show me that I am mistaken about kindness: some sorts of kindness kill the soul of the recipient, and so forth. Then I no longer think that the belief ought to tend to create the attitude. The propositional reflection of all these possibilities of error is that the belief that something is good, although I may hold it, may be false. And thus, if I am right, a theory based upon attitudes can encompass those elements in moral thought which make us reflect on how difficult it is to know what is right and wrong, good or bad.

Finally we may consider tenses. Tenses can certainly provide extreme difficulty for analyses which concentrate upon what is done when something is asserted to be the case now. Thus the Toulmin account of 'It is probable that P', according to which this is used to make a guarded assertion that P provides no account of 'It was probable that P would happen' – or, at least, no account which does not confuse it with the very different 'It is probable that P happened'. And if we consider 'X was a morally fine man', it might appear that we have no option but to construe this as 'The attitude of approval towards X was appropriate' – an analysis of the form which I claimed to be totally unhelpful. However, a device is available which, although it may look unnatural, appears to me to take account of tensed assertions without having to view them as applying tensed predicates to attitudes. The question we must ask is whether anybody who asserts 'X was a morally fine man' is expressing a moral attitude. It is from the supposition that he is not that difficulty arises, just as difficulty arises when it is realized that by saying 'It was probable that P would happen' I am not guardedly asserting anything. But anybody asserting 'X was a morally fine man' is expressing a moral attitude. Not, it is true, to X as he is, for X may in the interim have degenerated. But he is expressing the attitude to X as he was. Quite clearly, anyone saying 'X was a morally fine man' is sincere only if he approves of X as he was, morally, and in making his assertion it is that approval which he expresses. The difficulty is thus averted by realizing that the subject of approval when a tensed assertion is made is not, of course, the object as it is now, but the object as it was then.

I have now given several examples of the device of propositional reflection, the ways in which expressions of attitude and propositions concerning the interrelations of attitudes with each other and with beliefs are given a syntax which makes them appear to relate to facts in a peculiar, unobservable, moral realm. It must in no way be considered surprising that this device should exist. For disagreement in moral attitude is one of the most important disagreements there is, and working out the consequences of moral attitudes one of the most important subjects there is. The device of propositional reflection enables us to bring the concepts of propositional logic to this task. It enables us to use notions like truth, knowledge, belief, inconsistency, entailment, implication, to give moral argument all the structure and elegance of argument about facts.

But isn't the theory saying that there is really no such thing as moral truth, and nothing to be known, believed, entailed – only the appearance of such things? Not at all. It is a complete mistake to think that the notion of moral truth, and the associated notions of moral attributes and propositions, disappear when the realistic theory is refuted. To think that a moral proposition is true is to concur in an attitude to its subject: this is the answer to the question with which I began the paper. To identify further this attitude is a task which is beyond the scope of this paper, but which is the central remaining task for the metaphysic of ethics. To think, however, that the anti-realist results show that there is no such thing as moral truth is quite wrong. To think there are no moral truths is to think that nothing should be morally endorsed, i.e. to endorse the endorsement of nothing, and this attitude of indifference is one which it would be wrong to recommend, and silly to practise.

4 Evaluation and Speech
J. E. J. Altham

The emotive theory of morals, particularly in the classical form given by C. L. Stevenson,[1] was a bold attempt to break out of the epistemological impasse to which the moral realism of G. E. Moore and the intuitionists had led. But in its classical form, the theory was vulnerable to a large number of by now familiar objections, which have been marshalled very effectively by J. O. Urmson in his recent book.[2] There remains, however, a sense that the emotive theory is not completely wrong, and many of its guiding principles have survived, in one form or another, in works more recent than Stevenson's. The emotive theory, although primarily thought of as an account of *moral* judgement, extends beyond ethics to cover evaluation in general, and it is as a theory of evaluation that it will be considered in what follows.

It is worthwhile first to list, in deliberately vague formulations, some of the main suggestions of emotivism that survive after the correction or purgation of its more evident errors. The list is not exhaustive, nor are all its members either peculiar or essential to the emotive theory, but each principle is to some extent characteristic of the *general* outlook currently associated with the term 'emotivism'.

(1) There is an at least roughly distinguishable subclass of general terms any of which characteristically gives an evaluative element to judgements in which it occurs – a class which may be called the class of evaluative terms.

(2) The evaluative terms may be marked off from the others by their connection with distinctive kinds of linguistic act.

(3) The sincere performance of acts of speech belonging to one of these kinds is conceptually connected with the speaker's attitudes or emotions.

(4) The sincere performance of such acts is also conceptually

---

[1] Especially in his book *Ethics and Language* (New Haven, 1944).
[2] *The Emotive Theory of Ethics* (London, 1968).

connected, in at least some cases, with the speaker's desires or intentions concerning the emotions or attitudes of his hearer.

(5) The most general terms of evaluation, such as 'good' and 'bad',
are not unusually ambiguous.

(6) The descriptive basis on which the most general terms of
evaluation are applied varies enormously with the kind of thing
evaluated.

(7) The connection of evaluative terms with distinctive kinds
of linguistic act can be used to explain the univocity of such terms
in spite of variations in the descriptive basis for their application.

(8) The association of distinctive kinds of linguistic act with
certain evaluative terms belongs to the *analysis* of such terms, and
thus forms part of the explanation of their meaning.

Principle (1) assures us that evaluative judgement can be studied
through consideration of a particular class of distinguishable linguistic
items. Knowledge of the nature of such items is not the main *end* of
this branch of philosophy; linguistic studies are here a useful and convenient means for the attainment of a better understanding of evaluation – the human activity. But since this activity involves thought, and
frequently issues in judgement, end and means are closely tied up with
each other. Principles (2) to (4) indeed immediately bring us back from
the words to the performances of men. According to (2) it is not by
their subject-matter, whether it be value, items supposed to have value
or anything else, that evaluative words are to be marked off from
others, but by their relation to certain kinds of thing people may *do* in
using language. (3) draws attention to the connection between such
linguistic performances and what may broadly be called the affective
life of the speaker. Few people can ever have doubted that, as a matter
of psychology, there are strong connections between a man's affective
life and his evaluations. What he favours, admires or approves, and
again what he censures, reproves or despises, is in part determined
psychologically by his emotional dispositions. And conversely, how
he will *feel* about some person, fact or state of affairs will be affected
by his scheme of values. But it is characteristic of an emotive theory
to hold further that a tie-up between judgement and the judger's
affective life is institutionalized in the conventional force of certain
linguistic forms. (4) involves a connection between the speaker's judgement and the affective life of the hearer. It is a standard belief of emo-

tivists that it is one of the main functions of evaluative discourse to serve the cause of attaining and mutually recognizing a community of feeling or attitude towards some things, persons or states of affairs. These purposes are not always present. There are occasions of evaluative discussion – such as some discussions over matters implicitly agreed by the parties to be matters of taste – whose purpose may be no more than a comparison of reactions, and where failure of the parties to accord with one another is not taken to be unsatisfactory. This point explains the qualification 'in at least some cases' in (4). There are, on the other hand, evaluative discussions where failure to reach a community of feeling or attitude constitutes failure to fulfil the purpose of the discussion.

The importance of attaining a mutually recognized community of feeling or attitude should not need much emphasis. It is important in a wide variety of situations, and for many different further purposes. It is desirable for the stability of many personal relationships, and more widely for social unity in general, and it serves the objects of recognizing and maintaining a tradition in the arts. The emphasis on the search for agreement is characteristic of a subjective theory; the corresponding emphasis of an objective theory of evaluation would be rather on the search for truth. But to place the main emphasis on agreement rather than truth does not *require* subjectivism (although emotivism has historically been a subjective theory). The agreement is indeed an agreement in attitude rather than in belief, but there are still various ways in which the emotivist point might be incorporated into an objective theory. The emotivist point is that evaluative language has, built into it, features which make it serviceable for attaining a mutually recognized agreement in attitude, and this point is quite independent of whether or not there are objective conditions under which putting such language to this use is justifiable by reference to true evaluative belief. Emotivism, as it is used here, could be true whether or not an objective theory of evaluative – and in particular moral – judgement is tenable. It is a theory which, in its most general aspects, is neutral with respect to this great question, although it may impose *some* constraints on possible answers.

In evaluative soliloquy, the hearer is the speaker himself. The principle adumbrated in (4) may still have application in a modified form. The solitary thinker is not here aiming for a community of attitude with another, but he may be striving for a *harmony* among his own attitudes and feelings. For instance, his intention in arriving at an evaluative formula may be to resolve some ambivalence in his own attitudes. The processes of eliminating unwanted feelings, or reciprocal adjustment and modification of attitudes and affections, or of encompassing all that is confusedly felt in a unified judgement, may go on within a single person as well as between the members of a group.

This last reference to reciprocal adjustment and modification calls to mind the more co-operative occasions of evaluative discussion. It is tempting for philosophers to neglect these co-operative aspects, and to concentrate upon evaluative *disputes* between parties who at least initially have pretty definite views. But tentative exploration of possibilities, and mutual help towards agreed judgements, are no less typical of evaluative discussions, though they may be less striking. The philosophers' concentration upon disputes stems from their concern with the problem of how to bring other people round to one's own point of view, and in particular, the role of reason in such exercises in persuasion. Concern with this problem is itself some tribute to the emotivist's insistence on the important role of the search for agreement. But the problem of how to attain and settle a point of view is no less interesting – at least for those that eschew dogmatism. Consequently, it is important to consider, not only the linguistic performances involved in evaluative *judgement*, but also the performances involved in evaluative *suggestion* and *supposition*.

Principles (5) and (6) pose a problem, and (7) announces the lines along which the solution is to be found. A term such as 'good', although its uses are multifarious, has a unity of meaning which permits us to reapply it correctly without further instruction to kinds of objects other than those from examples of which its use was learnt. If a man has learnt to apply 'good' to food, for instance, he does not need to learn more about 'good' to be able to apply the term to pianos (though he will need to learn something about pianos). Yet the features of food in virtue of which it is 'good', such as being tasty, wholesome and nutritious, are quite different from and not even linked by a relevant chain of similarities with those in virtue of which a piano is a good one. So the unity of 'good' cannot be explained by reference to a unity in the descriptive basis for its application. So much is commonplace; the problem is to find wherein, in the light of the variation of descriptive basis, the unity of the term can lie. This problem is somewhat aggravated by the fact that, on some occasions, an account of something as good of its kind may not constitute a positive evaluation, but may function simply as a piece of information for the hearer. If I, who never fish, say to a guest of mine who is a keen angler, 'There's good fishing along by the woods below the weir', my utterance is informative, but probably not evaluative. In fact, a sentence containing a term such as 'good' is sometimes simply informative, sometimes simply evaluative and sometimes both, and the possibility of these alternatives requires an explanation consistent with the attribution of some unity of meaning to the term. (7) and (8) propose that the unity of meaning is to be found in the relationship to a distinctive class of linguistic acts – a class which, by (3) and (4), is specially connected with the speaker's and hearer's attitudes and emotions.

Principles (1) to (8) then, taken in accordance with these preliminary explanations, constitute a framework within which a plausible modern version of the emotive theory might be developed. The aim of this essay is to remove much of the vagueness from this specification of a framework.

JUDGEMENT AND THE SPEAKER'S ATTITUDES

It is appropriate to start with the relation between an evaluative judgement and the attitudes and feelings of the person whose judgement it is. According to emotivism, an evaluative sentence has, as part of its point in the language, the function of being a suitable vehicle for the *expression* of the speaker's attitudes or feelings. That is a rather cumbrous formulation; it needs to be. For we cannot simply say that an evaluative utterance expresses the speaker's attitudes and feelings, since such utterances are frequently merely informative of fact. The qualification '*part* of the point' is necessary, since, as we shall see, there are other functions of such sentences, functions specific to evaluation. One may compare the formulation with a similar one for imperatives: an imperative sentence has, as part of its point in the language, the function of being a suitable vehicle for the expression of a speaker's intention that somebody (generally somebody else) should do something. Again, imperatives have other functions, and further, they can be used in ways other than any of those which belong to their point in the language. For instance, one may give an order simply to provoke or annoy, with no intention of having it carried out. It is tempting to call such cases instances of abuse, but it seems more correct, and more suggestive, to describe them as cases of linguistic *exploitation*. Exploitation occurs when one makes use of features of a piece of language which belong to its point in the language for a purpose which does not belong to the point in the language. We use the word 'exploitation' in a similar way when we speak of exploiting tax legislation (within the law). Here one makes use of a provision in the law for purposes quite other than that for which the provision was intended. Purely descriptive uses of evaluative terms fall into this same category of exploitatory uses. Thus if an utterance of a sentence of the form 'That is a good X' functions simply as a description of the X in question, the speaker is making use of features of 'good' whose point is to enable evaluation for a purpose which does not belong to the point of 'good' in the language. We shall see later in more detail how this is done.

Where such exploitation is not taking place, then, utterance of an evaluative sentence to make a judgement will, *inter alia*, *express* an attitude or feeling of the speaker. This statement is perhaps unremarkably true, but it is also remarkably unhelpful. 'Express' is a term with many and diverse uses. Two problems in particular attend its employment in the present context. One is that of distinguishing the expression of attitude or feeling in evaluation from expression of feeling or attitude by other verbal means, for instance in exclamations. The other is that of distinguishing the notion of expressing an attitude from that of stating that one has that attitude, where the expression is by means of an indicative sentence. Clearly, expressing an attitude is in general distinct from saying that one has it. A person may express his disapproval of something merely by pulling a face, but that act is not one of stating that he disapproves. But where the expression of attitude takes place in language, the distinction between expressing and saying that one has it is not so easily seen. And when one considers that the expression of attitude in evaluative judgement is by means of an indicative sentence, using words part of whose point in the language is to serve the expression of attitude, the distinction seems tenuous indeed.

If a man states that he has a certain attitude to something, he normally intends that his utterance should have some weight in inducing in his audience a belief that he has that attitude. And following H. P. Grice,[1] we may say that he intends to produce this effect by means of the audience's recognition of his (the former) intention. The audience grasp the intention if they are familiar with the words of the utterance. Here

[1] H. P. Grice, 'Meaning', *Philosophical Review* (July 1957).

we have the basic point, together with the framework of the mechanism, of stating. But the same statement holds also of the expression of attitude in evaluative judgement. Here also a normal intention – in so far as it concerns the expression of attitude – is that the utterance should have some weight in inducing the belief that the speaker has that attitude. And the mechanism of recognition via familiarity with the words of the utterance seems to be the same.

An attempt might be made to distinguish stating from otherwise linguistically expressing an attitude by saying that the evaluative expression carries some implication of grounds, or a particular kind of grounds, for maintaining that attitude, whereas stating that one has an attitude carries no such implication. But such a distinction will not work. For the implication of grounds derives not from the concept of stating alone, but from the concept of attitude as such. The notion of someone's holding an attitude towards something which was not grounded in any beliefs about the object that could be taken as relevant to the attitude can be regarded as unintelligible. Here a distinction must be made to make this last assertion plausible. It is possible to take up an attitude, to pose as having it, without grounds, and in such cases we can speak as though the attitude is one the man who takes it up actually has. For instance, we may say that A's attitude to B at a party was hostile, even if A's behaviour simply arose from a whim. In such cases 'attitude' is used to express a straightforwardly behavioural concept. The determination of attitude is made entirely on what the person does, and the style or manner of his doing it. How A really feels towards B, for instance, would in this case be irrelevant. The ambiguity is brought out by the possibility of saying 'I adopted a respectful attitude, but my real attitude towards him is far from being one of respect. In fact, I despise him as a pompous charlatan.' It is not the behavioural sense of attitude, but rather the *genuine* attitudes, that concern this paper, and it is the genuine attitudes that must be based on features the object of the attitude is believed to possess. The genuine attitudes are primary. A behavioural attitude is called respectful when it is the kind of behaviour that would issue from an attitude of genuine respect.

The evaluative expression, then, does not differ from the statement of attitude by having an implication of grounds. Nor does it differ in having an implication of there being a particular kind of grounds. For it seems that the kind of grounds depends on the kind of attitude and the nature of the object, and not on the means whereby it is communicated.

There remains, however, a difference. The evaluative judgement is not always said to be false if the speaker does not have the attitude his judgement expresses. But a statement that he has that attitude is always false if he does not have it. So expression cannot here be the same as statement. The problem is to find the grounds for this difference with respect to attributions of falsity. My contention is that the grounds cannot be found by concentrating only on the ways in which the speaker lets it be known what *his* attitude is; it is necessary to consider the connection between the speaker's communication of his own attitude and his intentional relation to the attitudes of his audience.

Consideration of the speaker's intentional relation to the audience is also important for the problem of showing the difference between evaluative judgements and expletives, exclamations, use of derogatory words such as 'dago', etc., in their role as expressive of attitude.

THE HEARER'S ATTITUDES

The crudest and most unappealing form of subjectivism in the theory of evaluation is roughly this: an evaluative judgement is simply a statement by the speaker that he has a certain feeling or attitude. For example, 'This is good' means 'I am in favour of this', 'I approve of this', or still more baldly 'I like this'. The theory is, to put it gently, oversimple in many ways, and G. E. Moore produced a simple and powerful objection to it.[1] Suppose A says 'This is good' and B says of the same thing 'It's not good'. If each is merely making a statement about himself, then they are not disagreeing. But they are disagreeing. Hence each is *not* merely making a statement about himself.

Now so far as concerns the speaker's communication of his own attitudes, the objection from the facts of disagreement seems to apply whether the communication of attitude is by statement or by some other mechanism of expression. If *all* the speaker is doing were to communicate his own attitude, Moore's objection would be fatal, however the communication was made. The possible distinction between stating and expressing wanes in importance before the problem, for an analysis in terms of attitudes, of accounting adequately for disagreement.

If A has one attitude towards something, and B has a different one towards the same thing, that in itself does not amount to disagreement. A may have a hostile attitude towards C, and B have an attitude of

[1] G. E. Moore, *Ethics* (London, 1912).

respect. They differ, they may even know they differ, but it does not follow that they disagree. Disagreement, however, arises when one wants or hopes to bring the other around to having the same attitude as himself. There is also the case where A does not know what B's attitude is, but hopes or desires that it is the same as his own. This condition, of having an attitude towards something and wanting it shared, is of course a very common state of mind. It is obvious why it should be in such cases as those where a man is in favour of some plan of action for which he needs the help of others. It is sometimes less obvious why we should be so keen that others should share our attitudes, for instance to works of art, and so disappointed when we find they do not.

Now it seems plausible that it is a necessary condition of having the institution of evaluative discourse that human beings should be prone to this condition, that they should frequently both have an attitude and want others to share it. Unless there were a desire that our attitudes be shared, we should not be concerned with evaluation, but at most with communicating what our own attitudes were. The problem is to see how this prevalent desire for a community of attitude ties in with the actual features of evaluative language. Some early emotivists thought that the link was of a *causal* nature. An evaluative word was supposed as it were to carry an emotional charge, so that when it was spoken it would tend causally to produce an emotion or attitude in a properly conditioned hearer. If, then, A wanted B to share his feelings, he uttered the word most appropriate for triggering off that feeling, and hoped for the best. This is a caricatural presentation, but it is clear that the idea of a crude causal influence exerted by evaluative words is a myth, and open to empirical refutation. There is something like an emotional charge attached to some words which are nevertheless not evaluative, e.g. 'democrat', and no emotional charge attached to others which are evaluative, e.g. 'good'. But the early emotivists seem to have been entirely right to try to relate evaluation to the speaker's hopes or desires concerning the hearer's attitudes or emotions. It is their way of doing it that is wrong. Another objection to their idea is that if the hearer already agrees, the emotive power of the word is superfluous. If he does not, an emotive blast is insufficient to make him change his mind. It is not even the right kind of thing to get someone to change his mind, unless he is extraordinarily weak and fickle.

A better suggestion seems to be this: an evaluative *judgement* is, at least, a *request* or *invitation* to the hearer to agree to maintain or adopt a certain attitude, the attitude the speaker is at the same time expressing. An evaluative *suggestion* involves an invitation to the hearer to *consider* making the expressed attitude his own. An evaluative *hypothesis* is put up so that speaker and hearer may consider what the consequences would be if they were to make the attitude in question their own. Disagreement then has the following character. If A asks B to do something, but B refuses and in turn asks A to do something, and A refuses, then there is disagreement of a kind between them. The present idea is that the basis of evaluative disagreement is of this kind. It is not, however, all that disagreement amounts to, as we shall see.

Suppose A says, 'I am in favour of this, and I ask you to share my attitude'. Why should B grant the request? Indeed, how can we be assured that B is even in a position to grant the request? He cannot always just have whatever attitudes A may ask him to have. If the analysis stopped here, at the point of claiming only that an evaluative judgement was an expression of attitude, coupled with a request that it be shared, it would leave it entirely mysterious how an evaluative judgement could in general fail to be an absurd performance. It is absurd after all to invite or request somebody to do something, if you have no grounds for thinking he is in a position to do it.

Under what conditions, then, can the hearer respond positively to the request? An attitude is acquired, adopted or maintained towards something on the basis of the features that thing is known or believed to possess. An attitude is grounded in beliefs about the nature of its object. Thus the hearer is in a position to share the speaker's attitude when he has beliefs about its object which he can take as a basis for that attitude. But the speaker does not have to believe that the hearer already has such beliefs prior to the speaker's making his judgement. He has only to believe that there are features of the object such that, if the hearer knew of them, or believed the object to possess them, he would be in a position to share the speaker's attitude. This weaker condition suffices, because the speaker may follow up his judgement by pointing out the features he takes to be relevant, or, in certain cases, his judgement may itself convey the presence of such features.

The expression 'would be in a position to have an attitude' is used rather than the stronger 'would have an attitude', because whether or not a man adopts or has a particular attitude towards something is to some extent a matter for him to choose. This is not always so; a person may be antecedently committed in some way, or find himself willy-nilly having a certain attitude, but often he is able to choose what considerations to allow to weigh with him, and what to regard as unimportant. And the influence of another who desires him to share his attitude is sometimes not a negligible factor in determining the choice.

It is, however, a feature of the present account that if the speaker knows that, even when the hearer is in possession of the relevant facts, it will be quite *impossible* for him to share the speaker's attitude, then the speaker's evaluative judgement will be out of place, or at least will have only some secondary, and possibly exploitatory function, such as that of provoking the hearer, annoying him or challenging him. If a liberal says to someone he knows to be an orthodox Roman Catholic 'The free availability of abortion is a great blessing', he is not using evaluative language for its primary purpose. He is using the invitatory aspects of evaluation for some other purpose – perhaps he just intends to give pain. If the speaker knows that his hearer cannot, as he at present is, give weight to those features which determine the speaker's attitude, he may realize that the time is not yet ripe for the evaluative judgement. He must first try to alter the hearer's frame of mind. Specifically evaluative language may play only a small part, or none at all, in such a discussion, where the speaker is as it were preparing the ground, by putting the thing in an attractive light, contradicting beliefs he takes to be false, exploiting possible analogies and so on. A similar process is gone through if the parties discover they disagree, if the hearer does not respond positively to the invitation. Here again, one goes back behind the evaluation to the basis for attitudes. But if there is no point of agreement in attitude from which the parties can work forward towards a shared attitude on the main question at issue, and this is realized, the discussion is sterile from the evaluative point of view.

So far, therefore, we have the following suggestions as to what might form part of an account of evaluative judgement:

(1) The speaker is expressing an attitude, perhaps also an emotion.

(2) The speaker is requesting or inviting the hearer's participation in that attitude.

(3) The speaker believes that there are features of the object of the attitude such that, if his hearer knew of them, his hearer would be in a position to participate in that attitude.

STATING AND CONVEYING

Condition (3) of the last section is frequently satisfied in the following way. The speaker has general standards for taking up an attitude to a certain kind of thing. To take a mundane case, he may have standards for assessing central heating systems. He will look with favour upon such a system if, for instance, it is inexpensive, economical to operate, efficient, easily maintained, compact and not unsightly. The thing he is evaluating is a particular thing of that kind. Moreover, he believes his hearer shares those standards. Further, he believes his hearer knows what his – the speaker's – standards are. All these conditions are quite commonly satisfied. Let us illustrate their workings in the case of a judgement 'A is a good F'. We have

(1) S (the speaker) is expressing a favourable attitude towards A.

(2) S has standards for a favourable attitude towards things of the kind F.

(3) S believes that A meets these standards.

(4) S believes that his hearer H shares these standards.

(5) S believes that H has a correct belief about what S's standards are.

(6) S is expressing favour *on the basis of* his standards.

(7) S is inviting H's agreement to share a favourable attitude on the basis of the standards believed to be shared.

If S is correct in his beliefs about H's standards, then S has a *right* to expect that H will respond favourably to his invitation. For if H really does have these standards, then he has a commitment to favour Fs that meet them. S is thus inviting H to carry out his commitment to favour Fs that meet the standards by favouring A in the recognition that A *does* meet the standards.

Now where the condition exists, as it does, of mutual belief that the standards are agreed between the parties, and such belief is true, then the judgement 'A is a good F' *conveys* information about the features of A. For suppose H believes that S is sincere in his judgement. Then he can infer that S believes that the standards are met. And since he knows what the standards are, he acquires information as to the properties of A. In such circumstances, the judgement also functions as a description of the object evaluated. All this is plausible for such a case as 'This is a good central heating system'. But compare the judgement 'This is a good novel', made by one person to another who does not know his critical opinions. The judgement conveys virtually no information to the hearer about the character of the novel. The reason is clear. The hearer is not aware of the speaker's standards of goodness in novels. Nor can he make even a reasonable estimate, since standards of assessment in the criticism of fiction vary so markedly. Further, the speaker cannot reasonably intend that his utterance should convey such information, since he has no reason to believe that the hearer knows what his – the speaker's – standards are.

This account of the conveying of information allows for possibilities of misunderstanding. For suppose S is wrong in his belief about what H's standards are, and H believes that his own standards are the same as those of S. Then S will be intending to convey that his own standards are met, but H will take it that it is his – H's – standards that are met. He may then come to believe that the object has properties quite other than those that S intended to say that it had. Descriptively, then, the utterance will be a failure. But evaluatively, it may still be a success. For H may know independently of the utterance that the object does meet his own standards, and on that basis agree to participate in S's favourable attitude. Then S's utterance is an evaluative success in that it results in mutual recognition of a shared attitude. On the other hand, there remains a latent possibility of misunderstanding in that, although there is a shared attitude, there is no shared basis for that attitude. Evaluative agreement can therefore conceal a divergence in standards, and this can lead to severe disappointment at a later time.

The capacity of an evaluative judgement to convey information yields possibilities of exploitation. It may be that for some kind of thing the standards of evaluation are agreed and indeed have become somewhat ossified. One can perhaps take it for granted that the hearer will latch on to these standards. It may then become understood that these standards are purely conventional, and have ceased to carry any commitment to favour things that meet them. A judgement to the effect that a thing of that kind is good may then carry no evaluative force. It may express no attitude and invite no participation. It would function purely descriptively, and not even carry any commitment to any evaluation. So an account of this purely descriptive use of 'A is a good F' would go as follows:

(1) S *has in mind* certain standards for favouring things of the kind F.

K

(2) S believes that H will have the same standards in mind.

(3) S believes that A meets these standards.

(4) S believes that H has a correct belief as to what standards S has in mind.

Such a use simply to convey information properly counts as exploitatory. For it does not belong to the point of 'good' in the language that it should be so used. It results from the normal, non-exploitatory use involving mutual recognition of standards by dropping certain conditions and weakening others. The speaker is exploiting the features of the normal use that derive from the invitation to share attitudes. For it is the invitatory aspect of 'good', together with the fact that attitudes are related to beliefs on which they are based, which makes possible the conveying of information when the beliefs on which the attitude is based are standards. It is only once that standards are established and mutually agreed that the invitatory and expressive aspects can drop out, leaving only the purely descriptive function.

There is even a third case, where the speaker intends simply to convey information, but is employing standards which are in fact genuinely his own. In that case, his judgement is not itself an expression of attitude, but is such as to carry a commitment to attitude.

In the fully evaluative case, there is more than one kind of possibility of disagreement.

(*a*) S and H may disagree about whether the object meets the standards.

(*b*) S may be wrong in believing that H shares his standards. S's aim misfires as it were. He has different standards, and the object does not meet them, whereas it does meet S's.

(*c*) S and H have different standards, and the object meets both sets of standards. S and H agree in attitude, but disagree in the basis for their attitude.

Various combinations of these cases are also possible. For example, S and H may disagree both about the character of the object *and* have different standards, and this may be the case both where they agree in attitude and where they disagree in attitude. Together with the fact that in many cases a man's standards, the bases of his attitudes, may be elusive even to himself, these manifold possibilities go far to explain why evaluative disagreement is so highly liable to give rise to misunderstanding and argument at cross-purposes.

I have spoken of the speaker *conveying* information in an evaluation according to standards rather than *stating* facts about the object. The reason for this is a preference for retaining the locution 'stating that *p*' for the cases where what is stated is recoverable solely from the *meaning* of the sentence used to express that *p*. It is my contention that the information conveyed by 'good' in 'A is a good F', for instance, is *not* recoverable solely from the meaning of the sentence. This is to be construed as a denial that 'good' has any descriptive meaning, and is not a negligible claim. There have been a fair number of moral philosophers of whom C. L. Stevenson and R. M. Hare are but two, who have ascribed descriptive meaning even to such general terms as 'good'. This is a mistake, and leads inevitably to the ascription of an incredible ambiguity in the term. For if it has descriptive meaning, then this must vary with virtually every different kind of thing that can be said to be good. The present theory offers a more plausible alternative. If the hearer understands the judgement, he understands that he is invited to share an attitude. Attitudes are based on beliefs. Since he is invited to share an attitude, he understands that it is one the speaker has. The speaker must thus have beliefs on which he bases it. If the hearer knows what the speaker would, in such a case, base his belief on, he can infer what the speaker believes the character of the object to be. So he has reason to believe that the object has that character. This is information conveyed. The information is not *contained* in the evaluative judgement in a way that could be spelled out in an analysis of its *meaning*, but is conveyed through a knowledge of what is necessary for the judgement to have its specifically evaluative function, together with relevant knowledge of the speaker. As the example 'This is a good novel' indicated, more is required for information to be conveyed than an understanding of the meaning of the utterance. He understands the *meaning* if he knows English, but he gains no information unless he has a knowledge of the speaker's critical standards.

To make this matter clearer, it is useful to compare the conveyance of information not contained in the judgement in evaluative cases with the similar situation in descriptive cases. Thus, to take a definite case, I compare the relation between 'B is a good piece of steak' and 'B is tender, tasty and marbled' with the relation between 'John is a tall man' and 'John's height is at least six feet'. First, just as it is no part of the *analysis* of 'John is a tall man' that John's height should be at least six feet, so it is no part of the analysis of 'B is a good piece of steak' that

B should be tender, tasty and marbled. Secondly, a speaker, in saying that B is a good piece of steak, may convey to another that B is tender, tasty and marbled, and so also a speaker, in saying that John is a tall man, may convey to another that John is at least six feet tall. Thirdly, the mechanism of conveyance is similar (though not identical) in the two cases. The difference lies in the fact that in the evaluative case, the information is mediated by the speaker's standards and in the second, descriptive case it is mediated by an empirical belief. Both standards and empirical beliefs could vary without change in the meaning of the respective judgements.

That John is a tall man says that John is tall for a man, but this proposition by itself entails nothing about how tall a man has to be to be tall for a man. Spoken in contemporary Britain, it would most probably convey, though not entail, that John was at least six feet tall. But spoken in the Middle Ages, it might convey only that John was at least five feet six inches tall. Spoken in a community of pygmies, it would convey perhaps only that John was at least four feet six inches tall. This variation implies no change in the meaning of 'John is a tall man'. The variation stems from the fact that how tall a man has to be to be tall for a man depends on the distribution of heights among the male population the speaker has in mind. Without some belief on the part of the hearer concerning this distribution, the utterance will fail to convey an idea of how tall John is. And without some such belief, the speaker cannot be intending to convey an idea of how tall John is. If the information the hearer obtains is what the speaker intends to convey, then speaker and hearer must have (more or less) the same belief about the distribution of height. Further, if the speaker is to be confident that the hearer will acquire the intended information from the utterance, he must be confident that the hearer has a correct belief as to the speaker's belief about the distribution of height.

It is important that the communication can be a success with respect to conveying information even when the speaker's and hearer's beliefs about the distribution of height are wrong. For instance, let us suppose that for some reason S and H both believe (wrongly), that most men are around five feet four inches tall, and that relatively few reach five feet eight. Then suppose S, believing that John is five feet eight, says that John is a tall man. He may be sincere, but his judgement is false. But its falsity does not matter, since H will not get the wrong idea, if he has the same wrong belief about heights as S, and knows that S's belief is the same as his own. He will acquire the belief that John is at least five feet eight, and this is just what S intended to convey (though what he *stated* was false). In this way a truth may be conveyed, although what is stated is strictly false, because a false general belief is shared by the parties.

In this case, the meaning of 'tall man', together with the empirical facts alone, determine what the *true* general belief would be. But for the success of the communication in giving an idea of John's height, the truth of the general belief is unimportant. What is important is that the belief be shared (and if the belief is false, we have a case of *mistake*, not of exploitation). In the evaluative case, both the evaluative *and* the descriptive purpose can be successfully achieved, however crazy the standards of the parties for goodness in steak may appear to be, so long as speaker and hearer have the same ones, and the speaker is right in thinking that the hearer is right in his belief about what the speaker's standards are. For then the intended information will be successfully conveyed, and the hearer will respond positively to the speaker's request to share an attitude.

Now 'tall' is a normal case of an adjective with descriptive meaning. As has been shown, in its workings it is quite similar to 'good'. How then can it be denied that 'good' has descriptive meaning? The reason is this: the descriptive meaning of 'tall' does not lie in what is conveyed rather than stated. It lies in what is stated. But if 'good' has descriptive meaning, it seems that it would have to lie in what was conveyed. But what is conveyed forms no part of the analysis of meaning of the utterance. So 'good' does not have descriptive meaning. It is possible that sometimes all that is meant by talking of 'descriptive meaning' is that there must be some description upon which an attribution of an evaluative term is based. But it is very confusing to use the term in this way. It blurs the significant differences between 'good' and straightforward descriptive terms. It can also help to blur the distinction between what a speaker means on some occasion, and what the term means. The speaker may mean to convey some determinate description in using an evaluative term without the term itself actually having that meaning. It has been the point of this section to show how this can be so, and be so without exploitation.

Condition (3) of the end of the last section was that the speaker should believe that there are features of the object of his attitude such that, if his hearer knew of them, his hearer would be in a position to participate in that attitude. If this condition could be satisfied *only* by the conditions (1) to (7) of the beginning of this section, evaluation would generally be a far more amicable business than it is. Disagreement would arise only where the speaker had made some mistake, so that some of the beliefs (3) to (5) were false. There would also be the possibility of disputes arising from exploitatory uses, but these would form so large a class as to cast doubt on whether they were exploitatory after all, and hence cast doubt on the analysis. Now in fact condition (3) at the end of the last section is unnecessarily strong and requires weakening. It was put in the strong form to enable the discussion of conveying to proceed more simply. This was not vicious, since (1) to (7) frequently *are* satisfied, and in the interests of clarity it is justifiable to postpone certain complications and qualifications. All that is in fact needed, in place of (3), is that the speaker should think there is *some chance* of the hearer being in a position to share his attitude, when he knows the facts. The case of sterility mentioned was one where the speaker knew there was no such chance. As another example, consider an evaluation of the Government's record made by the Prime Minister speaking in the House of Commons to the Leader of the Opposition. There is no question of a positive response from the Leader of the Opposition and the Prime Minister is perfectly aware of this. As a remark to the Leader of the Opposition, the evaluation is entirely exploitatory. Its function is to needle, cross or anger. Its non-exploitatory function is entirely in relation to the uncommitted sector of the public, and any waverers or malcontents there may be on the back benches. It is an invitation to such people to agree to the Prime Minister's attitude – which is no doubt highly favourable.

Having weakened this condition, it is possible to consider modifications of (1) to (7). In the case of a judgement 'A is a good F' we frequently have a situation of the following kind:

(1) S is expressing a favourable attitude towards A.

(2) S has standards for favouring things of the kind F.

(3) S believes that A meets these standards.

(4) S does not believe that H is *immovably* committed to incompatible standards.

(5) S believes that H has a correct belief about what S's standards are.

(6) S is expressing favour on the basis of his standards.

(7) S is inviting H's agreement to have a favourable attitude

towards A by making S's standards his own, or by continuing to hold them (supposing they are already his own).

(4) may be called a non-sterility condition. The new (7) is a modification of the old which removes the presupposition by S that H's standards are already the same as those of S. The new conditions are weaker than the old, but they still enable S to be conveying descriptive information to H, by his utterance of 'A is a good F'. The previous condition (4) is unnecessary for doing this. That is, it is not necessary that H be believed to share S's standards. All that is required is that he know what those standards are.

In the earlier case, S can be described as *invoking* standards he believes to be shared. In the present case, he is *using* standards of his own, and *proposing* their acceptance by H. Let us call the earlier case the standard-invoking use, and the present case the standard-proposing use. In both uses, the relevant conditions (1) to (6), it turns out, can be derived as conditions for the sincere and pointful performance of an act of the respective type (7). Consider the standard-proposing use first. It would be absurd for S to invite H's agreement to have an attitude unless S himself had that attitude. H himself can hardly fail to understand this. This shows us how S is expressing his attitude. Expression here is that form of communication which occurs when the sincerity and propriety of a speaker's linguistic performance require that a certain proposition be true of *him*. In this way a statement is an expression of belief, since if S states what he does not believe, he is insincere. Yet his statement need not for all that be a statement *that* he believes it. We can thus link the relation to the speaker's own attitudes and his relation to the hearer's by deriving the former from the latter as a sincerity-condition of a kind the hearer can hardly fail to appreciate. That it should be easily appreciable by the hearer is important for the efficiency of evaluative language as a mechanism for the expression of attitude. Secondly, S's expression must be on the basis of his standards, otherwise there would be no point in his proposing those standards to H. This gives us (6) as well as (1). Further, (7) carries the immediate implication that S has standards, which gives us (2). Next, the expression of attitude would be clearly insincere unless S believed that A met the standards. So we have (3) as well. Unless H has a correct belief as to what S's standards are he does not grasp what S is proposing in a performance of type (7). S must realize this, so we can add (5). Finally,

(4) is a condition of the performance's being pointful. Thus, given that (7) is a type of performance that belongs to the point of evaluative language, (1) to (6) appear as no more than minimal conditions for sincerity and pointfulness. However, we must mention that a performance of type (7) may be proleptic. H may not *already* know what S's standards are. S may make his invitation in anticipation of a future explanation of his standards. This caveat, however, does not make any substantial difference. The same applies to the standard-using case, where, *mutatis mutandis*, the other conditions can be derived from the nature of the speaker's performance.

SUBORDINATE OCCURRENCES

So far four different functions of 'good' in an assertion about a particular thing have been isolated and distinguished. They are the standard-proposing use and the standard-invoking use, each of which is properly evaluative, and the use to convey information, either by means of merely conventional standards or by means of the speaker's own standards, without actual expression of an evaluative judgement. In all four cases, it has been only the *categorical* form of judgement 'This is a good X' that has been considered. The accounts that have been given require modification before they are applicable to judgements other than the simple categoricals. In a use of sentence of the form 'If this is a good X then *p*', as has frequently been remarked in the literature, the speaker is not actually evaluating the X in question. In terms of the present account, he is not actually expressing an attitude to the thing in question, nor inviting the speaker to share it, nor attributing properties to it via the mechanism of conveyance. The problem is to see how to fit an account of such subordinate occurrences into the general pattern of an emotivist theory.

First, the use of such a conditional in a purely descriptive way, exploiting merely conventional standards, presents no special problem. In effect, what is being hypothesized in such a case is simply possession by the X in question of the properties required for it to meet the standards. But the hypothesizing is done via the mechanism of exploitatory conveyance, as described previously, rather than in virtue of the *meaning* of 'this is a good X' in the context. Suppose the sentence is 'If this is a good watch, then we should buy it', and the conventional standards of reliably telling the time and being easy to read are all that is in question. Then the *function* of this sentence, in its context, is no different from the function of 'If this is a watch which is easy to read and tells the time reliably, then we should buy it', but the two sentences do not *mean* the same. For in the second case the function is performed simply by the words of the sentence having the meaning that they do. In the first case, the function is performed only in virtue of there being some presupposed conventional standards, mutually recognized by the parties.

The case is similar where the standards are ones the speaker has made his own, and the function is the same as that of a purely descriptive conditional. Other cases are a little trickier. Various possibilities may be distinguished. One is where the speaker has standards, and does not know that the object in question meets them. Another is where he knows the properties of the object, but does not know what standards to adopt. A third is where he knows neither the properties of the object, nor what standards to adopt. These possibilities are most conveniently illustrated by taking a question as an example, with a subordinate occurrence of 'good'. Consider the question 'Is it a good Picasso?', together with various contexts in which this might be asked.

(1) Suppose it is asked by one expert on twentieth-century art of another, whom he presumes shares his standards. The former expert, we suppose, has not yet seen the picture, the one to whom the question is addressed has. The question in this context is a request for information as to whether the picture meets the standards presumed to be shared.

(2) Suppose it is asked by a man who is as yet fairly naïve and ignorant in matters of modern art. He is standing contemplating the picture, and the question is put to a friendly connoisseur who is by his side. This man's problem is that of the acquisition of standards; he is not yet in a position to discriminate among Picassos, but desires to be so. He trusts the connoisseur's judgement, and his question is a request for guidance (though of a relatively naïve kind). It shows willingness to make the connoisseur's standards his own, at least for the time being.

(3) Suppose it is asked by a similar man, of a similar connoisseur, but before the questioner has seen the picture. Here the questioner knows neither the properties of the object nor what standards to adopt. If the connoisseur answers 'Yes, it is a good Picasso' his answer is a doubly proleptic invitation to share a favourable attitude, and as such requires a situation of trust, as does case (2).

In each of the three cases, the questioner, by asking the question, indicates a general preparedness to share a favourable attitude if the gaps in his knowledge are filled in in the right way. But what gaps there are vary from case to case, and context to context, in accordance with the general framework presented in this essay.

The situation is similar with conditionals. The content of the antecedent 'If this is a good X . . .' may vary. One case is where the utterer has standards, and is hypothesizing that the X in question has properties that would meet them. *That* there are standards, and that they are the speaker's, need not belong to what is hypothesized. This much may already be mutually recognized. Another case is where the properties of the object are known and what is hypothesized is that certain of *these* properties are sufficient to meet such standards as may be appropriate. Here the speaker is presupposing that there are standards he would be prepared to adopt, but is not presupposing that he *has* such standards already. A third case is that where neither the speaker's possession of standards, nor what the properties of the object are, belong to the background. Here the content of the antecedent is at its richest. In each case, the background plus the content of the antecedent together make up a set of sufficient conditions for the propriety of the categorical 'This is a good X', but how this set is divided between background to the conditional utterance and what is hypothesized varies from case to case. Thus no unique analysis of conditional occurrences is possible. The complexity and multiplicity of function of 'good' allows for various possibilities within a single general framework. But in spite of the variability of the content of the hypothesis, there is one thing that can be said of all the conditional evaluative cases; that if the content of the antecedent is fulfilled, the speaker should be prepared to invite his hearer to share a favourable attitude. For the content of the hypothesis is always such as to fill out the remaining conditions for a categorical judgement – the conditions other than those presupposed as background to the conditional utterance.

We now turn to consider negation, e.g. 'This is not a good X'. Here again 'good' has a subordinate occurrence, and here again there are various possibilities. One is that the speaker is presupposing a mutual recognition of agreed standards, and the content of his denial is that the X in question does not have properties that would meet them. Another is that the speaker has standards, but does not suppose the hearer to share them. His utterance would be a – possibly proleptic –

invitation to the hearer to refuse favour on the basis of making the speaker's standards his own, rather than, as in the former case, on the basis of standards assumed to be already the hearer's own. But the possibilities seem here to be more restricted than in the conditional or interrogatory cases. For there seems to be no propriety in a categorical denial of goodness where the speaker does not have standards of his own.

These remarks are no more than a sketch of how 'good' may function in subordinate occurrences, but they are enough to indicate how such occurrences can be shown to fit in with the general account.

MORE ABOUT STANDARDS

So far no requirement has been made that the standards invoked or proposed by the speaker in an evaluation should be the *correct* ones. In this respect the present account differs from a recent proposal of J. O. Urmson,[1] who suggests as a definitional schema:

This is a good X = This satisfies a description such that no one can *correctly* dissent from a favourable evaluation of it as of the kind X. (my emphasis)

Such a reference to correctness seems unnecessary. The proper functioning of evaluative language seems not to require, though it does not exclude, that the notion of correctness should have any general application to standards. Certainly somebody cannot with propriety evaluate something by saying 'By the incorrect standards that I am using, this is a good X', as Urmson points out, but this point does not establish that the speaker presupposes correctness for his own standards, since he may not believe that the notion of correctness has any application. There is *a* place for correctness, but it is rather special. For instance, suppose I am judging a vegetable show, which is to be judged in accordance with standards laid down by the Royal Horticultural Society. I may make mistakes about what the standards are, and give the prizes to the wrong marrows and turnips, etc. I should be applying standards, but they would be in some respects incorrect. And their incorrectness is in just those respects where they diverge from those of the Royal Horticultural Society. A man can thus be said to be using

[1] *The Emotive Theory of Ethics*, p. 142.

incorrect standards when there is agreement on what standards are to be used, but he is not using them, but others. Such cases are, however, only a subclass of standard-invoking evaluations. Normally the criticism of standards, if it takes place at all, is in terms of their appropriateness, realism, good sense and so on, rather than in terms of correctness. Even in judging such comparatively 'objective' matters as what would be a good instrument for a particular purpose, we do not speak of the standards involved as correct or incorrect. If someone disagrees with us, we might say that his standards were absurdly high, or perverse, unsuitable or eccentric. We should not say they were incorrect, except in such a special case as the one just mentioned. We do indeed frequently say that someone's standards are *wrong*, but this need not imply that there is just one set of correct standards. For there are at least the following alternative cases:

(1) A certain kind of misunderstanding. A man is using the wrong standards because he has not grasped the object of the evaluative enterprise in hand. For example, a thing may be both an X and a Y, and be a good X but a poor Y. If the purpose is that of judging it as an X, and the man, through misunderstanding, judges it as a Y, then, if the agreed standards of goodness of Ys are different from those for Xs, he is using the wrong standards.

(2) 'Wrong' can be used simply to mean 'unsuitable' or 'inappropriate'.

(3) There is the case where A says to B that a third person C has the wrong standards, where the object is to express disfavour of C's standards on a presupposed basis of B's agreement in standards with A.

(4) There is the case where a co-operative enterprise is being discussed, which requires for its success common standards among the parties. A says to B 'We can't have C, he has the wrong standards'. For instance, A and B are trying to form a quartet to play Mozart. C has quite different and incompatible standards of what counts as a good performance of Mozart. For A and B's quartet, he has the wrong standards – i.e., with him in it, the quartet is unlikely to be a success.

Urmson does consider the objection to his formula that if a hearer does not share the speaker's standards, he need not be incorrect in disagreeing with the evaluation.[1] But his answer is not satisfactory. His main point is one that I agree with, that a prevalent use of 'good'

[1] *The Emotive Theory of Ethics*, p. 143.

presupposes agreed standards. But this does not justify an implication that the standards supposed to be agreed are correct. Under such a presupposition, the formula could run '... no one can *consistently* dissent ...', meaning 'consistently with the standards on which agreement is presupposed'. But Urmson must mean more by 'correctness' than consistency, since he refers to the possibility of *erroneous* standards in the course of discussing the objection. It seems that he has not sufficiently carefully distinguished between the presupposition that standards are agreed, and the presupposition that standards are the correct ones. There is much to be said for the view that at least some common uses of 'good' involve the former, but it is at least doubtful that they involve the latter. For the various points of evaluative utterances involving 'good' seem to be achievable without the presupposition of correctness: the conveying of information, the expression of attitude, the invitation to share an attitude – these do not require a presupposition of correctness, or even the applicability of that notion. No doubt a speaker implies that his standards are reasonable, defensible ones, and, as we have seen, they are ones he would wish his hearer to share. But that still does not require that he believe that his standards have any sanction of correctness.

It also seems that Urmson exaggerates the generality of the presupposition of agreement in standards. He says[1] 'It would be deceitful, an abuse of speech, if, knowing that by your standards a thing would be bad which is good by the standards I recognize, I were to say simply and without qualification that it was good. It would be deceitful because you would be entitled to presuppose agreed standards.' This is too strong, since it may already be clear to the hearer what the speaker's standards are, in which case he will not be misled. Nor need the use of 'good' in such a case be extraordinary, non-standard or exploitative. The presupposition of agreement is normal, but easily cancellable. There *can* be cases of deceit such as Urmson describes. They will be cases where the speaker believes that the hearer does not know what the speaker's standards are, and where the hearer does not already have a description of the object sufficient for him to make his own evaluation of it. For if he already knows what the object is like, the speaker's evaluation will not deceive, but merely make clear the divergence in standards. And if he already knows what the speaker's standards are, again he is not deceived. Moreover, where there is

[1] Ibid., p. 144.

deceit, it is of a descriptive nature. The speaker will be relying on the hearer's belief that they share standards, so that what his utterance conveys to the hearer will be that the object satisfies certain descriptions that the speaker knows or believes it does not satisfy. There is no evaluative deceit so long as the speaker is judging in accordance with his *own* standards.

Urmson also goes too far when he says[1] 'Thus in all our use of the term "good" there is a presupposition that there is some correct set of standards, for every kind and from every point of view, and in discussions of whether certain things are good it is presupposed that we all share the correct ones.' This is an extraordinary view. It implies that 'good' cannot be used in a discussion between people who are trying to agree on standards. For instance, suppose a discussion of the theory of literary criticism is going on, concerning the appropriate standards of merit in novels. The parties are open-minded and puzzled and have as yet no settled standards. A claim, in such a context, that a particular novel is a good one need not be out of place just because it is not known what the standards are, and hence cannot be presupposed that they are agreed. Again, one may suggest an evaluation to test a proposed standard for reasonableness, prior to its being agreed. But what is more obviously wrong with Urmson's statement is its implication that once divergence in standards is recognized, the term 'good' must drop out of the discussion. Indeed he says explicitly 'We cannot discuss whether a thing is good, engage in standard-using discourse, without this presupposed agreement on standards.' This just seems to be obviously untrue. If it were true, all disputes over whether a thing was good would be over whether it satisfied agreed standards, or would involve misunderstanding through the presupposition of agreement being false. But there are disputes over whether something is good between people who *know* they differ in standards. The much weaker non-sterility condition I have proposed seems more plausible – that each party should not believe the other to be *immovably* committed to different standards.

Another problem for Urmson is this: how is he to deal with the occurrence of 'good' in a statement of the standard itself, e.g. a statement of the form 'An X is a good one if it satisfies conditions A, B, C'? Certainly a man who makes such a statement does not always presuppose that his audience already agrees with it. He is not *using* his

[1] *The Emotive Theory of Ethics*, p. 144.

standard, nor setting a previously non-existent standard. He is saying what his standard is. It is unclear how this fits in with Urmson's account. The application of his formula yields 'An X satisfies a description such that no one can correctly dissent from a favourable evaluation of it as of the kind X if it satisfies conditions A, B, C'. This can be reduced to 'If an X satisfies conditions A, B, C, no one can correctly dissent from a favourable evaluation of it as of the kind X'. Apart from the reference to correctness which I have already disputed, this does not look too implausible. But it does not seem to presuppose agreement. Moreover, if it does not, it would seem extraordinary if, upon moving from the general statement 'If *an* X . . .' to the particular case 'If *this* X . . .', we were to move from a sentence not presupposing agreement to one which *does*. Such problems do not beset my account, which is easily adapted to the general case of expression of standards themselves. The speaker will again be expressing an attitude and inviting another to share it, but since he is articulating the bases of his attitude in the utterance itself, certain of the other conditions drop out. The speaker does not have to believe that the hearer knows what his – the speaker's – standard is, for instance, since what he is doing is to *tell* him his standard. Hence also no information about Xs is conveyed, since the mechanism of conveyance works via the hearer's knowledge of the speaker's standards, and here no such knowledge is presupposed antecedent to the utterance, nor is the utterance proleptic.

In so far as an evaluation of a particular object is in accordance with standards, it can be said that the speaker has reasons for his expression of favour – giving the reasons would consist in citing the properties mentioned in the standards. And in so far as the standards themselves are judged to be appropriate, the reasons may be said to be sound ones. This feature – the availability of reasons – is often thought to be one that helps to mark out evaluation from the mere expression of personal preference. It is thought to be a necessary condition of an evaluative judgement that the question 'Why?' should be in place, but not necessary that it should be in place if the judgement is a mere expression of personal preference. It seems unclear whether this condition can be used to distinguish the two classes of judgements, but it certainly seems to be a necessary condition of evaluations. Indeed it is a requirement that can be derived from the invitatory aspects of evaluative judgements. We have seen that a man cannot at will just take up any old attitude he may be invited to. If the speaker's invitation is to be in place, he must believe there are considerations which would put his hearer in a position to respond positively to it, and sincerity demands that they also be considerations which weigh with himself. These then are his reasons. Urmson puts the matter the other way round. He says, 'In so far as it is the case that "This is good" and "I approve of this" do solicit the agreement of others, it is because we are entitled to use such language only if our attitude is a reasoned one, so that divergence from it may count as disagreement.'[1] This raises the question why we should be entitled to use such language only if our attitude is a reasoned one. Also, divergence in attitude is not always disagreement. What is it that makes it disagreement if you do not share my attitude in a matter of evaluation? Even two divergent *reasoned* attitudes are possible without disagreement. These questions are not easy for Urmson, but they virtually answer themselves if we put the matter the other way round, and derive the necessity of reasons from the speaker's wish for others' agreement.

MORE ON INVITATION

Following the *Oxford English Dictionary*'s definition of 'good', many philosophers have identified *commendation* as the characteristic linguistic act performed in a non-subordinate use of 'good'. But it has also seemed to some that commendation is itself a concept in some need of analysis. It seems to me that the attraction of commendation for an analysis of 'good' lies in its suggestion of just the sorts of invitatory features on which I have laid so much stress. For it seems to belong to the primary point of acts of commending that they call for a response – a response of favour towards the thing commended. A man who commends does not thereby primarily intend to indicate or manifest something about *himself*; his primary intention is that his words should have some weight in inducing a favourable attitudinal relation of the hearer towards the object commended. The association of commendation with the speaker's expression of attitude is indirect, as in the case of judgements of goodness; if the speaker wishes his commendations to carry weight, they must be commendations of things or people he himself favours. But 'commend' seems to be rather specialized in its contemporary use; the things one can sensibly commend are a smaller class than those one can favourably evaluate. One can say that

---

[1] *The Emotive Theory of Ethics*, p. 63.

the weather is good, but is it sensible to *commend* the weather, for instance? Commendation is just one, and not an especially common one, of the ways whereby a speaker may try to fulfil his desires that others should have certain attitudes towards things.

'Invitation' is the word I have most commonly used for a linguistic act performed in an evaluative judgement, but there is no intention of excluding others. The desire that others share our attitudes is the central fact, and it can be served in other ways. An evaluative judgement may involve no more than a suggestion, but it can be a request, or an exhortation, or it can invoke a known commitment of the hearer. Different cases will demand different descriptions; there seems to be no single word which covers every case of the intentional relation to the speaker's attitudes I have in mind.

Throughout the later sections, it has always been attitudes rather than emotions that have been spoken of as the objects of the speaker's concern in relation to his hearer. This also is not essential; it is not only attitudes that a speaker can invite his hearer to share, although attitudes are the most frequent objects of such evaluative invitations. The place of emotion in the description of an attitude varies from attitude to attitude, and from person to person, but in many evaluative contexts, particularly moral ones, the relevant attitudes are ones in which the emotional content is quite high. Relevant attitudes in moral contexts may include such attitudes as sympathy, admiration, love, scorn, contempt, horror, disgust, hostility, awe and reverence. It may be the emotions involved in such attitudes that the speaker most wants his hearer to share.

There is a ready objection to bringing emotions into the picture in this way. It will be said that I cannot sensibly invite another to have or to share a particular emotion, and that this is because emotions are largely beyond control or influence by such means. This objection seems to be wrong, and especially wrong when it is used to buttress a distinction between emotion and attitude in the interests of a thesis that it is with attitudes that evaluative discourse must be concerned. For first, the attitudes mentioned in the previous paragraph have a high emotional content, so that to call upon someone to maintain, adopt or share such attitudes involves a call upon his emotions. Secondly, it should not be forgotten that people have emotional dispositions, and that they can, over a period of time, maintain or modify these dispositions. Thirdly, it is easy to underestimate the

L

degree to which at least some people's emotions are amenable to reason. If a person who is not neurotic is shown that one of his fears is groundless, it will normally disappear, and this can be a case of reasoning someone out of his emotions. Fourthly, the ascription of a particular emotion to someone often involves ascription to him of a belief of a particular type. For instance, resentment seems to be essentially a reaction to the nature of another's will towards one, as manifested in his behaviour. If I resent what someone did, I must believe that it showed some ill-will or lack of respect. If I become convinced that there was no such ill-will or lack of respect, my nettled feeling can no longer be described as resentment. These points make it possible for a man to have standards of feeling, as he can have standards of judgement and standards of behaviour. A standard of feeling is an emotional disposition deliberately maintained; an evaluative invitation to share a feeling invokes the actualization of such a disposition in accordance with the standard.

It is particularly clear with the moral emotions that we have standards of feeling. People have standards for feeling such things as gratitude, remorse, indignation and shame, for instance, and those are feelings one can call upon others to share. Standards of feeling play a large part in evaluation, and the classical emotivists were mistaken only in *over*emphasizing emotion and ignoring the more dispassionate attitudes. They were not wrong in giving it an important place.

NOTE

I have eschewed current terminology, in not using such words as 'illocutionary' and 'perlocutionary'. This is because such words belong to a theory which is as yet in an unsettled state, and use of them gives an appearance of technical precision, which is deceptive because of the variety of non-equivalent explanations of them that occur in the literature.

5 Actions and Consequences[1]
John Casey

Many moral philosophers and most moralists have insisted on the absolute character of morality. It has even been taken as a proof that a man's principles are *moral* that he thinks of them as absolutely binding, and that he is unwilling to give them up even when obeying them will lead to painful consequences. For Kant the moral law must be valid, 'not merely for men, but for all rational creatures generally, not merely under certain contingent conditions or with exceptions, but with absolute necessity'.[2] A moral principle which based itself upon the desirability of certain consequences would not really be a moral principle at all, but merely 'a rule of skill, or counsel of prudence'.[3]

Against this a minority of philosophers have argued that any moral principle which is not finally related to the production of certain consequences is either irrational or immoral. According to this view, moral principles in the end make sense or have authority only if they are connected with human happiness and unhappiness, human wants and needs. I shall call philosophers who take the first view 'absolutists' (although there is also a good case for calling them 'deontologists'), and philosophers who take the second view 'consequentialists' (although there also is a good case for calling them 'utilitarians').

Absolutism will typically hold certain types of action, or certain states of affairs – such as telling the truth, being brave or honourable and so on – to be absolutely good; that is to say, it will treat them as ends. The consequentialist will typically judge the goodness of actions and states of affairs in terms of their relation to some final end – such as human happiness. The consequentialist might wish to argue that if some of the ends proposed by an absolutist conflict with what he con-

[1] I am very grateful to Mr J. E. J. Altham, Dr S. W. Blackburn and Mr Q. R. D. Skinner for helpful criticism. I am particularly indebted to Mr Roger Scruton, whose criticisms and amendments have greatly clarified the structure of the argument.

[2] *Fundamental Principles of the Metaphysic of Ethics*, translated by T. K. Abbott (London, 1965), p. 30.

[3] Ibid., p. 42.

siders to be the ultimate end, then to continue to adhere to these ends would be irrational. The accusation of 'irrationality' might take several forms. *Prima facie* it amounts to the view that absolutism must propose a moral system without giving any rule as to how such a system can be brought to bear upon a recalcitrant or changing reality. Suppose that certain virtues define ultimate moral ends; then they will do so independently of any changes in the world which might lead to the exercise of these virtues having disastrous results. An absolutist who holds, for instance, that the traditional virtues of courage, wisdom and liberality are necessarily a part of moral goodness must continue to do so even if the world becomes such that the exercise of these virtues is likely to lead to misery. It is just not possible for a man to be good through being cowardly, stupid and mean.

It is at this point that the disagreement between the two sides becomes clearer. The consequentialist will argue that the virtues and virtuous action are connected with moral goodness simply as a matter of common experience – for example, as a result of their frequent connection with happiness – not as a matter of logic. This would be enough to show that the consequentialist does not treat, say, the virtues as ends; for him, if the virtues ceased to contribute to happiness, they would cease to be good, or would cease to be virtues. This will be, for the absolutist, the fundamental error of the whole consequentialist approach. In his view if courage, wisdom and liberality began, for some reason, either to make people miserable or to lead to results which made people miserable, this simply could not be a reason for thinking that courage, wisdom and liberality had ceased to be good, or for thinking that a man could be morally good while lacking these virtues. This is a position that lends very natural support to that idealism of Virtue which is so characteristic of the ancient moralists: we recall Horace's picture of the just man who, 'were the vault of heaven to break and fall upon him, its ruins would smite him undismayed',[1] or the description in Cicero of Regulus who 'of his own free will and under no compulsion except that of a promise given to an enemy, returned from his native land to Carthage; yet virtue proclaims that when he had done so he was happier while tormented with sleeplessness and hunger than Thorius carousing on his couch of roses'.[2]

Here an impasse seems to have been reached between the conse-

---

[1] *Odes*, III.iii.
[2] *De Finibus*, II.xx, translated by H. Rackham (1951).

quentialist and the absolutist. The absolutist insists that it is of the essence of moral principles, of the virtues, or of moral duties, that they be treated as ends, or as referring to ends. It is of the essence of morality that it should be so treated for the simple reason that it is precisely on this basis that we decide which, among the many rules which govern a man's conduct, are *moral* rules. We might call a man's principle moral, partly *because* he refused to justify it in the light of consequential considerations. From the point of view of the absolutist, then, it follows that the consequentialist is either proposing an alternative moral *code* of the same logical status as the absolutist's, or else he is proposing that we replace morality with something else. The former alternative is, in many ways, uncongenial to the consequentialist, since it suggests a view of virtues and duties which is remote from ordinary human experience, in a way in which the typical absolutist virtues and duties are not.

In reply to this the consequentialist could argue that in that case morality in its traditional form really is irrational. This reply might not be based only on the failure of an absolutist code to change in the light of changes in the world, but on a deeper objection. He might claim that only a consequentialist theory gives rise to a coherent notion of *moral reasoning*. That is to say, the consequentialist might say that an absolutist scheme, with its plurality of logically independent ends, may produce irresoluble dilemmas (where obeying one principle may entail disobeying another) without providing any means for resolving them. He might also suggest that an absolutist is likely to find himself in a situation in which adherence to a particular principle will produce misery for a large number of people. So far, however, nothing has been said that suggests that the absolutist can be convicted of a fundamental, logical mistake. The impasse would be resolved in the consequentialist's favour if he could show that absolutism necessarily rests upon a simple, basic mistake about moral reasoning, such that any absolutist principle must (*a*) not exhibit genuine moral reasoning, or (*b*) not exhibit reasoning of any sort. In the following I shall take as my starting point one very interesting and powerful attempt to show that absolutism necessarily does rest upon a simple, basic mistake.

I KILLING AND LETTING DIE

In an article entitled 'Whatever the consequences'[1] Jonathan Bennett
sets out to show that *no* moral principle of the form 'It is always
wrong to do X whatever the consequences of not doing so' can possibly commend itself to a normal person unless (*a*) he is merely confused about its implications, or (*b*) he is 'passively and unquestioningly
obedient to an authority'. These categories are intended to be exhaustive: 'Conservatism, when it is not mere obedience, is mere muddle.'[2]
Now Bennett does not advance a *general* argument against the
rationality of absolutist principles, but he analyses a particular case
in which, he suggests, such a principle could only be defended by a
false moral weight being given to the distinction between *acting* and
refraining from action. Bennett's argument, if successful, would certainly be conclusive. We cannot take a moral principle seriously if it
necessarily places moral weight upon trivial differences between actions
or states of affairs. If it can be shown that any absolutist principle must
do this, then it could be shown either that it is not a genuinely *moral*
principle, or that it is irrational. I shall accept the stronger claim that
it would be irrational, and I shall assume that if this were so then it
could not be taken seriously as a moral principle. Moral principles of the
form 'It is always wrong to do X whatever the consequences of not
doing so' are of the kind I have called 'absolutist'. Moral schemes in
which such principles are central will characteristically claim that if
there is a moral difference between two courses of action, then this will
be because they do not both fall under the same moral principle. Since
on this view moral differences in particular cases result from the application of principles, it will be crucial for the rationality of the principles that they do not treat insignificant differences between actions
as morally crucial. If it can really be shown that *any* absolutist principle must inevitably claim that there is a moral difference between two
courses of action where the normal conscience simply could not see
any such difference, then it will have been demonstrated that no ab-

---

[1] *Analysis*, vol. 26, No. 3 (January 1966).

[2] Ibid., p. 102. 'Conservative' is the term which Mr Bennett has coined, in preference
to the terms 'absolutist' or 'deontologist', for one who adheres to principles of the form
'It is always wrong to do X whatever the consequences of not doing so'. I prefer the more
traditional term 'absolutist' which, for present purposes, I do not wish to distinguish from
'deontologist'. I realize that these terms are apt to be misleading, but so, I think, is 'conservative'.

solutist principle is rationally defensible. It seems likely that we *can* settle the question whether there is always a decisive moral difference between doing something and refraining from doing something (for instance, refraining from preventing something). So if Bennett's arguments are right, he will have shown how the dispute is to be resolved; and he will actually have resolved it by disposing of a whole tradition of moral philosophy, including the central tradition of Catholic moral thought.

The case Bennett takes is that of a woman in labour who will certainly die unless an operation is performed to kill the unborn child, while if the operation is not performed the child can be delivered alive by post-mortem Caesarian section. In this case, according to Bennett, the obstetrician is presented with 'a straight choice between the woman's life and the child's'.[1] The moral absolutist who holds to the principle 'it is always wrong to kill the innocent, whatever the consequences of not doing so' would condemn the operation on the obvious grounds that it involves killing an innocent child. Of course the non-performance of the operation would also involve the death of an innocent – the mother – but for the absolutist the dilemma is asymmetrical

> because the two alternatives involve human deaths in different ways: in one case the death is part of a killing, in the other there is no killing and a death occurs only as a consequence of what is done.[2]

Assuming that the absolutist does not subscribe to the principle 'It is always wrong to kill the innocent, whatever the consequences of not doing so' simply out of obedience to a moral authority, then, in Bennett's view, he must think that the premise, 'In this case, operating would be killing an innocent human being while not operating would involve the death of an innocent human being only as a consequence of what is done', gives *some* reason for the conclusion 'In this case operating would be wrong'.[3] Bennett's contention is that it gives no reason whatsoever.

Bennett advances an account of the distinction between killing and letting die. He envisages a scale with 'the only set of movements which would have produced (the death)' at one end, and 'movements other than the only set which would have produced (the death)' at the other:[4]

---

[1] Ibid., p 83.   [2] and [3] Ibid., p. 85.   [4] Ibid., p. 95.

This, then, is the conservative's residual basis for a moral discrimination between operating and not-operating. Operating would be killing: if the obstetrician makes movements which constitute operating, then the child will die; and there are very few other movements he could make which would also involve the child's dying. Not-operating would only be letting-die: if throughout the time when he could be operating the obstetrician makes movements which constitute not-operating, then the woman will die; but the vast majority of alternative movements he could make during that time would equally involve the woman's dying. I do not see how anyone doing his own moral thinking could find the least shred of moral significance in *this* difference between operating and not-operating.[1]

If no moral weight can be put upon the distinction between killing and letting die, then the fact that not-operating would only be letting the mother die, whereas operating would be killing the child, gives no reason for the conclusion 'In this case operating would be wrong'. Bennett thinks that, in its application to the obstetrical case, the moral principle 'It is always wrong to kill the innocent, whatever the consequences of not doing so' can *only* be commended to the normal conscience if the distinction between killing and letting die always does mark a decisive moral difference. Since there is no such difference, the absolutist who wishes to base his moral principle on reason rather than authority has failed to do so.

Later I shall try to show that the distinction between killing and letting die has been formulated in such a way as to beg the question against the absolutist. Certain considerations of agency and responsibility which any moral principle must take into account if it is to be rational seem to have been overlooked (Parts II and III of the present paper). First, however, I shall argue that there is another way in which Bennett has overlooked considerations of agency and responsibility, and has thus produced what looks like a general argument against absolutism, when really he is criticizing a principle which no intelligent absolutist should wish to defend. An absolutist who pays due attention to notions of agency will *admit* that there is no moral difference (at least in some cases) between killing and letting die; and this is because killing and letting die are both ways of being responsible

[1] *Analysis*, vol. 26, No. 3 (January 1966), p. 96.

for a death. The same state of affairs – a death – is necessarily the result both of killing and letting die. The concept of killing and the concept of letting die are connected in such a way that they must necessarily fall under the same moral principle whatever moral scheme one has. So a moral principle which forbids the killing of the innocent must, if it is to be rational, be construed as forbidding both killing and letting die.

Nor does this apply only to killing and letting die. It would, for instance, obviously be odd to condemn killing and yet not to condemn being an accessory to a killing. This is recognized by criminal law, which attaches a degree of guilt to being an accessory to murder which is sometimes as great as that which attaches to actually carrying out the killing. We *could* describe the criminal law as employing two quite independent principles, one covering murder, the other covering cases of being an accessory to murder. But a criminal code which punished murder but did not also punish being an accessory to murder, would be irrational (and unjust). It would also be irrational not to regard certain cases of being an accessory to murder as being as bad as murder, as involving a guilt as great as that of actually carrying out the killing. This is because to hand a murderer the gun which he is to use to carry out his crime may, in certain circumstances, be to participate in what he does to such an extent that two persons are equally involved as agents, and share equal responsibility.

Such locutions as 'He let X happen' and 'He failed to prevent Y' normally involve a man in the production of a state of affairs by as-cribing responsibility to him for it. They may involve him in the state of affairs as surely as if it had been the result of his direct agency. It is for this reason that any moral scheme must include both doing some-thing and being responsible for the same state of affairs under the same moral principle.

Let us take, for example, the case of slander. Strawson[1] has given an analysis of moral attitudes which connects them with such feelings as resentment and remorse. Resentment at being slandered, and remorse at having slandered someone else seem to be necessary conditions for genuinely believing slander to be morally wrong. A man who resented being slandered, but who never felt remorse at having slandered some-one else could scarcely be said to believe that slander was morally wrong. He would be evincing hostility to certain cases of slander, but not moral

[1] Cf. 'Freedom and resentment', in P. F. Strawson (Ed.), *Studies in the Philosophy of Thought and Action* (Oxford, 1968).

disapproval. And even if he does feel remorse at having slandered some-one, this would not be sufficient for saying that he holds, as a genuine moral principle, that it is wrong to slander. If he is ready to feel remorse at having slandered, then he ought also to be ready to feel indignation at hearing someone slandered. This 'vicarious analogue of resentment' (as Strawson calls it) is, as much as remorse, part of what it is for a man to hold as a genuine moral principle that it is wrong to slander. But if a readiness to feel indignation is an important criterion of a man's sincerely holding such a moral principle, then we seem to be moving towards saying that a person in a position to prevent the promulgation of a slander who feels no disposition whatever to do so – experiences no desire to contradict it, for instance – can only doubtfully be said to hold that slander is wrong. The doubt would be much stronger if he never felt any regret at having failed to prevent or contradict the slander. Such a man, we might say, cannot see what is wrong with slander, what is the harm of it. But if it is a criterion of a man's sincerely holding that it is morally wrong to slander that he should feel remorse at having slandered, indignation at hearing someone else slandered or regret at having let someone be slandered, then it must be a sign of his sincerity in holding the principle that he should feel remorse or regret at being *responsible* for a slander – either through conniving at it, or through remaining silent. One could have no proper grasp of a principle forbidding slander without seeing that it also covered cases of being responsible for a slander. Nor, without seeing how it covered cases of being responsible for a slander, could one really understand how, as a moral principle, it applied to cases of actually slandering.

However, a definition of slander such as 'the malicious misrepresenta-tion of a man's actions so as to defame him' contains, among other things, a reference to the state of affairs necessarily produced by a suc-cessful slander; if the slander is believed, the man is defamed. It is hard to imagine how someone could feel indignation or remorse at a slander unless he considered the situation which results from a successful slander was bad. The wrongness of slander must at least be connected with the wrongness of a man's being defamed. It is only if one deplores a man's being defamed – only if one sees that as an evil – that one can feel indignation or remorse at slander. So if one thinks that it is morally wrong to slander, one must also think it wrong for a man to be defamed; and one must also think it wrong to be responsible for a man's being defamed – for instance, by letting him be slandered.

Similarly, any moral principle which forbids the killing of the innocent must involve the condemnation of some state of affairs – such as
someone's deliberately depriving an innocent person of life. So given
such a principle, any act of commission or omission which falls under
the generic description 'being responsible for the death of an innocent'
will define an action covered by the principle. This will include having
someone killed, aiding and abetting a murder, and all courses of action
covered by the quasi-legal fiction of an 'act' – such as an 'act of omission'. One may let someone die, neglect someone such that he dies, or
refrain from preventing a death. These are all ways of being responsible
for a death. This analysis applies to a principle which holds that it is
always wrong deliberately to deprive an innocent person of life, just
as much as to any other.

Thus the obstetrical example can be faced by the absolutist. To say
that there is no decisive moral difference between killing and letting
die is to say that there is *one* moral principle which covers both.
To say that there *is* a moral difference is to say that there are two
principles. Now the irrationality of assuming a sharp moral distinction
between killing and letting die is connected with the oddity, in certain
cases, of denying that doing X and letting X happen involve a man in
the same degree of agency,[1] or of failing to see the close conceptual
connection between murder and being an accessory to murder. Therefore in saying that a person who holds that it is always wrong to kill
the innocent should also, if he is not to be arbitrary or irrational, hold
that it is wrong *in the same way and to the same degree* (in certain cases)
to let the innocent die, one is surely saying that in a moral scheme in
which the first principle were asserted, but in which all cases of letting
die were always regarded and judged quite differently, it would actually
be difficult to be sure that notions of agency were fully connected with
moral principles – in which case it would be impossible to see how, in
such a scheme, morality connected with responsibility. There could
not be a moral scheme which made such arbitrary distinctions without
involving itself in radical confusions about agency and responsibility.
Now to deny, in certain cases, that there is a decisive moral difference
between doing X and letting it happen is to point out that there is a

---

[1] I find it useful to use the term 'agency' to cover cases of responsibility. If a man directly
kills, he is guilty in respect of the death as agent; if he lets die, he is guilty in respect of
the death as being responsible. Furthermore, as we shall see, the nature of a man's agency –
what sort of agent he is – may determine the degree and nature of his responsibility.

conceptual connection between doing something and allowing it to happen which is revealed in the notion of responsibility (this explains the logical difference between the claim that 'Do not kill' includes 'Do not let die' and a claim that 'Do not kill' includes 'Do not drink beer'). The same applies, for instance, to telling an untruth, allowing an untruth to be believed, not correcting a falsehood and so on. Those cases, coming under the second and third descriptions, which are 'as bad as' telling a lie are also cases which are as good as telling a lie – which are the moral equivalent of lying. There are not three, logically independent principles covering the three types of case. To relate the second and third to the first is to engage in casuistry, not in the production of new moral principles.

Returning then to the obstetrician, we see that he is involved in a *dilemma*: The premise 'In this case operating would be killing the child . . . not operating would be letting the mother die' gives *some* reason for the conclusion 'In this case operating would be wrong' (indeed, taken with the relevant principle, it entails it). But similarly this premise gives an equal reason for the conclusion 'In this case, not operating would be wrong'. Thus there is a dilemma irresoluble by the principle. From the fact that the premise counts towards the conclusion 'In this case operating would be wrong' it does not follow that it must count against the conclusion 'In this case not operating would be wrong', or for the conclusion 'In this case, not operating would be right.' Whether or not the production of an irresoluble dilemma is to the discredit of the principle is scarcely to be settled in the abstract. That a principle give rise to irresoluble moral conflict does not *ipso facto* refute it; certainly nothing has yet been said against the possibility of such dilemmas. There might well be reason for adhering to a principle other than a belief that it is unlikely to give rise to tragic dilemmas, and the fact that in this particular case it is (perhaps) impossible to act in obedience to the principle, whichever course of action is decided upon, does not of itself refute it. A moral principle is not *ipso facto* better the fewer dilemmas it produces.

Now if the killing/letting die distinction did mark a moral difference, it would show that in this case adherence to the general principle does not produce a dilemma. The dilemma is avoided because it becomes clear that the obstetrician should save the child and let the mother die. But this result can only be counted as giving support to the principle itself if, first, the less a principle can be convicted of producing a dilemma the better it is, or secondly, we have some other grounds for holding that it is better that the mother should die than that the child should. What is clear is that this particular absolutist principle under-stood in the way I have suggested – the only way which does not involve radical confusions about action concepts – ceases to be vulner-able to Bennett's argument.

II ACTING AND REFRAINING

In the light of what has been said, it certainly seems odd that the abso-lutist or deontological moral tradition should base itself upon the plainly false view that there is always a decisive moral difference between doing something and letting it happen. In so doing it would be basing itself upon a plainly irrationalist view of moral principles, a view which would also, as I have said, reveal some radical confusion about agency and action concepts. That it should base itself upon such obvious confusions is altogether too strange. It is so strange, in fact, as to suggest that there are further ideas about agency – ideas which are, perhaps, characteristic of such a tradition – which we have so far over-looked. Some of these ideas I shall now try to explore.

I have not so far questioned the assertion that the absolutist could only have a reason for thinking that the child should be saved *rather* than the mother if there were a decisive moral difference between killing and letting die. It would then be of the first importance that the death of the child results from a 'killing' and that of the mother only from a 'letting die'. I have agreed that there is no such moral difference, al-though on grounds which remain compatible with some form of abso-lutism – i.e. the absolutist principle must be interpreted as covering cases of killing *and* letting die. So the absolutist has, as yet, no reason for saving one life *rather* than the other.

The question we must now ask is: could there be some other asym-metry in such a case which could give a reason for saving the child rather than the mother? We have so far assumed that the only possible asymmetry is between killing and letting die; and this has no appli-cation in the present case. But there are, in fact, two other ways in which the absolutist could argue to show that there is an asymmetry. Both of these arguments depend, again, on notions of agency.

(1) It might be that the obstetrician neither kills the woman nor lets her die. So the absolutist principle, in its properly wide in-

terpretation, can give a reason in this case for acting in one way rather than the other.

(2) Whether or not the obstetrician 'lets the woman die' there could be certain features of the case which create an asymmetry of a kind which any normal conscience must see to be morally relevant – whatever might be the moral principles that govern such a conscience.

If (2) is true then it is relatively unimportant for present purposes that (1) should also be true. My main concern will be to show that (2) *is* true, in the light of considerations which will suggest that the inflexibility of absolutist principles need not lead to an inflexibility in their application of an absurd kind. I shall try to show that the absolutist might well wish to describe the two courses of action open to the obstetrician in terms which would bring them under separate moral principles. I shall then argue that his grounds for claiming that there is such a moral difference are ones which any normal conscience could recognize, however the two courses of action are to be described. I shall begin by illustrating (1) since that is the best way to introduce those considerations as to agency on which (2) finally rests.

The description of the case so far seems to rest on the assumption that we can pass from the statement 'The obstetrician does not operate, with the (clear, immediate and foreseen) result that the woman dies' to such statements as 'He refrains from saving her life' and 'He lets her die'.[1] We have so far given no attention to the possibility that the first type of statement may not imply the second, or that one cannot in every case properly replace the other. Yet it is here that a distinction of great importance for the absolutist's case might come.

To illustrate, let us imagine an ideally conservative view of the obstetrical role. According to this view, it is the function of physicians to assist certain 'natural processes' selected and defined in some traditionalist, natural law fashion (it might be said that this conception of the medical profession can be understood partly in terms of its history, partly from the type of training given to medical students, partly from certain oaths doctors might take and partly from certain expectations which patients are encouraged to have). Physicians in general, and

---

[1] Some of the things Bennett says in describing the obstetricial case are as follows: 'This presents a straight choice between the woman's life and the child's' (op. cit., p. 83); 'He does not kill her, but he *lets her die*' (p. 93); '. . . he knowingly refrains from preventing her death which he alone could prevent' (p. 93); and in another context '. . . X chose to conduct himself in a way which he knew would involve Y's death' (p. 96).

obstetricians in particular, are not expected to make decisions in the course of their medical practice derived from social, political or any other than 'medical' considerations. This view of the medical profession, while accepting that it is the duty of physicians to procure health, would set strict limits on the means that could be used to do so. It might, for instance, say that were an obstetrician to kill a healthy foetus (in a case such as the present one) in order to procure the life of the mother, he would not be simply curing a disorder of the mother's body (as he would be if, say, he removed a dangerous tumour) but doing something else. He might be deciding which of two lives was more valuable, or who had the better right to life. Whatever the merits of his decision, that would be outside his role as an obstetrician.

Now I do not wish to *defend* this view, but simply to entertain it, on the supposition that it is not unintelligible, and not lacking in precedent. Let us suppose also that this view of medicine is set against, or goes with, certain ethical beliefs. Among the moral principles will be one which runs: 'It is always wrong to kill the innocent, whatever the consequences of not doing so'. This view of the medical function is not obviously totally irrational – whether or not it commends itself to the liberal conscience – and it can perhaps commend itself to intelligent, morally sensitive men. We can at least entertain it.

Given this conception of the role of physicians it is clear that there can be no question of killing the child in order to save the life of the mother. This simply does not present itself as a possible course of action. To say that it *is* a possible course of action is to assume that the medical function is different from what we are imagining it to be. For example, it might be said that there is here 'a straight choice between the woman's life and the child's'.[1] But a straight choice for whom? If our understanding of the obstetrical role rules out the possibility of the child's being killed in order to save the mother, then we would certainly not agree that such a choice is open to the obstetrician; nor would the obstetrician think that such a choice was open to him. Killing the child is out of the question. The phrase 'there is a choice between . . .' is being used in an oddly neutral way. If I meet in the street a friend whom I respect and admire, it would obviously be absurd to say 'I am presented with a straight choice between slapping his face and not slapping his face'. There is simply no question of my slapping his face. The assumption that there is a

[1] Ibid., p. 83.

choice open to the obstetrician either to save or not to save the woman's life goes with the view that in not operating he lets the woman die: 'He doesn't kill her, but he *lets her die*'.[1] But the traditionalist wishes to say that certain means of procuring the mother's life are outside the obstetrician's scope as a doctor. Killing the child, he insists, is not an option that can be regarded as presenting itself. The result is that the woman will die. Does it follow that the obstetrician 'lets her die'? Does he 'refrain from saving her life'?[2]

To suppose that it does follow is simply to propose some other conception of the obstetrical role. We cannot use terms which describe actions in this role-neutral fashion. Our conception of the role in which a man is acting, or our assessment of his character will considerably affect what we can describe him as doing in a particular situation. For example, if a man who is not an habitual thief goes into a bookshop, browses for a time, buys a book and leaves, it would be wrong to say that he refrained from stealing the book. That would imply that he *was* an habitual thief, or at least that on this occasion he had really been tempted to steal. It might have been, as it were, physically possible for him to have stolen the book, but since he is not a thief no such option or choice, or, for that matter, opportunity for refraining from theft, presented itself. Suppose, again, that I am travelling in the front passenger seat of a car. It might be easy for me to seize the wheel and turn the car into a ditch. Given the absence of certain contingencies and personality traits, I do not do so. Nor do I *refrain* from doing so. Turning the car into a ditch is not one of a multitude of untoward things I am refraining from doing.

The view we take of a man's character, or of his role in a certain type of situation, sets limits not only on what we can regard him as responsible for in that situation but also, as we have seen, on what we can properly describe him as doing or refraining from doing. Thus it is by no means obvious that an account of what the obstetrician does, and what is his responsibility, will be neutral as regards his role or function. The traditionalist might well quarrel with what he might regard as a covertly role-determined account of the obstetrician's actions which poses as role-neutral. 'He lets her die' is slipped in as though it were merely a different – perhaps more pointed – version of some such statement as 'He does not operate, with the foreseen result that the woman dies'. The point at issue comes out well where Bennett dis-

[1] and [2] Bennett, op. cit., p. 93.

tinguishes 'Joe killed the calf' from 'Joe let the calf die' in terms of 'relatively few' or 'almost all' the movements Joe made resulting in the death of the calf. The formula for 'letting die' is:

> Of all the other ways in which Joe might have moved, *almost all* satisfy the condition: if Joe had moved like that, the calf would have died.[1]

The context of this passage strongly suggests that this is intended to express the sufficient conditions of Joe's letting the calf die (Bennett leaves out of account considerations about immediacy, intention and so on, since he wishes to arrive at the residual basis of any attempted distinction between killing and letting die in the obstetrical case). But let us slightly alter the example and imagine that Joe happens to notice a fly caught in a spider's web, and about to be devoured by the spider. Joe observes this unmoved, and passes on. Of all the ways in which Joe might have moved, *almost all* satisfy the condition: if Joe had moved like that, the fly would have died. The fact is, unless there is some reason to say that Joe was concerned in what was happening (either in terms of some role, or on moral or religious grounds, or out of 'reverence for life'), then that formula could give no more than necessary conditions for 'Joe let the fly die'. Stripped of all these implications, the statement 'Of all the other ways in which Joe might have moved, almost all satisfy the condition "if Joe had moved like that the fly would have died"' could never aspire to mean more than 'Of all the other ways in which Joe might have moved . . . etc.' For it to issue so unexpectedly into the economical and pointed remark 'Joe let the fly die' some implications would have to be restored. If, on the other hand, Joe, who was well supplied with water, came across a man dying of thirst, merely regarded him unmoved and passed on, we might, all other things being equal, say that Joe let the man die, because we might consider that he has a relationship to a man beyond any that he can be supposed to have with a fly.

Given the traditionalist account of the obstetrical role, a course of action which would save the mother's life is certainly possible and, in a neutral sense, presents itself. It is clear (and he may be presumed to know it) that if the obstetrician were to kill the child the mother would live. In this sense various courses of action are 'presented' in all the

---

[1] Ibid., pp. 94–5.

other cases. We know what would happen if the car passenger were to seize the wheel, and we know that it would be easy for the man in the bookshop to steal a book (and they also know it). Killing the child, however, does not present itself as possible in any sense stronger than this: it is not a live option. So, the traditionalist might argue, to say that the obstetrician who does not operate 'could have (was in a position to have) done otherwise' is to use 'could' in an over simple, role-neutral fashion, and to ignore the sense in which, as an obstetrician, he could not have done other than he did. It was within his power to kill the child, but as an obstetrician there was no question of his doing so. His conclusion might be that, given this conception of the obstetrical role, the obstetrician is not 'presented with a straight choice between the mother's life and the child's', he does not 'let her die', nor does he 'refrain from saving her life'. Needless to say, he doesn't kill her either.

But now we must assume that this particular traditionalist is an intelligent man, and that he does not think that an adequate account can be given of a man's various roles simply by his being brought under the description of his profession. Unlike the carpenters and cobblers of the *Republic* we can hardly feel that in regarding a man as an *obstetrician* we have totally defined his responsibilities in life, or totally accounted for the sorts of option that are open to him. And here a grave objection against the traditionalist immediately arises. Surely, it will be said, there is one consideration which overrides all others – that derived from moral principles. And it has already been asserted that the 'traditionalist' scheme we have been entertaining goes with, or is set against, certain moral principles, one of which runs: 'It is always wrong to kill the innocent, whatever the consequences of not doing so'. Since, by the arguments of the first section, 'kill' must draw in its moral train cases of letting die, then the obstetrician is back in a dilemma: in operating he kills, and in not operating he lets the mother die.

The traditionalist's reply to this might be as follows. The conception of role gives certain action descriptions, which in turn can be the objects of moral assessment. It is not a question of whether moral principles are overriding, but, given that roles govern the use of action concepts, and are hence in some sense pre-moral, of whether, accepting the moral principle, this case falls under it. We must raise, in the first place, the question of the relationship of the obstetrician to the woman. It is essentially a contractual relationship, with certain moral upshots (such as the obstetrician's being guilty of bad faith towards her if, having received her as a patient, he simply neglects her) and this determines the action description upon which the moral principle must be brought to bear. To take another example: it might be the case that a patient will certainly die unless a particular drug is administered which would certainly save her. This drug would be immediately available at the cost of one thousand pounds, which the woman does not have. The doctor, under whose care she is, has just this amount in the bank. He does not devote it to buying the drug, on the grounds that to spend his own means to procure the life of a patient, while it would be morally admirable, goes beyond what can strictly be considered a duty. This might or might not be callous of him (so the argument might run) but it would not be a case of letting the woman die, even though her death is the direct, foreseeable result of his not paying for the drug. By contrast, if the woman's *husband* had a thousand pounds, and refused to spend it to buy the drug, he *would* be letting her die – even though there might actually be a less immediate causal chain, between her death and his refusal, than in the other case. This is because a husband's relationship with his wife is not narrowly contractual, but involves a very general concern for her welfare. So even given adherence to the moral principle 'It is always wrong to kill the innocent . . .', it is possible that the obstetrician's behaviour does not conflict with it.

Yet we are now brought to the point at which the consequentialist's argument is most powerful against this way of thinking. I have been concentrating on the traditionalist's refusal to accept such locutions as 'He lets her die', 'He refrains from saving her life', etc. But to deny these locutions is to deny the application to this case of only a weak version of what we may call the 'no moral difference' thesis – the version, in fact, for which I argued in Section I. There would be a great deal of point to this in very many cases, since in general the propriety of these locutions is linked with the propriety of ascribing responsibility for what happened. However, the 'no moral difference' thesis can be reformulated in a stronger version, as follows: these arguments may have shown that the obstetrician cannot correctly be described as 'letting his patient die' or as 'refraining from saving her life'. But all this is irrelevant; it does not refute the claim that what the obstetrician does, however it may be *described*, is not morally different from killing. No more moral difference attaches to these distinctions than attaches to the original distinction between killing and letting die. The case can be redescribed in terms of a stronger version of the 'no moral difference' thesis, which would hold that 'letting die' in *Bennett*'s sense is morally indistinguishable from killing; or, as we could put it: 'The obstetrician so conducts himself that, as a foreseen but unwanted and unintended consequence, the woman dies'.

I think that this is a very powerful argument, and is, I imagine, what a consequentialist would ultimately wish to say. The obstetrician, according to this argument, so conducts himself that the woman dies. Her death results in a way different from that in which it would have resulted, had he killed her, in that it is a consequence of his action – or rather, inaction. Yet this distinction does not, for the normal conscience, carry moral weight. Therefore his course of action is morally indistinguishable from one in which he killed her. Killing is wrong, therefore this course of action is wrong to the same degree.

So the first line of reply to the assertion that an absolutist principle cannot here give a reason for acting in one way rather than in another, once more comes up against the argument that there is 'no moral difference' between the two courses of action, *however* they may be described. Is there any rejoinder to this? Only, I think, in terms of the second line of argument which I mentioned earlier.[1] It must be shown that the absolutist's way of describing the two courses of action *could* be based upon some genuine difference between them.

It is immediately obvious that an analysis of the distinction between killing and letting die purely in terms of bodily movements produces results which are at least as paradoxical as those which are supposed to arise from absolutism. Taking again the case of a doctor who does not spend his personal fortune on a drug which will save the life of his patient, it might be said: On the strong 'no moral difference' thesis, the doctor 'so conducts himself' that as a foreseen (albeit unwanted) consequence, the woman dies. There is a distinction between his doing this and his killing her, but this carries no moral weight. Therefore on the strong 'no moral difference' thesis, he is guilty of her death. Yet, however callous some people might consider this man to be, *this* conclusion surely does not commend itself to the normal conscience.

A second example: One member of a pair of Siamese twins becomes seriously ill because his liver ceases to function. He will certainly die unless a new liver is transplanted into him. This, however, is impos-

[1] On p. 166.

sible because he is of an extremely rare blood group, or tissue type (if and when he dies, an operation to separate his brother from him will be quite possible). There is, however, one way in which his life could be saved: his twin brother is of the same blood group and tissue type. Being of a ruthless nature, he implores a doctor to procure the death of his brother, and save his own life by transferring his brother's liver into him. The doctor refuses the request. On the strong 'no moral difference' thesis, the doctor, in refusing to kill the healthy twin, is doing something morally tantamount to killing the unhealthy one. The case is obviously very close to that of the mother and child, and a more preposterous conclusion could scarcely be imagined.

These counter-examples suggest a point of very general significance. If we take, as a central formulation of the strong 'no moral difference' thesis, the statement 'The obstetrician so conducts himself that (as a clear, foreseen and immediate consequence) she dies', then we can schematize the points at issue as follows: We have, on the one hand:

(A) All cases of responsibility for a death. This includes killing, and all *genuine* cases of letting die – such as, for instance, the refusal of the husband of a sick woman to pay for a drug necessary for her recovery. It also, incidentally, includes cases of being an accessory to a death, incitement to murder, etc. (this list includes types of responsibility for a death which would make the guilt less than that of killing – differences marked in criminal law by such concepts as manslaughter, criminal neglect, etc.; so obviously a case of letting die is merely one member of a class of cases which is itself part of a larger class of 'cases of responsibility for a death').

On the other hand we have:

(B) All cases of 'so conducting oneself that X dies' (as a clear, immediate, foreseen consequence).

Now all cases of A are cases of B; but not all cases of B are cases of A. Cases of B give the *necessary* conditions for cases of A. But for the conditions to be *sufficient* some consideration as to agency (e.g. role) is required. Or we could say, the criteria for A are (1) B, and (2) something to do with agency (e.g. role).

To assert that there is no moral difference between (B) and killing

M2

is to suppose that (B) alone is sufficient to attribute responsibility for a death, and that (B) gives a genuine description of a man's action, and not just of his behaviour (in the sense of bodily movements). Yet there is no simple relation between action and behaviour, and considerations of agency are very often essential if we are to proceed from a statement about a man's behaviour to a statement about what he actually did. The relations of responsibility which authorize the passage from one kind of statement to the other are complicated – in the next section I shall discuss exactly how they affect the description of what a man does. But it is on these relationships that an absolutist would have to rely in order to prevent the inflexibility of his principles leading to morally insensitive decisions. If moral principles cover *behaviour* – as many consequentialists seem to assume – then it will, of course, be impossible to draw a line between behaviour which should fall under a particular principle and that which should not. Wherever the line be drawn, there will be a difference between behaviour on one side of the line and behaviour on the other side which will not seem morally significant to any normal conscience. This is simply because the difference is one of behaviour. Moral principles apply to *actions*, and a judgement as to someone's agency or responsibility in what is done is necessary before any moral principle can be brought to bear. So there is, on an absolutist basis, just as much scope for casuistry and for fine moral distinctions between courses of action, as there is on a consequentialist basis. Responsibility admits of degrees, and the extent to which what a man does is wrong will be decided on the basis of the correct description of what he does.

There can, then, be two actions which, from a certain point of view, are not differentiated one from another by features upon which the normal conscience could base a moral difference. For instance, given a sufficiently narrow description of the case, the doctor who does not spend a thousand pounds on purchasing a drug for his patient, such that she dies, is not doing anything different from her husband who also declines to spend the money. So far there is nothing in the features of the two cases upon which the normal conscience could base a moral distinction. But in fact these cases are central examples of morally different *kinds* of case, and the kind is given by the role or agency in each case. What is morally relevant is the feature of each case which affects the action description and so determines under what moral principle the action is to be brought. Thus if a feature is morally relevant it is because it is a feature which leads to one action being brought under one description, and another being brought under another description, when no principle applies equally to each description. Both cases might have what we might call their non-relational properties or features totally in common, so that on these no reasonable man could seek to base a moral distinction. These features do not give the kind of moral difference which is required. The *kind* of difference is between instances of two radically different action concepts, each carrying different ascriptions of responsibility and each ascribable or defeasible on different grounds. The difference is given by the action being related to (for instance) the role of the agent.

This seems to bring us fairly naturally to the sort of case typically covered by the Doctrine of Double Effect. Imagine the following case: a woman is dying of cancer. A drug which will relieve her pain is available, and of all the pain-relieving drugs it is by far the most efficient, and, indeed, the only one which will really remove the pain in a case such as hers. It is, consequently, the one which doctors always prescribe, and its use is according to the best medical standards. At the same time, and as a side effect of its removal of pain, it reduces physical resistance and hence, to a measurable degree, shortens life. This example reveals one important way in which the actions/consequences distinction can have moral significance, apart from considerations of immediacy, intention and so on. For what the doctor is doing is relieving pain rather than shortening life – even though the shortening of the patient's life is a foreseeable result of his action. Reflection on the grounds for our describing the action in this way suggests that, in classing something that happens as a consequence rather than as part of what was *done*, we may intend thereby to defeat an ascription of responsibility.[1] An argument about whether the shortening of the woman's life is a consequence of what the doctor does, or whether he 'shortens the woman's life' might well *ipso facto* be an argument about whether he can be held responsible for the woman's life being shortened. Can a sharp line be drawn between those descriptions of his actions which ascribe responsibility to the doctor for the woman's earlier death, and those which don't? It is clear that descriptions employing such phrases as 'lets her die' ascribe responsibility. But if we put these descriptions at one end of a scale, and descriptions of

[1] Cf. H. L. A. Hart, 'The ascription of responsibility and rights', in A. G. N. Flew (Ed.), *Logic and Language*, I (Oxford, Blackwell, 1960).

the form 'He so conducts himself that she dies'[1] at the other, then in between will be a whole range of descriptions shading into each other, those carrying an ascription of responsibility only subtly distinguished from those which do not. Sometimes we distinguish cases where a consequence is within the sphere of a man's responsibility (i.e. where it is part of what is *done*), from cases where it is *merely* a consequence, by the use of 'the consequence' rather than 'a consequence' to refer to it. Thus:

(*a*) 'He relieved her pain. A consequence was that her life was shortened.'

(*b*) 'He relieved her pain. The consequence was that her life was shortened.'

This slight verbal difference reflects a superficial similarity between the cases – a similarity and perhaps identity in their non-relational properties. However, although these expressions function similarly as descriptions of what (crudely) is going on, they are not both correct as descriptions for the simple reason that the relational properties of the doctor's action which would lend support to the use of the first are different from those which would lend support for the second. So although they describe the situation similarly, they *ascribe responsibility* in different ways.

Such differences in description could reflect different implications as to the doctor's role (not, of course, in the sense of his moral role) in the case. These implications as to role will give us a reason for preferring one sort of description of his action over another. So we might say that a view of his role or agency which accepts as a matter of course that in administering the drug he is acting in an accepted, recognized role – that of physician – will necessarily lead us to give descriptions of what he *does* of type (*a*). A view of the medical function which holds that it is an essential part of a doctor's role simply to prolong life to the utmost will necessarily lead to descriptions of type (*b*). Now (*a*) simply gives one of a whole cluster of descriptions, some of which (like (*a*) itself) do not obviously carry moral weight. But this is because it may not be immediately obvious to which *kind* of description either (*a*) or (*b*) belongs. We see to which kind either description belongs in

[1] In fact it is by no means clear that such a neutral, technical sort of description as this would be on the same scale at all.

seeing how it falls naturally into one of two groups, the central or para-digm cases of each being:

(1) 'He relieved her pain' and
(2) 'He shortened her life'

Given its membership of each kind, we see how even the slight dif-ferences distinguishing such descriptions from each other can carry implications as to the doctor's role, and, hence, his responsibility. It is in virtue of these implications that the differences of description carry moral weight.

The criteria of relevance which will govern our selection of *the* consequences of an action are intimately connected with such notions as role and, hence, responsibility. For instance, supposing that the pain-relieving drug which also shortens life has a further effect, which is to induce a certain colour in the cheeks. We should not normally mention this as *the* effect of the drug, not simply because we are not, as a matter of fact, interested in this particular effect, but because we are describing the actions of a doctor, not of some sort of cosmetician.[1] Now if someone were to insist on a description of the doctor's actions such that the shortening of the woman's life came closer and closer to being something like *the* effect, he would also be bringing his descrip-tion closer and closer to one of the form 'He shortened her life' rather than of the form 'He relieved her pain'. He would be bringing the shortening of the woman's life into the centre of the area of the doctor's concern. He would be saying that it is a natural part of the description of the doctor's action, either as a doctor or as some other sort of agent. And in so bringing it into the area of the doctor's concern or role or agency he would be *ascribing responsibility* to the doctor for the woman's earlier death.

The drawing of the actions/consequences line, and the selecting for mention of some consequences and not others, will in many cases be at the same time a determination or assessment of role or agency, thereby establishing implications for the ascription or rejection of responsibility.

---

[1] One could, incidentally, distinguish between 'effects' and 'consequences'. It is an effect of the drug that it induces colour in the cheeks, but its inducing colour in the cheeks is not a consequence of the doctor's action in administering it. The idea of a consequence already implies certain criteria of relevance. I do not think that my ignoring of this distinction affects the argument.

III ROLE AND RESPONSIBILITY

It is worth distinguishing three senses of 'responsible':

Responsibility (1):

This is the sense in which a *person* can be responsible for something, such that he can be held responsible or admit responsibility. Sometimes 'responsibility' can be replaced by another term; for instance, where what is done is wrong, to be responsible (1) for it is to be *to blame* for it. Responsibility (1) is fundamentally connected with praise and blame and other moral notions.

Responsibility (2):

Responsibility (1) is to be distinguished from the sense of 'responsible' in which a man has, or takes on, or accepts a responsibility. For instance, as a father I have a responsibility for the welfare of my children. As a doctor I accept, or take on a responsibility towards my patients. Responsibility (2) involves the idea of a duty or obligation to bring something about, to prevent something, etc.; it is frequently connected with a particular role, occupation or relationship. To neglect a duty or obligation arising out of some responsibility (2) may result in one's being responsible (1) for any result which ensues.

Responsibility (3):

This is the causal sense of 'responsible'. An ulcer may be responsible in this sense for the pain a man feels; the motion of the moon is responsible (3) for the ebb and flow of the tides. It is also important to notice that a man's *action* may be responsible (3) for a state of affairs. For instance, my action in mopping my brow may be responsible (3) for the death of a small insect without *my* being responsible (1) for it – unless, say, I have some sort of responsibility (2) to prevent it. Responsibility (3) is, by itself, insufficient for praise and blame, and hence for such moral notions as 'holding responsible'.[1]

An examination of the relations between these senses of 'responsible' is necessary if we are to clarify the absolutist's argument. If the absolutist is not invoking merely arbitrary distinctions between courses of

---

[1] For an excellent discussion of types of responsibility, cf. H. L. A. Hart, *Punishment and Responsibility* (Oxford, 1968), p. 124. See also Joel Feinberg, 'Action and responsibility', in A. R. White (Ed.), *The Philosophy of Action* (Oxford, 1968).

action, then this must be because his notion of how moral principles apply to actions is governed by a particular theory of responsibility.

I shall begin with responsibility (3). It seems to be a necessary condition for someone's being morally responsible for something that it be the result of something he does or fails to do. Responsibility (3) – causal responsibility – seems to be what is invoked in the attemptedly neutral description of the obstetrician's behaviour in the original example: 'He so conducts himself that she dies'.

Does this in fact give a description of the obstetrician's behaviour which is neutral as regards his role? Can descriptions in terms of responsibility (3) provide a neutral basis on which to ascribe moral responsibility? Let us revert to the case of the car passenger who, I suggested, cannot properly be said to 'refrain' from turning the car into a ditch. Now the locution in this case, analogous to that used in the 'strong' no moral difference thesis, would be: 'He so conducted himself that the car did not go into a ditch'. This immediately strikes us as very improper. We could not, I think, properly say that a passenger who does not seize the golden opportunity presented by his position in the front seat and turn the car into a ditch 'so conducts himself that (as a foreseen and wanted consequence) the car is not turned into a ditch'. Even if it were true it would still be improper to bring it into an ordinary description of an ordinary drive. 'John and James went for a drive. The weather was fine; they visited various country churches. During the drive John so conducted himself that the car was not turned into a ditch.' We seem to appeal to some criterion of conversational propriety to rule out the intrusion of a statement such as the last, which is certainly irrelevant and misleading.

Even the statement 'John did not turn the car into a ditch', though perfectly true, would be a thoroughly improper and misleading intrusion into a description of the drive. The statement that John so conducted himself that the car was not turned into a ditch is even more improper, since it implies that the car's not having gone into a ditch was the result of something John did not do. Now John's not having turned the car into a ditch may be a necessary condition for the car's not having gone into a ditch. But does it follow from this that the car's not going into a ditch *results* from (among other things) something John did not do? Take an analogous example: If I help a blind man across a road, his reaching the other side in safety could only very oddly be said to result from such things as my not treacherously pushing him under a lorry, or of a chasm not suddenly opening up under our feet, even though it is true that these things did not happen, and that we could not have arrived safely if they had. A pattern of normal expectations inhibits the introduction of certain negative statements into the description ('I did not push him under a lorry . . .', 'A chasm did not open up . . .') and also prohibits certain causal statements which rely upon the propriety of the introduction of these negative statements ('He crossed safely because I did not push him under a lorry'). The introduction of a statement which claims to give the *cause* of some event presupposes a pattern of normal expectations, such that what will count as the cause of the event is, as it were, an intrusion into the pattern of expectations.[1] This is particularly clear in the case of an alleged negative cause of a negative event – as in the car example; here one cannot imagine what pattern of expectations is presupposed.

If a man does not do X, we cannot properly say that his not doing X is the cause of some result Y unless, in the normal course of events, he could have been expected to do X. Responsibility (3), like other causal notions, relies upon certain criteria of relevance.

But what determines our criteria of relevance? Let us take the case of a mother who neglects her child, so that it dies. Medically the child's death might result from malnutrition. Yet we would still want to say that morally (and, presumably, legally) it is the mother's neglect that is responsible (3) for its death. Now these two causes are not incompatible; both lack of food and neglect by the mother are connected with the child's death by an appropriate causal law. Each can be spoken of as *the* cause of the child's death; and there are many other events any one of which might count as the cause of the child's death according to other criteria of relevance. None the less it would be extremely misleading to assert that the child's death was caused by lack of food in a context where the assumed criteria of relevance are not medical but moral. That would imply that our normal expectations about how mothers behave in this situation are satisfied, when they are not. For the mother *neglected* her child.

To assert that the mother neglected the child, and that this neglect was the cause of its death clearly involves certain assumptions as to how we can expect mothers to behave to their children. Our judgement as to what is to be expected will be governed by some conception of

[1] Cf. J. L. Mackie, 'Responsibility and language', *Australasian Journal of Philosophy*, vol. 33, No. 2 (August 1955).

what the relationship is of a mother to her child, and what are the duties and obligations that arise out of it. In other words, what is to be expected will be defined in terms of the mother's *responsibilities* in sense (2).

So even the ascription of responsibility (3) may not be neutral as regards role, for the criterion of relevance which enables us to say of any action or non-action that it is responsible (3) for some result may derive from some notion of what is to be expected in terms of some role or relationship.

Returning to the obstetrical case: the assertion 'He so conducted himself that she died' must *at least* mean that her death resulted from something he did or failed to do. It could perhaps be expressed as follows:

(*a*) 'The mother would have lived if (and only if) the doctor had killed the child'.

(*b*) 'He did not kill the child'.

(*c*) 'She died'.

Now it is surely clear that this does not amount to the assertion that the doctor's conduct is responsible (3) for the woman's death. Since the assertion that the doctor's conduct is the cause of the woman's death is not meant to *compete* with the medical hypothesis – which also offers a sufficient cause of her death – then the point of the assertion must be to involve the doctor in her death. Now the conjunction of (*a*), (*b*) and (*c*), which gives a perfectly correct account of what happened, does not amount to the assertion 'He so conducted himself that she died' without the further implication that the doctor's acting otherwise is at least not out of the question, and, in fact, is what could be expected. If a description attributing the woman's death to some action or omission of the doctor's is preferred to one which refers merely to a medical cause, then there must be the implication that he could have been expected to act otherwise. And what can and cannot be 'expected' may be determined by our conception of his responsibilities (2).

In other words, the most appropriate description of what a man does, and hence what is to be taken as *the* effect of what he does, will very often depend upon a notion of his responsibilities (sense 2). This can be illustrated in the case of the pain-relieving drug: it would be decidedly odd to say that the doctor 'so conducts himself that colour comes into his patient's cheeks' (supposing the drug to have that effect). Bringing colour into his patient's cheeks would be no part of what, as a physician, he is doing. The oddity of such a description of his action lies in its supposing some sort of scientific context, in which this effect would be an object of study. But to attribute this effect to the doctor's action would be to presuppose a criterion of relevance derived from his medical role. The statement therefore has two, conflicting, implications, which produces an inevitable oddity about its use.

By contrast, to say 'He so conducts himself that she dies sooner' (assuming that the drug shortens life as well as relieving pain) at least has the merit of being based upon a perfectly comprehensible view of the medical role – of what kind of thing a doctor has a responsibility (2) for. For instance, it might be thought that the aim of medicine is simply to keep a patient alive for as long as possible. If we choose our criteria of relevance differently, then the obstetrician who so conducts himself that his patient dies can also be said so to conduct himself that all sorts of other things happen: he 'so conducts himself' that his wife has more of his company than usual, that the national television audience is increased by one person, and so on. But of all these possible consequences only one seems relevant – the death of the woman. Why is this? Because there is some question that the death of the woman concerns the obstetrician; there is some question as to his responsibility (2) for her.

So the attribution of causal responsibility – responsibility (3) – for the death to some action or omission of the doctor's depends upon certain implications as to his responsibilities (2). Now it is true that our notion of what it would be normal to expect, etc., which will govern the propriety of attributing the death to his inaction[1] need not go so far as to be an assertion of his responsibilities in the full sense, since it might also be derived from an assessment of character or psychology. But if killing the child is *ruled out* by the medical role, then this will prohibit our taking his killing the child as something we could

---

[1] The place responsibility (2) can have in ascriptions of causal responsibility is particularly clear where an effect is attributed to a negative cause. If the doctor so conducts himself that the woman dies, then her death is not the result of anything he does, but of something he does not do. That is to say, her death does not result from everything he does rather than kill the child, but from his not killing, or from his failing to kill the child. It is rather obvious that we can only describe him as failing to do something when there is some question of his doing it.

reasonably expect. Hence the correctness of our ascribing causal responsibility in the present case will depend upon the acceptability of some particular conception of the doctor's role.

We can go further than this. The attribution of causal responsibility to someone's actions still does not amount to an attribution of responsibility to *him*. When we talk of a person, rather than his actions, as responsible for something we invariably mean to ascribe responsibility in a more full-blooded sense (sense (1), for example). It has been suggested that this is not so, and that a person can be causally responsible for an event. For instance: 'Disraeli was responsible for the fall of Gladstone's government'.[1] It is certainly possible so to use this phrase that 'Disraeli was responsible for the fall of Gladstone's government' follows from 'Disraeli did X and Y which caused the downfall of Gladstone's government'. But this would, I think, be misleading, since it would obscure the evident gap between an attribution of causal responsibility and a final judgement as to personal responsibility. The statement that Disraeli was responsible for the fall of the government is usually taken to have a different meaning, such that it does not follow analytically from 'Disraeli did X and Y which caused the fall of the government'. It could be analysed as follows: 'Since Disraeli's having done X and Y led to the fall of the government, Disraeli was responsible for the fall of the government'. In the first case the fall of the government is ascribed to certain actions of Disraeli's; in the second case responsibility for the fall of the government is ascribed to *Disraeli* on the grounds that certain of his actions caused it to fall.

So we could say that causal responsibility is never ascribed to a person, but only to his actions. At any rate, when a person is described as being the cause of something, either this is elliptical for a statement attributing causal responsibility to his actions, or even to certain states of his body, or else 'cause' is being used in a way which connects it with responsibility (1). In other words, a person can be a cause of something in just those circumstances in which he might properly be said to be responsible (1) for it. The point in ascribing responsibility to a person rather than to certain of his actions, or certain states of his body, is to link the ascription of responsibility with moral praise and blame. By contrast, to say that his actions were the cause, rather than that *he* was the cause, may be to attempt to inhibit praise and blame. One praises or blames a *person* on account of what he did or failed to do.

[1] Cf. Hart, *Punishment and Responsibility*, pp. 214–15.

This brings us to an important point. Although I have been using as typical examples of locutions which ascribe responsibility (1) such phrases as 'let X happen', 'refrained from preventing Y' and so on, the most general term for 'being responsible for' is 'being the cause of'. We could say that in describing someone as letting something happen, failing to prevent something or neglecting someone such that they die, we are in different ways asserting that he is the cause of something and is therefore responsible (1). Now if it is true that his *actions* are the cause of some state of affairs, under what circumstances will it follow that he is the cause? I think first that the state of affairs must be noteworthy in some way, even if it does not actually have to be a matter of praise or blame. For instance, if I shut the door, a perfectly proper and true causal statement could be framed which makes my action in pushing the door the cause of its shutting. But this would not be sufficient for saying, on the basis of my action being the cause of or responsible for, the door's shutting, that *I* am responsible for its shutting. This is because the shutting of the door is a matter of complete inconsequence. There is no question of praise or blame, or of any sort of assessment or evaluation of my part in shutting the door. I cannot admit or claim responsibility for it. There is thus no point in involving me, as a person, in the shutting of the door, since nothing is thereby added to a description of the door's being shut as a result of my *actions*. On the other hand, it would be proper to ask 'Are you responsible for these hideous decorations?' because there is some question of a personal assessment of me in respect of the decorations. One way in which a result of an action can have the kind of significance required for the attribution of responsibility (1) is the agent's acting in some role or relationship which confers on him some responsibility (2) for a state of affairs. For instance, it immediately makes sense to ascribe responsibility (1) to someone for the door's being shut if – say, as Keeper of the Gate – he has some responsibility (2) for keeping it open.

All that needs to be added to this condition is that there should be no features of the situation which excuse the agent – such as involuntariness, unforeseeability of consequences and so on.

Now if these conditions are all satisfied, then I think it follows that a person is the cause of something, and therefore responsible (1) for it. So in a situation where a man's actions or omissions are the cause of something, to go on to say that *he* is the cause is to imply that these conditions are in fact satisfied and that he is therefore a proper object of personal assessment in regard to the production of the state of affairs, a proper object of, for instance, praise and blame.

The locutions 'letting X happen', 'failing to prevent Y', etc., each describe a man's actions as the cause of something, and they describe *him* as the cause in all cases where no excusing conditions are present to reject the ascription of responsibility (a man may let something happen unintentionally, and we cannot, therefore, claim that there is a conceptual identity between 'letting something happen' and 'being responsible (1) for its happening', even though the first will always amount to the second in cases where excusing conditions are absent).

It follows that if it is clear in advance that we have grounds – which are not merely excusing conditions – for holding that someone cannot be responsible (1) for something, then it must be improper to accuse him of 'letting it happen'. Imagine, for instance, the scene around a gallows as a condemned felon is about to be hanged. We assume that, apart from the hangman, a doctor, a priest and, say, the prison governor are present. The doctor's function is to feel the condemned man's pulse and report when he has expired; the priest has to whisper the last comforts of the dying; the prison governor has to witness the execution. We imagine also that any one of these persons would be able, should he so wish, to interfere in such a way as to prevent the execution, and that the penalties for such interference are small. Now some opponents of the practice of capital punishment might want to say that the practice is so evil that everyone has a duty to interfere to prevent it who is in a position to do so. On these grounds they might say that the doctor, priest and prison governor in not interfering are letting the felon die. It might even be said that their doing their usual jobs, performing in their usual role *instead* of interfering, amounts, in these circumstances, to letting the man die. The priest, in telling his beads instead of preventing the hanging, involves himself in the man's death.

Now if, on the contrary, we hold not only that hanging is not always evil, but also that it is no business of the people present to interfere in the judicial processes of the state, then we would reject the description of their behaviour as 'letting die'. We see how the introduction of 'letting die' adds something new to the description of the scene. On a conventional, non-reformist view, we would have a scene in which the doctor waits to inspect the body, the priest whispers his comforts, the governor witnesses the hanging; at the same time, a man is being hanged. There is no connection in terms of responsibility, so far, between these different elements in the scene. Nothing connects the activities of these people (except in the minimal sense in which their not interfering might be said to be a necessary condition of the hanging) with the death of the felon. But as soon as someone says 'They were letting him die' everything changes. They are, after all, involved in his death. Because they ought to have prevented it, but did not, their non-intervention is a cause, or even *the* cause, of his death, and they bear some or full responsibility for it.

Even if we were to agree that they let the man die, but plead that they could not be expected to do otherwise – because of the penalties, or whatever – then although we would be invoking excusing conditions which would exonerate them from moral responsibility (or at least reduce their responsibility) we would still be conceding a large part of the reformist's claim. We would be agreeing that the man's death came within the area of their responsibility (2). Whereas if we say that a man's being hanged was in no sense their responsibility – they were present in a certain professional capacity – then we would be arguing that the locution 'letting die' was improper, we would be *defeating*[1] the ascription of responsibility, not excusing them from responsibility. We would be rejecting the reformist's characterization of their behaviour which was so framed as to make possible the ascription of responsibility.

So the conditions that must be fulfilled before we can properly say that a man lets someone die (is responsible for the death) are, at least in very many cases, precisely the conditions which are contextually or conversationally implied in saying 'He so conducted himself that X died' (i.e. his actions were responsible (3) for the death). In the obstetrical case, then, we cannot give the supposedly role-neutral description of the doctor's actions (in such a way as to ascribe responsibility (3) to them) without covertly ascribing, or presupposing that we could ascribe, responsibility (1) to *him* for the woman's death. In other words, if we assume that it is proper to describe the doctor either as 'letting the woman die', *or* as 'so conducting himself that she dies', this can only be because we presuppose some reformist conception of the doctor's role.

[1] Cf. Hart, in Flew (Ed.), *Logic and Language*, I. I mean that we would be claiming that there are features in the situation which would defeat an ascription of responsibility.

We may now summarize these conclusions about responsibility and relate them to the obstetrical case. A man is responsible (1) for something if (and only if)

(*a*) His actions (or omissions) are responsible (3) for it.

(*b*) The outcome has some importance in terms of what he might be expected to do; in general, that is, in terms of a pattern of responsibilities (2), in the context of which he acts.

(*c*) Normal conditions (i.e. no excusing conditions).

So in order to ascribe responsibility to the doctor for the woman's death we must show that conditions (*a*) and (*b*) are satisfied. Anyone who wishes to ascribe moral responsibility to the doctor must think that (*a*) is satisfied. This would be reflected in the use of such terminology as 'He so conducted himself that. . .'. The consequentialist does not raise questions relating to (*b*), and he really seems to argue as though responsibility could be attributed to the doctor on the basis of (*a*) and (*c*) alone. In a sense this is right – but only because the correctness of saying that condition (*a*) is satisfied relies upon a rule of conversational propriety which is equivalent to the assertion of condition (*b*). His argument seems to require that (*a*) should both carry an implication as to the doctor's responsibility (1) *and* remain neutral as to his responsibility (2). But this, I have tried to show, is not possible. We may schematize the argument as follows:

(*a*) As a result of what he did (or did not do), the woman died (causal responsibility, sense 3).

(*b*) He was responsible for the woman's death – i.e. he let her die, was an accessory, procured her death (in 'normal' conditions).

The propriety of both (*a*) and (*b*) rests upon the truth of certain presuppositions as to the doctor's responsibility (2); this is the case with (*a*) because to *say* (*a*) implies certain things with regard to these presuppositions, and with (*b*) because (*b*) entails certain things with regard to these presuppositions. To say *either* is therefore to suppose that we have a good reason for saying that there is no moral difference, or that there is, at least, a moral similarity, between what the doctor does and killing. Hence:

(1) If we describe the case in a neutral way (such that there is a

non-relational equivalence between what the doctor does and killing, according to the argument of Section II),

(2) and if we assume the propriety of these locutions (*a*) and (*b*),

(3) then we are assuming or asserting a relation of responsibility (2) which is other than that ascribed by the traditionalist conception of the doctor's role which we have been envisaging.

We have not, then, produced an argument against the doctor's acting as he does, but have simply asserted a different notion of what he ought to be doing (in terms of his role). So the consequentialist case can only be sustained as part of an argument in favour of a particular conception of the medical role. The absolutist's position, on the other hand, amounts to this:

(*a*) The principle to which the doctor adheres ('Never take innocent life') really means 'Never act so as to be responsible (1) for a death'.

(*b*) If the idea of acting according to a role is accepted, then a man will not be held responsible (1) for just *any* (causal) result of his action or inaction, even when the result is clearly foreseen, etc. It will limit the sphere of a man's responsibility (2), and will there-fore make it possible for him to apply his moral code, by giving him a clear picture of *what*, in a particular situation, he is doing.

It is also possible that without some notion of a role which allows a man to see in advance what he may and may not be responsible (1) for, it would be difficult, and perhaps even impossible, to apply a moral code at all. In this sense roles are pre-moral, which explains why they govern the description of what a man does, rather than support a moral judgement of him on the basis of a description of what he does. So the absolutist can maintain that the correctness of his redescription of what is *done* by the obstetrician when the woman dies gives a reason for saving the child's life rather than the mother's.

Of course, the man who does not accept anything like the tradi-tionalist's view of the medical function will find much of the foregoing absurd. For example, the analogy with cars not being turned into ditches will seem peculiarly grotesque because although there may be in general no question of passengers doing such things, there *must* always be a question of killing the child in order to save the mother. However, it is no part of my argument to assert or deny the traditionalist's scheme. The wrongness of any particular scheme would not affect the logical points I have tried to raise, nor would it damage absolutism as a view of the status of moral principles. None the less, the traditionalist's scheme, placed side by side with an explicit absolutism, reveals very clearly the logical presuppositions upon which an absolutist position may rest.

Once we raise the question as to whether or not the traditionalist's scheme is tenable, we move out of the realm of purely philosophical argument. To say that there *is* a live question of killing the child in order to save the mother, such that the doctor who does not do so can be said to be the cause of the mother's death, is to claim that certain upshots are the doctor's business, are relevant to his role as a doctor or as some other agent, do fall within his sphere of responsibility. We cannot then settle the argument by looking for a description of what the doctor does which is neutral as regards his role or responsibility, but only by deciding what we think *is* the medical role and its relation to the various other roles and responsibilities a man may have.

IV   ROLE AND INTENTIONS

In Section I, I discussed the logical connection there must be between the moral condemnation of killing and the moral condemnation of being responsible for a death. This was described as the 'no moral difference' thesis. Any moral principle must apply to all actions which involve a man as an agent in a state of affairs judged by the principle to be morally good or bad. I have suggested that there is a way in which absolutism can admit the 'no moral difference' thesis, and at the same time provide for decision-making in particular cases. Killing[1] and letting die must, for an absolutist who believes in the sanctity of human life, be morally similar. This similarity was elucidated by way of an exploration of the conditions that have to be fulfilled if someone is to be described as sincerely accepting such a principle as 'It is wrong to kill'. The logical connection indicates a connection between the moral guilt of killing and the moral guilt of letting die. Nevertheless, to establish a moral *connection* is not yet to establish a moral *equivalence*. We have not yet given any idea of the circumstances under which there would be *no* moral difference between the two courses of action, even though we have shown how it is possible for absolutism to admit that there are cases where there is no such moral difference.

[1] By 'killing' I always, of course, mean 'deliberate killing'.

For example, supposing a mother neglects her young child such that it dies – say of starvation – then there certainly seems to be some sort of connection, in terms of responsibility for a death, between such behaviour and killing. Of course the connection may be remote, since the neglect may be the result of negligence or laziness; but there nevertheless *is* a connection. It is not as though she is criticized merely for 'neglecting her responsibilities'. No doubt to neglect one's responsibilites is wrong, but the gravity of this case comes from the quite particular responsibilities which she neglected – towards the life of the child. Any moral judgement will therefore involve an attitude to the death of the child. So the mother's moral guilt arising from her responsibility for the child's death will at least exist on the same spectrum or scale as the guilt that would attach to killing, or being an accessory to a death. The case will, at any rate, be in this moral area.

Yet even if it is on the same spectrum or scale, or in the same moral area as killing, can neglect leading to a death be the moral *equivalent* of killing? Let us imagine a case where neglect really does seem morally equivalent to killing. Suppose for instance, the mother shows no sign in her general behaviour of laziness or incompetence, but is, on the contrary, remarkably efficient, knows perfectly well how much and what sort of nourishment is necessary for children. Nor has anything diverted her attention from the child. Perhaps, on the contrary, she shows a definite interest in it; but she simply does not feed it, or consistently gives it less than is required to keep it alive. Here we certainly seem to have a plausible case of neglect such that the child dies being the moral equivalent of killing. The trouble is that it is rather too plausible, because although it certainly is a case of neglect, it is not neglect proceeding out of laziness, inadvertence or negligence. It seems, in fact, a case of murder by deliberate neglect. In looking for a description of the mother's actions which will suggest the highest degree of culpability, we have succeeded in describing her as *intending* the child's death. It is in just such a case that it is unimportant whether we describe her as killing or letting die, because such a case of deliberately letting die is obviously morally equivalent to deliberately killing.

Now in describing the obstetrical case we have all along deliberately avoided the question of the doctor's intentions in order that we might explore any residual basis there might be for a distinction between killing and letting die on the one hand, and doing nothing with the result that the woman dies, on the other. Indeed, we have allowed that even if the woman's death were properly to be described as the consequence of the doctor's conduct, it would be the 'unwanted and unintended' consequence of his not killing the child: 'He so conducted himself that as a foreseen but unwanted and unintended consequence she died'.

In fact to describe the woman's death as foreseen but unwanted and unintended is rather odd. Take first 'unwanted'. To describe a consequence as unwanted implies either that you did not in fact want it to happen, or that you wanted it not to happen. No doubt before he decided not to kill the child the obstetrician wanted both the child and the mother to live. But after he took his decision, which he knew would certainly save the child and lead to the death of the mother, he can no longer properly be said to *want* the mother to live, but only to entertain an idle wish that she might, despite everything. Having taken the decision, he cannot properly be said to want the mother not to die, but only to wish that she could live. So if, in this case, he 'lets the mother die', her death can only be an 'unwanted consequence' if we understand 'unwanted' to mean simply 'not wanted'. But the only point in describing it as 'not wanted' would be to indicate that *before* he made his decision he would have preferred the woman (as well as the child) to live. And this would have no obvious moral relevance, except in telling us about his motives.

The case is even odder with 'unintended': Can the woman's death (again assuming, for the sake of argument, that he 'lets her die') properly be described as an 'unintended consequence'? An unintended consequence, surely, is one produced through inadvertence, carelessness or lack of foresight. A 'consequence which was not intended' still seems to mean a consequence which was overlooked, not foreseen or not thought of. If the consequence, far from being neglected through inadvertence or oversight, is both clearly foreseeable and, in fact, foreseen, then it can hardly be described as 'unintended'.

In describing a consequence as unintended we reduce or even take away blame for it. The extent to which blame is reduced will depend upon whether the consequence was, or should have been foreseen, or whether it was the result of negligence or inadvertence. Negligence can be so gross and culpable as to be criminal, but it cannot amount to the moral equivalent of a deliberate act. But a man cannot just withdraw his intention from an act or its consequences. If the consequence is foreseen with certainty and immediacy, and there is no question of inadvertence or negligence, then it is difficult to see what is being added to a description of it by also calling it 'unintended'. So if we can properly describe the doctor as 'letting the woman die', and if this is not the result of inadvertence, negligence, lack of foresight and so on, then he *intentionally* lets the woman die.

However, intentionally letting her die is not yet the same thing as *intending her death*. If it were, then the doctor in letting her die would be as responsible for her death as if he had deliberately killed her – as responsible as the mother who deliberately neglected her child such that it died. There would genuinely be *no* moral difference between such a letting die and deliberately killing. But in fact intentionally letting someone die is not necessarily intending his death. In the case of the mother neglecting her child there was a palpable case both of intentionally letting die and intending a death. That this is so is indicated, I think, by the ease with which we could say 'She starved the child' or 'She killed it by neglect' rather than 'She neglected it such that it died'. That is to say, the passage from 'X intentionally let die' to 'X intended the death' corresponds to the difference between being responsible for something by letting it happen, and being responsible for something by bringing it about by a deliberate action. We have already seen that there is a moral similarity between these two, since they are both ways of being responsible for a death. There is, however, a *prima facie* moral difference between intentionally letting an evil come about and intending an evil, corresponding to the difference between allowing a course of events which is already in train to proceed to its culmination, and actually initiating it oneself. Such a difference reflects, perhaps, an *overall* difference in the intentions of one who intends an evil and one who merely allows an evil to come about. It would usually be reasonable to suppose that if one intends an evil one wants or desires it, either as an end or as a means to an end; whereas, although one may intentionally let an evil come about because one desires or wants it, one may equally well let it come about out of indifference, incontinence or weakness of will. This helps, perhaps, to explain why one wishes to say that there is *always* a moral difference between killing and letting die. The one case seems *always* to be evidence of a 'guilty mind', the other not always. And it is worth mentioning that this seems to correspond to the difference in criminal law between deliberate murder and such crimes as 'manslaughter by neglect'.

It is clear, then, that if the doctor 'lets the woman die', then he does so intentionally. But it need not be the case that he intends her death. Nevertheless, her death certainly could not be described as an 'unintended consequence' – even if he only intentionally lets her die. It makes no difference that he would be very happy if, by some miracle, both mother and child could survive. He cannot avoid a situation in which he intentionally lets the mother die while, at the same time choosing a course of action – or making a decision – which will infallibly result in her death. What he *can* do is deny that the mother's death *is* something that he brings about – i.e. that he can properly be considered responsible (1) for it. We might here recall Miss Anscombe's example of a man pumping water which he knows to be poisoned into a house, such that the people in the house will be poisoned.[1] If pumping the water is the man's usual job, and if he plausibly insists that all he is doing is carrying on with his usual job, caring only about earning his pay, and not bothering about the fact that the water is poisoned, then it could be said that 'poisoning the household' is not a description under which he acts, not a description of what he intends. However, it would seem that he is intentionally letting the household be poisoned, and therefore is to some serious degree responsible for their death – guilty, say, of manslaughter rather than of murder.[2]

In the obstetrical case, there is no question of negligence or inadvertence. Either the doctor is as responsible for the death as if he killed, such that 'letting die' gives his intention in acting as he does – 'intending her death' – or else he is responsible for her death because he intentionally lets her die. He can only be *completely* relieved of responsibility for her death if he neither intentionally lets her die nor intends her death – if, in other words, 'letting die' is excluded as a description of his behaviour. It must be that the question of his intentions in respect of the woman's death simply does not arise; it must not be true that he intended her death, nor that he intentionally let her die, nor that her death was the 'unintended consequence' of his actions. All such descriptions of his behaviour involve the assumption that her death is something he could be held responsible for.

We can see now the connection between the doctor's denying that he intended the woman's death (to take the stronger version) and his denying that he 'let the woman die'. It is not that her death was unintended, but that the question of his intentions does not here arise.

---

[1] *Intention* (Oxford, Blackwell, 1957), section 25.
[2] Ibid. Miss Anscombe, however, thinks that he is guilty of murder.

It does not arise not because he withdraws his intention from her death (like Pilate) but because his relation to her is (in his eyes) determined by his role as a doctor, and that role excludes such things as killing the child in order to save the mother. Let us take an analogous example: Suppose a priest, who adheres to the absolute rule of the secrecy of the confessional, learns from a penitent that he has committed a crime. In failing to divulge the crime to the authorities he might be accused of 'letting the criminal escape unpunished'. But to say this would be to decide in advance against accepting the rule of the absolute secrecy of the confessional. In terms of that rule the priest can certainly deny that he was 'letting the criminal escape punishment', because his relation to him was one which excluded any possibility of revealing what he had learned, whatever the consequences. He might insist that he wasn't letting a criminal escape, but rather respecting the secrecy of the confessional – just as the doctor might say that he wasn't letting the woman die, but rather not killing the child. The insistence that the one description of his action is the right one, and the other the wrong one, is not merely the product of an arbitrary preference, but is governed by a particular idea of what is the capacity or role in which the priest and doctor act. But similarly, for the priest to deny that he 'intended' the criminal to escape, for him in fact to deny that he had any intentions in respect of the man's escaping, and for the doctor to deny that he intended the woman's death, is not for either of them merely to prefer one assessment of their intentions over another, but for them to see that a notion of their role or agency (and hence responsibility) governs the descriptions that can be given of what they do and refrain from doing, and hence also governs what they can be thought of as intending *in* what they do.

So not only will our conception of a man's responsibilities govern what we can properly describe him as doing and refraining from doing, in a case such as this, but *his* conception of his role and its duties will determine the description for him under which he acts. However much we may wish to redescribe his actions, in terms of some reformist view of his role, *his* conception of his role can govern what he can be said to intend in acting as he does. Even if we wish to reject his role, therefore, we cannot convict him of a crime. In the obstetrical case a connection has to be made between the two statements 'He did not kill the child' and 'The mother died'. I see no way in which a connection which involves the obstetrician in the woman's death can be made which does not make certain questionable assumptions about his role, his responsibilities or his intentions.

V   'WHATEVER THE CONSEQUENCES'

Given the part that notions of role play in descriptions of action and ascriptions of responsibility, it may be that a description of the obstetrician's behaviour can be given which would support rather than simply be derived from a moral judgement. Whether or not one inincludes certain consequences as part of a description of what is *done* may well depend upon the view one takes of a man's role or agency, and hence his responsibility. Including or not including certain consequences as part of what he does will involve defining his role and responsibility.

There is a sense in which the defining of a man's role or agency is pre-moral. Although moral approval or disapproval may in fact tend to influence one towards including certain consequences as part of a description of what is done, the properly decisive factor will be a judgement about agency and responsibility. A moral judgement cannot of itself determine an action description, or an assessment of responsibility, independently of all other considerations; and an attitude to the consequences of what a man does (or does not do) is not by itself sufficient for holding him responsible for those consequences.

However, to say that the defining of a man's role is pre-moral is too simple, since one's willingness to accept or take seriously a particular pattern of human activity, as a 'role' having bearing on a man's moral responsibility, may already presuppose a judgement of value. To accept that there could be a role of 'father' or 'physician', and at the same time to deny that there could be a role of 'sadist' or 'Jew-baiter' presupposes some sort of moral approval of fathers and physicians and disapproval of sadists and Jew-baiters. It may be that one cannot speak non-paradoxically of a good doctor without presupposing that a doctor is a good sort of thing to be,[1] or that it is a way of being, or at least does not conflict with being, a good man.

Now it is by no means self-evident that the moral judgement in favour of a particular role can always be expressed in utilitarian terms –

[1] Cf. Austin Duncan-Jones, 'Good things and good thieves', *Analysis*, vol. 26, No. 4 (March 1966).

that the exercise of a particular role has, for instance, socially desirable consequences. It might rather be based upon the view that a particular role, a particular pattern of activity embodies certain characteristic human excellences or virtues. The acceptance of a role might, then, involve certain moral presuppositions, but might nevertheless not be vulnerable on moral grounds to re-examination in the light of particular consequential considerations. In other words, we have here an analogy with absolutist moral principles. I suggested in the first section that one way of regarding moral absolutism is as a theory about ends, and it may be that absolutist moral principles are most plausible when they define what sort of man it is, in the last resort, desirable to be. It might be possible for a role, as defining a type of human activity or character judged good in itself, to be treated as an end. In reacting to a moral situation, a man may think in terms of the duties and obligations of a particular role which is already fully developed and does not, as it were, spring out of an open-minded assessment of what would be the best results to realize on the whole. In so doing he could reasonably be described as basing his judgement upon authority – the authority of a particular role.

This is the point at which to bring out certain presuppositions of the consequentialist's argument. For the consequentialist, the paradigm moral agent is one who 'does his own moral thinking', engages in 'independent moral thought'; whereas the absolutist is 'helplessly' or 'passively' obedient to a moral authority.[1] The concept of role that I have been discussing seems prior to any particular case, and determines how the particular case is to be described. It is thus analogous to a moral judgement that does not spring from an open-minded response to the particular case. To allow a prior conception of role so to determine the description of the obstetrician's action – like deciding on where to draw the actions/consequences line in the light of a prior moral judgement – would be to fail to engage in genuinely independent reasoning. A consequentialist would hold that if a role simply rules out certain actions which we know would produce good effects, and enjoins others which we know will have tragic results, then so much the worse for the role. Not to agree to modify it in such a case – in the face of a clear choice between the worse and the better consequences in terms of predictable human happiness – would be irrational, or callous, a passive surrender to a received notion, a failure to do one's own moral

[1] Cf. Bennett, op. cit.

thinking. There would, then, be an analogy with the resort to an absolute moral principle. The normal conscience would need to be satisfied, on this view, that a received conception of a particular role, or a received moral principle, does not frustrate a clear human good.

What I have called a man's 'role' defines what sort of agent he is, and what are his responsibilities and obligations, *prior* to any particular case. To suggest that a man must accept responsibility for all the foreseen consequences of what he does or refrains from doing is really to refuse to accept the notion of a 'role' in this sense at all. For the consequentialist or utilitarian there is really only one sort of 'role' – that of the ideally rational man (in the words of John Rawls[1]) 'seeking case by case to realize the best on the whole'. The consequentialist would hold that a moral principle which did not allow itself to be refuted, or a role which could not be discredited, by the consequences in a particular case would be either irrational (in the sense that no one who persisted in it would be doing his own moral reasoning), or immoral. We seem to have two polar concepts: on the one hand is the man with a normal conscience, the man who does his own moral reasoning. On the other is the man who is passively and unquestioningly obedient to authority, and who has therefore opted out of moral thinking altogether. The philosophical implications of this contrast are obscure, although what it would not be unfair to describe as its ideological point seems rather clearer. A number of issues seem irreducibly entangled here, but perhaps we could concentrate on one: Does the contrast make a strictly philosophical point about the *rationality* of a moral principle, or does the distinction come down to the distinction between the absolutist or deontologist, and the consequentialist or utilitarian? In other words, does it in the last resort reduce to the assertion that the absolutist is after all, as we should expect, an absolutist rather than a consequentialist? And is the underlying thesis not that consequentialists are rational, whereas deontologists are not, but that consequentialists are better (is a consequentialist dissatisfied better than a deontologist satisfied?)?

Now a principle such as 'It is always wrong to kill the innocent,

[1] 'Two concepts of rules', in Philippa Foot (Ed.), *Theories of Ethics* (Oxford, 1967). Rawls distinguishes between a 'practice' conception of rules, in which the rule is logically prior to any particular case, and determines how what happens in that case is to be described, and a 'summary' conception of rules, in which moral rules are simply a good prudential guide to conduct, justifiable on utilitarian grounds.

whatever the consequences of not doing so' may be the expression of a very general set of values. To modify or abandon it may involve a fundamental redrawing of a moral scheme, an extraordinarily far-reaching change in feeling. Such a principle – or ideal – might not be primarily a rule of prudence or utility, and might not be held in such a way as to be refutable by the sad consequences of a particular case. That is to say, it will not be an empirical generalization vulnerable to any or all counter-instances. Indeed, the very idea that a counter-instance could be brought would involve refusing to see the principle as a constitutive ideal – as part of a scheme which determines the sort of moral judgements that can be made – and might be to suggest a reform or change in terms of values which may not exist in the present scheme at all. The present scheme might resist challenge by reference to ends because it contains within itself an evaluation of ends; nor may it be easy to challenge it in a particular case with reference to consequences, since the existing moral scheme might already provide a particular evaluation of the consequences. As a man's role determines the sorts of description that can be given of his actions, so the basic principles or ideals which constitute a moral scheme may not only determine how someone is to behave in a particular case, but also how he is to regard the consequences of his behaviour. In looking for the justification of such a principle as 'It is always wrong to kill the innocent, whatever the consequences of not doing so', we might take account of its scope, its richness, the place it has in a particular scheme of values. This would bring out its meaning for the people who adhere to it – and perhaps its role in a particular culture. To understand it may involve understanding the culture. Understanding the role such a principle plays in a culture or value scheme may often be indistinguishable from coming to see its justification – in the sense of seeing how it can commend itself to civilized, intelligent people, how it is impressive and worthy of respect, although alien, etc. (so that the justification of the principle would not provide a motive for *me* to adopt it). The justification will not be primarily consequential because the evaluation of the consequences may only make sense against the background of the particular scheme (this is a way of saying that such fundamental principles or ideals function as *ends*, and to justify them is to give a full picture of the scheme of which they form a part). Of course, changes in society or the general environment may cause a particular moral principle to lose its rationale, so that adherence to it could be callous,

obtuse or a blind legalism. Although this might appear in the consciousness that adherence to the principle had a constant tendency to produce tragic consequences, it might rather be that the principle has
become fossilized or obtuse. This part of the picture could, in all sorts
of ways, have ceased to be illuminating rather as a particular literary
style might outgrow its expressiveness.

But it is not easy to lay down in advance the criteria for such conservatism being irrational or, say, inhumane. The insistence upon a
moral principle, particularly when it has the character of an ideal, such
as the sanctity of human life, could be carried to heroic lengths (and
thus treated as an *end*) without becoming absurd or grotesque (for
example, Regulus' return to the Carthaginians in order to keep a
promise). In one case the refusal to take innocent life might lead to the
death of another innocent. Put thus starkly, with the baldly stated
principle as the only justification, this might seem irrational, inhumane
or just unquestioningly obedient to authority. Nevertheless, the choice
is not just between the principle's leading, in such a case, to consequences we could approve of, and its being simply authoritarian. Tragic
consequences might result from the insistence, in a particular case,
on an ideal about the sanctity of innocent life. Among the questions
to be asked about such an ideal, some will be about probable consequences, but some also will be of the following sort: Does it seem to
express a more or less profound response to experience? Is it an ideal
which in general we can understand and respect? Can it commend
itself to sensitive and intelligent men? Or could it be adhered to only
by callous, unimaginative people? Can it express feelings, a moral
imagination, which can be related to values of our own? Could it be
seen as the expression of values which, in our own moral scheme, take
a rather different form? Related to this last question, can it be the expression of certain *virtues*? Apart from probable consequences, there
might be a difference (to name but a few qualities) of scope, seriousness or dignity between two moral principles.

Of course this is only the vaguest sketch of a way of regarding a
moral ideal which is not primarily consequentialist, such that 'justifying' it would be more like persuading oneself of the admirableness
of a particular *end* rather than calculating the best means to a further
end. Now the man who adheres to a moral principle in this fashion, such
as 'It is always wrong to kill the innocent, whatever the consequences
of not doing so', and who refuses to modify it in the light of a tragic

case, is presumably not 'doing his own moral reasoning'. That is to say, he treats this principle as an end, and does not constantly measure it against its tendency to produce human happiness. In that sense his judgement of the particular case will be 'authoritarian' – that is to say, he will not judge what to do in the particular case according to some expectation of what will produce (for example) the greatest human happiness and the least human pain, but he will simply subsume it under the principle. Now this may, of course, mean that he will find certain cases far less agonizing (morally, at any rate) than will the consequentialist. If to do one's own moral reasoning *is* just to be ready to examine each particular case in the light of its contribution to human well-being or happiness, or if to adhere to a moral principle in an ideally rational way is to refuse to treat it simply as a *donné*, but always to be ready to re-examine its rationale, lest following it becomes entirely a matter of legalism, then no one who holds to such a principle as 'It is always wrong to kill the innocent, whatever the consequences of not doing so', and who holds to it in the fashion I have sketched, will be doing his own moral reasoning, or will be ideally rational. But so far this has not got beyond saying that he is an absolutist rather than a consequentialist. It might even be – although this is certainly not self-evident – that consequentialism is a better policy in general than absolutism. Yet even this would not be enough. What is needed is to show that consequentialism is rational, and that absolutism is irrational.

Clearly it is here of the first importance to be aware to what extent 'rational' and 'irrational' are being used as terms of value. We might, for example, consider that a course of action which is inevitably (in the circumstances) self-defeating is of its nature irrational. For instance, the Roman Republican virtues may be admirable in all sorts of ways but if to insist on them leads to the breakdown of the framework in which this ideal could be pursued, such insistence would be absurd or irrational. Here the model of irrationality is the self-defeating action. But the move from an obvious and trivial case of a self-defeating action (a man who wishes for a long life refuses to eat any more food) to this complex ethical and political case is by no means unproblematic. In Addison's *Cato*, for instance, we have a tragic hero who is the supreme case of just such an unprofitable insistence upon the Republican virtues. When, in total defeat, he is offered life and liberty and the friendship of Caesar if he will surrender, and is asked to name his terms, he replies:

Bid him disband his legions,
Restore his commonwealth to liberty,
Submit his actions to the public censure,
And stand the judgement of a Roman senate.
Bid him do this and Cato is his friend.

Cato well knows that the result of his intransigence will be that compromise will not be possible, and the collapse of the Republic is inevitable. The point of the drama is that the Republic could only have been preserved if the Republicans had stooped to actions unworthy of their ideals. If Cato refuses to compromise his ideals, even though such a compromising might preserve the framework in which they could be pursued in future, all this shows is that (so far as individual behaviour is concerned) he is treating them as *ends*: the type of man who behaves in this way is virtuous and honourable, not because his behaviour leads to certain consequences, but because *this* is honourable behaviour. To say that, in this case, he should be prepared to jettison his ideals is to say that he should not treat them as ends, that he should be a teleologist with respect to them rather than a deontologist. In terms of a bourgeois utilitarian ethic we might consider Cato's behaviour quixotic; but it is not 'irrational' unless an extremely restricted sense is being given to 'rational'. It is obvious that a code of honour will involve its adherents in what, from a more utilitarian standpoint, will be irrational positions. The adherent of such a code who is faced with the choice either of abandoning it on one occasion, with the result that he will be able to adhere to it in future, or of refusing to abandon it now with the opposite result, is faced with a dilemma which the consequentialist or utilitarian might well escape. On the one hand, he wishes to comply with the code, on the other he wishes the situation to obtain in which the code can in general be complied with. The two wishes are as a matter of fact inconsistent – but there is nothing irrational about that. The course of action he chooses will demonstrate the extent to which the code defines his conduct as an end – defines, for instance, the sort of person who, *tout court*, it is desirable to be, whose actions are the actions of 'an honourable man'. If he decides to adhere to the code whatever the consequences, then we might say that he prefers to be a certain sort of man, even though he can only be this amid the ruin of the state of affairs which in general makes it possible. The extent to which this code is itself worthy of respect and rational, and the point at which adherence to it could become simply absurd and irrational, would be a matter of judgement in the particular case. Cato, for instance, resolves to spend the short interval left after his rejection of Caesar's offer

> With resolution, friendship, Roman bravery,
> And all the virtues we can crowd into it;
> That heaven may say it ought to be prolonged.

Simply to call this absurd or irrational would be merely to express a distaste for the ethic of honour.

Now if (reverting to the original obstetrical case) one were to insist that the doctor does, after all, let his patient die,[1] one would be saying that he really is presented with a difficult moral choice – between the mother's life and the child's – to deny the reality of which is to rely upon an excessively legalistic notion of what is a man's concern. It seems to limit his concern to a very narrow idea of his duties or obligations 'as an X' (doctor, lawyer), rather than 'as a man' or 'as a rational agent'. A distaste for this sort of morality is, perhaps, fundamental to the Protestant moral consciousness, and is well expressed by Mommsen in a scathing attack upon Roman Stoicism and its leading feature, 'the casuistic doctrine of duty':

> It suited the hollow pride of virtue, in which the Romans of this period sought their compensation amidst the various humbling circumstances of their contact with the Greeks, and put into formal shape a befitting doctrine of morality; which, like every well-bred system of morals, combined with the most rigid precision as a whole the most complaisant indulgence in the details.[2]

As a 'delightful example' of such casuistry Mommsen mentions a passage in *De Officiis* (III. xii, xiii) where Cicero discusses at some length a dispute between Diogenes of Babylon ('a great and highly esteemed Stoic') and his pupil Antipater ('a most profound scholar'). The dispute comes down to the distinction between 'concealing the truth' and 'not revealing the truth', and concerns the scope of one's moral responsibilities:

> Suppose a time of dearth and famine at Rhodes, with provisions at unheard of prices; and suppose that an honest man has imported a

---

[1] I.e. is responsible for her death.

[2] *De Officiis*, Bk IV, translated by W. P. Dickson (London, 1863), ch. 12.

large cargo of grain from Alexandria, and that to his certain knowledge also several other importers have set sail from Alexandria,
and that on the voyage he has sighted their vessels laden with grain
and bound for Rhodes; is he to report the fact to the Rhodians? Or
is he to keep his own counsel and sell his own stock at the highest
market price?

According to Antipater all the facts should be disclosed, that the
buyer may not be uninformed of any detail that the seller should
know; according to Diogenes the seller should declare any defects
in his wares, in so far as such a course is prescribed by the common
law of the land; but for the rest, since he has goods to sell, he may
try to sell them to the best possible advantage, provided he is guilty
of no misrepresentation.[1]

Now according to Antipater such behaviour would amount to 'concealing from your fellow-men what relief in plenteous supplies is
close at hand for them'.

'It is one thing to conceal', Diogenes will perhaps reply; 'not to
reveal is quite a different thing. At this present moment I am not
concealing from you, even if I am not revealing to you, the nature
of the gods or the highest good; and to know these secrets would
be of more advantage to you than to know that the price of wheat
was down. But I am under no obligation to tell you everything that
it may be to your interest to be told.'

Antipater's final reply to these, and like arguments is that a man *is*
under a moral obligation to tell other men what it is in their interest to
be told, and that any man must admit this when he thinks of 'the bonds
of fellowship forged by Nature and existing between man and man'.

Antipater is arguing that moral duties transcend any particular
obligations, and follow simply from one's being a man. He is opposing
to Diogenes' 'casuistry of duty' a universalist notion of a man's responsibilities. It is in virtue of *this* that 'not revealing' the truth can
amount to concealing it. Similarly, whatever view we take of the medical
role it would be perfectly meaningful to insist that the obstetrician does
'let the woman die', that he is responsible for her death; but this would
be a reformist insistence, an insistence, in the light of some view of
human solidarity, that this would be a better way to describe his

[1] *History of Rome*, translated by W. Miller (Loeb ed., Cambridge, Mass., 1956).

behaviour. It would express a preference for a universalist notion of a man's responsibilities, one not significantly affected by profession or caste. This is, of course, a very widespread modern view, and can even be taken as an orthodoxy. It is, nevertheless, the expression of a particular *moral* outlook and does not advance a purely philosophical argument about the nature of moral reasoning.

And this, surely, is the fundamental point. If we base an ascription of moral responsibility (or an action description such as 'concealing the truth' or 'letting die' carrying certain implications of moral responsibility) upon 'the bonds of fellowship forged by Nature and existing between man and man', then our argument is a moral one. The dispute between Antipater and Diogenes, far from being a trivial example of scholastic casuistry, is a paradigm case, not of a contrast between genuine and spurious morality, but of a clash between different *moralities*. Similarly, the parable of the Good Samaritan is not simply a conceptual analysis of the notion of 'my neighbour', but an attempt to persuade to a universalist view of certain moral responsibilities.

If we accuse the man who takes the narrower view of being irrational, the assumption that we seem to be making is that men are only genuinely rational in their moral outlook in so far as they are prepared to treat their roles and principles as 'summary'[1] – that is as rules of conduct which have in general proved their reliability in terms of their consequences, but which should be abandoned if some other way should turn up of realizing the best thing on the whole. In other words, the assumption is that men are only rational in ethics if they are consequentialists or utilitarians. Yet the conservatism or even obstinacy which may be characteristic of 'the man of honour' (such as Addison's Cato), or of Diogenes' merchant, or of the obstetrician in the original example, is entirely 'rational' in some more neutral sense of the word. There is no doubt that if a man can only follow the course of action that he does at the price of being blind, callous or simply uninformed, then we should have grounds for accusing him of being irrational, or of not doing his own moral thinking (not that these would be the most important charges that could be brought against him). Yet to call ethical conservatism irrational *as such*, and to suggest that the normal, rational man should only hold principles in such a way that they will be modified or overthrown by, for instance, tragic cases – so ruling out

[1] Cf. Rawls, op. cit.

any principle of the absolutist sort – is to use the words 'rational' and 'irrational', and the notion of 'moral reasoning', in an obviously evaluative and, indeed, partisan way, and to mount not a philosophical but a moral attack upon absolutism.

CONCLUSION

To describe it as a moral attack is not, of course, to dismiss it, but rather to suggest that it could not be carried through by means of an *a priori* argument. One must use a moral argument. A man may believe that one should always aim at being a certain sort of man, whatever the consequences. One should always be a man of honour, or *kalos kai agathos*, or magnanimous, not just as a means to an end, but because that is the right sort of man to be. He might adhere to this with all the self-sacrifice and sense of duty which are the characteristic criteria of someone's adhering to a moral principle. Any argument for or against his stance would have to be *persuasive*; it would involve the weighing up and appreciation of one sort of character, of one sort of life as against another. It has rarely been thought, except by the most simple-minded utilitarians, that consequentialism or utilitarianism provides an entirely satisfactory model for arguments of this sort. Certainly the man who aims at being a certain sort of person, whatever the consequences, is not *ipso facto* irrational. However he may go wrong, he is not making a fundamental mistake about the nature of moral reasoning.

Index